African Brain Circulation

International Studies in Sociology and Social Anthropology

VOLUME 105

African Brain Circulation

Beyond the Drain-Gain Debate

Edited by

Rubin Patterson

BRILL

LEIDEN • BOSTON
2007

Originally published as Volume 5 no. 3 (2006) of Brill's journal
'Perspectives on Global Development and Technology'

Cover design by Sandra van Merode

This book is printed on acid-free paper.

Library of Congress Cataloging-in-Publication Data

A C.I.P. record for this book is available from the Library of Congress.

ISSN 0074-8684
ISBN 978 90 04 15885 6

PRINTED IN THE NETHERLANDS

CONTENTS

Introduction

*Rubin Patterson**

GOING AROUND THE DRAIN-GAIN DEBATE WITH BRAIN CIRCULATION

The decades-long heated brain-drain versus brain-gain debate that has been intense among scholars, government officials, and emigrants from the global South, while still highly charged even today, will likely become increasingly irrelevant. The source of the growing irrelevance is twofold. First, Internet-Age emigration is fundamentally different from all of the preceding eras of emigration, due in large part to transnational societies that emigration engenders today. Transnational societies are those in which imagined communities straddle borders, and citizens not only possess intimate emotional attachments to multiple societies, but they engage more than one society materially in a dynamic fashion. Internet-Age emigration circumvents one being simply eviscerated from one's homeland and replanted in a new host society. Emigrants today can read daily newspapers, watch and listen to local television and radio programming emanating from the homeland while in the host society, and communicate throughout the day just as if they were ensconced locally back home. Citizens of the global South increasingly have the option of maintaining dual citizenship; therefore, as they gain citizenship in a rich society, their birthright citizenship remains in tack. Second, labor of varying quantity and quality from many countries, while it will never be as mobile as capital, will likely find its mobility facilitated through immigration arrangements designed to be matched with capital within countries to optimize production, market-share, and profits. The new global networked knowledge economy has sparked a new global competition for talent. Putting these two together—the ability of individuals to be engaged in both the home and host countries continually as well as to take advantage of economic opportunities across borders—provides a context for sustained brain circulation.

* University of Toledo; Sociology & Anthropology; Toledo, Ohio.
Email: rpatter@utnet.utoledo.edu.

Talent can be defined as "individuals of high impact. That impact can be in science and technology, business, culture, and politics" (Kuznetsov 2006:viii). Unlike in past years, top scientists, technologists, and other intellectuals from elsewhere are not automatically choosing to come to the United States, as nations such as Australia, Canada, New Zealand, and others are actively wooing the talent of such individuals (Florida 2005). The policy shift by Australia on how the country handles students studying under the Colombo Plan and subsequent programs is telling in this regard. Under those plans, students from poor Asian nations used to be required to return to their homeland for at least two years after completing their studies in Australia. Now that globalization forces nations to place a premium on talent, Australia has ended that policy, which was originally designed to help developing Asian nations build up their human capital (United Nations Population Fund 2005).

The brain-drain versus brain-gain debate has been about two questions: Should talented individuals emigrate from the global South to the West? And would it generate a brain drain for the homeland? As scholars, we cannot put the benefits and burdens of emigrated talent from Africa on a scale to determine precisely if it is an overall gain or a drain for the individual sending countries or for the continent as a whole. All we can do is document how cases in which individuals staying in a poor country versus emigrating to a rich country are helpful or harmful in specific instances, and from there we essentially extrapolate what the impact might be in the aggregate. Employing this sort of "aggregated individual accounting" methodology of the benefits and burdens of specific instances of emigration versus non-emigration could not truly simulate what would have been if there were no fleeing of talent, and also if all those who wanted to flee had managed to do so. Thus, such a methodological approach could not determine the impact of a "critical mass effect." In other words, those more sympathetic to the view that fleeing yields a brain drain suggest that African nations are robbed of the benefits that would accrue from a critical mass of talent that is needed to trigger an explosion of new economic activity and enormous gains in productivity. Reaching this conclusion from actual evidence, alas, requires a leap of faith. Historical sociology does not bear out the "all-talented-Africans-have-to-do-is-remain-engaged-at-home" school of thought. Conversely, it is also possible, as those more sympathetic to the brain-gain thesis suggest, that retaining essentially all of the African talent at home when it cannot be productively utilized will simply generate brain waste. What we do know is that an incessant flow of talent out of Africa to the West, left to its own devices, results in a collective brain drain at home. Perhaps the most vexing illustration of this concerns the fleeing of health care professionals.

When limiting the arguments to the extremes of each side of the debate, we can deduce that they are both right. Thus, if "all" of the talent were to flee, then those who remain would become significantly poorer than otherwise. Alternatively, if "all" of the talent were to remain in place, the population on the whole would generate more wealth than if "all" the talent were to flee. We can never know the answer empirically as "all" the talent will never stay in a homeland country, just as "all" the talent that wants to emigrate will never do so. The political and economic environment will affect both the quantity and quality of talent that flees as well as the overall outcome of the fleeing. Among the second-tier questions to answer include: What are the prospects of those who emigrate subsequently investing some of their capital built up in the West back home? And how productive will that capital be? So the fundamental question of whether emigrant talent generates an overall drain on a gain does not have a singular, automatic answer, for it is always contingent on a number of factors. This emerging area of study needs much more and better research to flesh out the contingent factors, their interrelations, and their impacts.

It is true that a critical mass of talent is necessary to trigger productivity gains and economic transformation, but a certain quality and quantity of talent is needed as is a certain type of enabling environment. Is it really possible to trigger the economic transformation poor nations are after with the quality of a critical mass of talent that has never engaged the highest foundational and cutting-edge science and technology (S&T) and industrial production centers? Knowledge, genius, and talent are socially produced, and that social production can be created today transnationally, not just nationally. These social products are stored up, built upon, transmitted to future generations and diffused to different societies, where the process recreates itself ad infinitum throughout time and space. The whole point of brain-circulating talent out of countries in the global South is for nationals to venture out and obtain some of this socially produced cutting-edge knowledge, genius, and talent (i.e., human capital); gain high compensation for mobilizing that intellect (i.e., economic capital); penetrate social and business networks to sustain further access (i.e., social capital); then bring some of this complex of capital back to their homeland via different modalities. Despite both the hype and the hope of the Internet, it is no substitute for some talented youth from a pre-high-tech Southern society studying and working in frontier economies. The point is that the Internet as a tool for learning and a platform for economic production is necessary, but not sufficient for poor nations seeking to close the technology gap. It turns out that migration of talent to frontier technology centers in sufficient numbers and strategic collaboration with the homeland are also necessary.

Throughout the industrial age, human talent has increasingly moved around the world to gain the most productive and gainful employment. And with this new, more intense wave of globalization, where the commercial elite in the West influence immigration procedures in order to have the quantity and quality of talent they seek (Wong 2006), the emigration of African talent to the West will only increase; to wit, US immigrants from Africa doubled in the 1990s, and more than 1.7 million Americans now report Sub-Saharan Africa as a place of birth.

Social scientists throughout the world have debated and government officials in the global South have explored various methods of curbing the socially debilitating aspects of fleeing talent from poor countries. Ideas have ranged from the so-called Bhagwati (1977) tax—the idea was for rich nations to tax the immigrant laborers from the South not only for their own public coffers, but also to collect funds to be sent to the immigrants' respective homelands—to restrictive and even draconian measures. Some analysts have even called for the emergence of an international regime to control the flow of individuals from the South to the West, and what the later must do on behalf of the former.

Though none of these proposed measures will ever come to pass, Bhagwati's compensatory policy idea at the time was at least an acknowledgment that talent from the South would continue migrating to the West, and that the prudent course to take was to use tax and subsidy tools to potentially transform this negative into a positive. The brain-circulation thesis, like the Bhagwati tax, rests on the same principle of the universal inevitability of fleeing talent for greener pastures. What makes brain circulation capable of moving from a mere thesis to a course of development practice is that it does not require any action by Western states.[1] Thus, without the West's acquiescence on imposing such a tax on immigrant labor and disbursing those funds to Southern homelands, there simply would be no tax and therefore no structured gain for the emigrant-sending nation through "compulsory remittances"—which is where we are today. With brain circulation, however, the power resides not with Western states, but with the transnational societies, which com-

[1] It is true that the South depends on Western nations opening their borders to their talented would-be emigrés. But this dependence is equally matched by the dependency of Western corporations on talent from the South. Silicon Valley as we have known it could never have been without talent from the South.

prise governmental, commercial, and civil society leaders in the South and their diasporas in Western nations. They have the capacity to work together for mutual success. Homelands can help their nationals be successful in the West by—among countless ways—subsidizing capital investments for their nationals in Western countries, and creating enabling environments back home so that talented individuals who hail from the South would be more inclined to invest some of their economic, human, and social capital back into their respective homelands, thereby increasing the odds of it collectively helping to transform the broader economy.

Again, the brain-circulation thesis is premised on both what we know—human migration in pursuit of greater opportunities abroad is an eternal human phenomenon—and on what we can easily project—human migration of talent will increase with today's new wave of globalization. The prospect of this thesis being supported rests fully with the transnational peoples in Southern homelands and their diasporas in the West. It is not a matter of attempting to get the West to provide more, say, foreign aid; rather it is a strategy to allow Southerners to be in control.

"Brain circulation" is distinguishable from the "brain gain," as the latter was conceived during the debate from years past. For starters, brain gain was viewed as an automatic overall outcome for poor nations when talented individuals emigrated to rich nations. The brain-circulation thesis, unlike that of brain gain, emphasizes the contingent nature of the process. Emigrant talent from the South to the West can be either an overall brain drain or a brain gain, for it is totally dependent on the extent to which the complex of human, economic, and social capital of the new immigrants from the South is accumulated, the extent to which it is courted by leaders in the homeland in a strategically coordinated manner, and the extent to which there exists an enabling economic and political environment in the homeland for the capital to be put to productive use. There have been some ad hoc automatic brain-gain aspects in the African context (e.g., the repatriation of Nkrumah, Nyerere, eminent scientists such as Dr. Chetsanga of Zimbabwe, and thousands of less well-knowns), but no overall brain circulation to date. Even some authors in this volume construe brain circulation as automatic brain gain. Brain circulation has yet to take place among African transnationals as it has among some East and South Asians. Only ad hoc brain gain has occurred to date as opposed to systematic brain circulation in Africa because of the absence of systematic, institutionalized coordination between homeland states and other organizations with diasporas in rich countries. As a literature develops on the contingent nature of brain circulation, its possibility of huge gains for African transformation and best practices and comparative case studies are documented, and policies and institutions among African transnationals in the homeland and in diasporas in the West established, then, finally, African brain circulation can be triggered.

Perhaps the most vexing challenge to overcome with respect to brain circulation is in the context of health care professionals. Africa has a quarter of the world's disease burden but less than 2% of the world's health care professionals. As the relative small number of health care professionals flee, what happens to the remaining population? Is it possible for fleeing African health care professionals to accumulate the complex of capital and invest it back home fast enough and in sufficient quantity and quality to contribute to the health aspects of life in their homeland more so than if they had stayed? In 2002, more than half of the new registered nurses in the UK were from foreign countries, five of the top ten source countries were Sub-Saharan African: South Africa, Nigeria, Zimbabwe, Ghana, and Kenya (UN Population Fund 2005). In 2003/2004, South Africa lost nearly 1,700 nurses to the UK alone (Mensah, Mackintosh, and Henry 2005). Although these middle-class health professionals send remittances to kith and kin, "It is pointless for an African household to receive remittances to pay for...health care costs when there are no...[physicians] and nurses" (UNECA 2006:13). Are health care professionals the only exception to the brain circulation model? If they are not an exception, what are the special provisions necessary for Africans to make up for the loss, beyond spending $4 billion a year for over 100,000 professionals (including health care), primarily from the West, but increasingly from China also, as Getahun reports in this volume?

Another distinction between the contingent nature of brain circulation as I describe it and the notion of automatic brain gain from emigrating talent from the global South to West as most see it centers on the question of what constitute the "gain" in brain gain when it does occur. For me, potential gains for the homeland from brain circulation are threefold: political, technological, and financial. The gains are explained in the following passage:

> The first measure of strategic diaspora-homeland collaboration is the level of influence the diasporic community has with the host state on behalf of the homeland. Leaders of some diasporic communities work collaboratively with the homeland state in attempts to affect the host state's domestic public policy (e.g., immigration) and its foreign public policy (e.g., foreign aid) in a manner perceived to be advantageous to the homeland. Another measure of this strategic collaboration is technology transfer. The type of technology transfer here involves diasporic technologists in rich, technologically-advanced countries investing in technology enterprises, contributing to research and development, and teaching science and engineering courses in universities, all in the homeland. Some homeland states work

> strategically with their technologically-talented nationals in rich countries to facilitate this technology transfer while other states do not. The final strategic collaboration measures is financial contribution. Aggregate financial contributions can be of two types, namely, remittances and [commercial] investment. Remittances are financial contributions from workers in foreign countries to relatives and friends; such funds are mostly always from rich to poor countries. Seventy percent of the world's $216 billion official international remittances in 2004 were from rich to poor countries.... Investments by diasporans into their homelands can be critical. Such investments help to accelerate growth and upgrade the homeland economy. (Patterson 2006:1896)

Most scholars, on the other hand, including some in this volume, who are sympathetic to the notion of an African brain gain accruing from Africa-to-West migration of talent attempt to account for the gains almost exclusively through remittances. As I indicate above, remittances are only one of many ways in which brain circulation can actually become an overall gain for African nations.[2]

While the eight chapters in this volume are concerned with the African diaspora, the migration of talent from the continent to the West, and diverse investments by the diasporans back into Africa, the foci of the chapters are quite diverse. Three of the chapters analyze issues associated with long-term African diasporas in the United States and Colombia; two chapters pick up the intellectual cudgels to debate whether the emigration of African talent is a collective burden or a benefit. The authors of one chapter did yeoman's work in pointing out our desperate need for more effective methodologies, including better conceptual and operational definitions of "brain drain." Another chapter, starting with the view that migrant talent to rich societies can be a decided benefit at home under the right conditions, attempts to apply brain circulation to the promotion of eco-industrial growth in Africa. The final chapter is an exploration of the impact of talent emigrating out of Ethiopia and not only how to stem the negative outcomes, but also how to derive positive gains from the emigration for Ethiopia. While the focus of each chapter is quite different, what the papers collectively share is a sense of the grappling among scholars as to how to make African transnational communities, stretching around the world, work for the benefit of Africa's development on the continent, primarily, but also in the diaspora. The chapters underscore different challenges, different potential benefits, and different strategies for minimizing the former and maximizing the latter.

---

[2] It is recognized that remittances can exacerbate preexisting problems, not the least of which is inequality. The literature regarding the impacts of remittances—both when left to its own devices as well as in the context of policy interventions—is accumulating.

In the first chapter, Hewitt makes two contributions to the literature. First, she provides initial statistical evidence supporting the brain-circulation thesis. Regression analysis of data on the size of diasporic populations in the United States and the level of foreign direct investment into their respective homelands, covering some 231 developing areas around the world, demonstrates an overall positive relationship: the larger the disapora, the larger the FDI in the homeland. Second, she argues that the brain-circulation model could possibly assist in bringing about the goals of pan-Africanism—21st century-style—which has been historically seen as cultural unity, decolonization, political unification, and economic integration. Utilizing combined perspectives of Nkrumahism, world-systems theory, and the perspective of the African sociologist, Cheikh Anta Diop, concerning the cultural unity of black Africa, Hewitt develops a framework for modeling the best practices of any pan-ethnic or transnational community for promoting development in semiperiphery and periphery countries.

Chapter two, by Sikod and Tchouassi, continues the theme established by Hewitt that the migration of talent from Africa to the West generates positive results on balance. Their chapter is one of the clearest arguments to date on why the emigration of African talent should not be scorned but supported. In addition to the clear conceptual argument, their focus is on eight francophone African nations. Focusing on the francophone nations is particularly a much-needed contribution, given that only a relative fraction of the brain-drain/brain-gain and brain-circulation literatures examine the situation for those nations. After all, far more nations in Africa are officially English-speaking than French-speaking, which results in far less scholarship on the francophone nations. Better than perhaps any other, these two authors provide the analytical foundation of the new brain-gain thesis as well as analysis concerning francophone African nations.

Akakpari's thesis in chapter 3 counters the ascendancy of the brain-gain scholastic tide. To his great credit, Akakpari laments the decline of a subject of crucial importance into polemics, each side cleverly constructing arguments in a manner that simply shows scholars talking past one another as opposed to engaging one another to get at the actual impacts of African emigration within countries and on the continent as a whole. As for his position on the subject, Akakpari provides a clear and ferocious argument as to why the emigration of African talent to the West has always been and still amounts to a costly brain drain for a continent that can ill afford such loss. He provides a litany of statistics to convey the gravity of the problems in Africa. Such an approach is not merely to suggest that as many well-developed minds as possible are needed to tackle the legion of weighty problems on the continent, but he also attempts to directly connect those problems to the emigration of talent from the continent. For instance, he points out that the International Organization for Migration (IOM) estimated in previous studies that at least 60% of doctors trained in Ghana during the 1980s have left the country. The emigration of such talent causes African countries, he notes, to spend approximately $4 billion to employ about 100,000 non-African expatriates. But, because Akakpari is interested in dealing with the issue honestly so that effective policies can be formulated to solve the problems at hand, he also acknowledges the issue of possible brain waste if all of the talent is unable to be absorbed productively into the mainstream economy. To take just one vexing example, there are many thousands of Ghanaian academics in the United States and Canada, if all of them were to attempt to return home and ply their trade of imparting higher education knowledge, the university system could not accommodate them all. Hard-headed analysis, not polemics, is needed to solve such vexing issues.

Chapter 4, by Dodoo, Takyi, and Mann, represents the type of insightful reflection for which Akakpari is calling. Contributions to the literature in this chapter are what we need to get not only more but far better data with which we can confidently work. Most scholars on the subject rely on international data from institutions such as IOM and the World Bank. These institutions provide important statistics, such as 20,000 skilled Africans leave every year for jobs in the West, while Africans spend $4 billion a year on recruiting Western expertise. But, just who are the skilled and talented emigrés from Africa? What are the criteria for consistent use in order for us to know if the 20,000 figure is correct, too low, or too high? Dodoo, Takyi, and Mann point to some of the operationalization of brain-drain variables and other methodological shortcomings of the important World Bank volume on the subject, entitled *International Migration, Remittances, and the Brain Drain*, edited by Schiff and Ozden (2005). Such a careful, dispassionate analysis by these three coauthors allows for a persuasive argument that the methodological approach used by the Bank most likely overestimates the true magnitude of the brain drain.

In chapter 5, Humphries focuses our attention directly on efforts by the US-based African diaspora and others who work on behalf of the Africa. The idea, in part, is to help raise Africa's visibility and also provide a more accurate framing among the US public and policy-makers. She suggests that, left to its own devices, the US government will see its national interests in Africa through the narrow prism of resources extraction and in geostrategic terms. The belief is that the prism can be broadened with more voices. At the heart of her study is the question: To what extent were members of arguably one of the most influential civil society advocacy groups for Africa—namely, the National Summit on Africa, which was organized to broaden that prism for the US government on behalf of Africa—capitalizing on the available democratizing tools of ICT? Using statistical analysis of primary survey data, Humphries examined the extent to which ICT was assisting political and grassroots organizing efforts to access and influence the foreign policy arena, specifically US policy toward Africa. Whereas works by Akakpari; Sikod and Tchouassi; and Dodoo, Takyi, and Mann are more concerned with the African diaspora in rich societies contributing to Africa in terms of remittances almost exclusively, Humphries's views of such contributions are more so in terms of the diaspora affecting US policy in a manner that generates more favorable outcomes for Africa. Ironically, as Humphries learns from her original research, the largest section of Africa's diasporic group in America is the one least disposed to utilizing ICT to communicate with fellow organizers and policy-makers in their work on behalf of Africa. Hence, the US digital divide is adversely affecting the prospect for better policy toward Africa in ways largely unexplored prior to Humphries's contribution.

Whereas Humphries examines an important aspect of the US-based African diaspora, Moreno-Zapata in chapter 6 examines a different aspect about another large African diaspora in the Americas, namely, Colombia. Moreno-Zapata brings to our attention the necessity of integrating the literatures of African diasporic studies and ecological development studies. Curiously, she notes, African Colombians get relatively little scholarly attention despite their being the largest African descendant population in Latin America, after Brazil, and their possession of land rights to 5,000,000 hectors of one of the world's richest biodiversity hotspots. Paradoxically, notwithstanding this potential source of ecologically induced economic wealth, not to mention actual source of their sustenance for previous centuries, 80% of African Colombians live in extreme poverty, have shockingly high levels of malnutrition, and have the nation's lowest coverage of public services. African Colombians are very similar to their counterparts back on the African continent, as they both live in areas endowed with economically valuable and life-sustaining natural materials but presently possess inadequate scientific and technological knowledge and skills to add value to those resources by producing products for sale in domestic and world markets. After analyzing key historical and contemporary facts of the case, Moreno-Zapata provides some suggestions on how African Colombians may move forward in their endeavors to take advantage of their mega-biological-diversity.

Like Moreno-Zapata in chapter 6, I also examine, in my chapter, the ecological basis for economic advancement, but I focus on the African continent rather than on an African diasporic community. That said, the thesis of my chapter is certainly applicable to African Colombians. What I focus on is the fact that industrialization to date generates unsustainable ecological destruction, and yet it only provides a high standard of living and comfortable existence for a mere 15% of the world's population. The global industrial edifice pioneered by the West is not accommodating for a future of industrial production for Sub-Saharan Africa. China's intrepid economic ascendancy of nearly 10% a year for some 25 years, to say nothing of India's steady, consequential economic advancement, has caused prices of dwindling commodities to rise sharply as well as severely impacted the environment. Because of Africa's ecological comparative advantage and because Africans have gone down the destructive form of industrialization the least, it is possible for Africans to consider being among the pioneers and early adopters of a new ecological industrial economy. The gap between Sub-Saharan Africans and the established and emerging economic powers is significantly smaller with regard to eco-industry than to the physical smokestack (e.g., steel and automobiles) and digital (ICT hardware and software) industries. To do this, I argue, Africans can start early by sending large numbers of their talented youth to the United States and Western Europe for advanced education and employment at universities, R&D institutes, and corporations related to ecological engineering, industrial ecology, ethnobotany, materials engineering, biology and related fields. In order to increase the likelihood that this will be a systematic brain circulation experience rather than a one-way brain drain, or just some ad hoc brain-gain experiences, leaders of African states, the private sector, and civil society institutions would have to structure strategic relationships with leaders of their diasporas so that the diasporas would be inclined to, not just send remittances, but to also invest some of their human, economic, and social capital back home to help pioneer the new eco-industrial economy in African countries.

The future is an appropriate and legitimate subject matter for both sociology and history. As Wagar (1999:xiv) states in *A Short History of the Future*: "the assumption of future studies is that responsible efforts to see what lies ahead give *Homo sapiens* more control over its destiny than if the attempts were never made.... Awareness of these possibilities improves the chance that public planning, policy-making, and personal decision will bring the real future into congruence with the desired future, whatever that might be."

In the final chapter, Getahun, before analyzing elements of brain gain development underway in Ethiopia, discusses what can only be characterized as a brain drain with respect to the emigration of talent from the country. On the UNDP's human development index scale, Ethiopia is the eighth poorest country in the world, yet it is providing the Western world with highly educated professionals. In 2003, life expectancy was 47.8 years and adult illiteracy rate was 58.5%, and in 2002 public expenditure on health was only 2.6% of the GDP, yielding a population per physician ratio of over 33,000. It was recently reported that there were more Ethiopian trained physicians practicing in Chicago than in all of Ethiopia. And what we find with professionals in the health care sector is being replicated among academics and military officers. An important point conveyed by Getahun is that the emigration of talent from Ethiopia is not necessarily synonymous with a brain drain. If there is high level, coordinated investment of some of the human, economic, and social capital of diasporans in rich countries back into Ethiopia, the chances of a brain drain occurring are reduced. The greater the coordination and the quantity of the investment back, the lower the prospect of a brain drain. Getahun points to new contributions back home by such diasporic groups as the Association for Higher Education and Development (AHEAD) and Ethiopian North American Health Professional Association (ENAHPA) as new Ethiopian transnartional civil society groups working to bring some ad hoc brain gain into existence. But thus far, according to Getahun, the government is not only failing to work strategically on behalf of brain circulation, it is working chiefly to restrict the emigration of talent from Ethiopia.

Though groups such as AHEAD and ENAHPA are making some brain-gain contributions, those contributions do not amount to brain circulation. Brain circulation requires strategic collaborative activity by the homeland state and other institutions working in partnership with the diasporic community to systematically improve the quality of life in the homeland and elevate its economy within the global economy, activities expressly not occurring in the Ethiopian case.

As a concluding note, it is worth reiterating that a few nations over the past few decades—via brain circulation in large part—have moved themselves out of a sea of poverty, improved the quality of life for citizens, transformed the domestic economy, and elevated their respective economy within the global economy. These nations, such as South Korea, China, Taiwan, and India, have had far more citizens to emigrate to the West than Sub-Saharan African nations, yet only the latter has suffered an overall brain drain. The problem is not that talent leaves; rather the problem is that the complex of capital that they generate abroad does not get systematically invested into their respective homelands. African governments have used the carrot and stick approach when it comes to emigration, though with precious little to show for it. They use restrictive measures to deter emigration and they occasionally use incentives to attract back to the homeland those who do emigrate. Another approach, following what has worked with brain circulation, is for those governments to redouble their efforts not to seek repatriation *en mass*, something that is not going to happen anyway and would cause a wave of new problems even if it did, rather governments should seek to have those diasporas to invest back home.

The African Union (AU) and New Partnership for Africa's Development (NEPAD) are two institutions capable of fostering brain circulation on the continent. AU encourages active participation of the diaspora because members have an indispensable role to play in building a true African Union. As for NEPAD, which sees itself as helping to "bridge the gap between Africa and the developed world," it contends that diasporans must constitute a substantial share of the bridge builders. Rhetorically, the AU and NEPAD are on point, but practically, many contend, they need to show more leadership and follow through in this area. Brain circulation is quintessentially an opportunity for the AU and NEPAD to develop since all African nations would stand to benefit from a development strategy that, as a few other nations have demonstrated, gives them more control over their progress.

This book on African brain circulation should be viewed as an early forerunner of a new literature that will surely grow in size and sophistication.

REFERENCES

Bhagwati, J.N. 1977. *The Reverse Transfer of Technology (Brain Drain): International Resource Flow Accounting, Compensation, Taxation and Related Policy Proposals.* New York: United Nations Conference on Trade and Development.

Florida, Richard. 2005. *The Flight of the Creative Class: The New Global Competition for Talent.* New York: HarperBusiness.

Kuznetsov, Yevgeny, Ed. 2006. *Diaspora Networks and the International Migration of Skills: How Countries Can Draw on Their Talent Abroad.* Washington, DC: World Bank.

Mensah, K., M. Mackintosh, and L. Henry. 2005. *The Skills Drain of Health Professionals From the Developing World: A Framework for Policy Formulaation.* London: Medact.

Patterson, Rubin. 2006. "US Diasporas and Their Contributions to Homeland Development in the Global South: A Study of Transnationalism." *Social Forces* 86:1891-1908.

Schiff, Maurice and Caglar Ozden, Eds. 2005. *International Migration, Remittances and the Brain Drain.* Washington, DC: World Bank. United Nations Economic Commission for Africa. 2006. *International Migration and The Achievement of MDGs in Africa.* Addis Ababa, Ethiopia: UNECA.

United Nations Population Fund. 2005. *International Migration and the Millennium Development Goals*. New York: UNFPA.
Wagar, W. Warren. 1999. *A Short History of the Future*. Chicago: University of Chicago Press.
Wong, Carolyn. 2006. *Lobbying for Inclusion: Rights Politics and the Making of Immigration Policy*. Sanford, CA: Stanford University Press.

1. Pan-African Brain Circulation

*Cynthia Lucas Hewitt**

ABSTRACT

This paper presents a quantitative analysis of the relationship between the number of immigrants from a country and the amount of U.S. direct investment into that country, showing a direct relationship supportive of the emerging brain-circulation model, and discusses the possible use of this model to assist in bringing about the goals of Pan-Africanism. The principles underlying Pan-Africanism are considered in respect to the outcomes of the movement, given the recent political economy of capitalism. Brain circulation provides one focused approach to designing policies and projects for sustainable development in Africa that will impact the lives of Africans there and globally. The transnationalism paradigm, which provides analysis of immigrant communities' identification and allegiance both with their homeland and their U.S. communities, is useful in highlighting factors important to the global Pan-African networking that is required for a successful African/African American brain circulation.

INTRODUCTION

This article provides statistical evidence supporting the brain-circulation thesis, and suggests ways in which the transnational movement of Pan-Africanism can adopt effective brain-circulation strategies for African socioeconomic development. It also reviews the historical background of Pan-Africanism and presents an analysis of the socioeconomic structures that present challenges to successful development. Brain circulation is a newly developing sociological framework for modeling the best practices of transnational communities promoting development in semiperiphery and periphery countries. This study investigates the processes whereby migration of substantial numbers of migrants from a developing country

* Morehouse College, Department of Sociology, Atlanta, Georgia.
Email: chewitt@morehouse.edu.

is associated with development of a significant flow of capital—financial, organizational, and human—back into the country. While the concept of brain drain associates out-migration with the dead end of lost human capital, the concept of brain circulation suggests that the outward flow is not without a return flow, and that the larger the outward flow the larger the potential inward flow, if the methods of promoting circulation are understood and employed. Out-migration is not conceived as a one-way street but rather as part of a current, which has been seen to return and build upon itself when the conditions along the way are propitious.

Pan-Africanism is a nationalist movement of African heritage people in the African Diaspora and in Africa, which has been growing since the mid-1800s, based on an understanding of the pivotal importance of the liberation and political unification of Africa to create an economically strong homeland for African people. A liberated and unified Africa would be the base for political empowerment globally to impact the cultural, social, and political freedom of African people everywhere. Contemporary social scientists attest to the importance of this conception (Henry 1999). The movement has been through many permutations and can count the political liberation of all the African continent's lands, culminating with South Africa in 1994, as the fulfillment of one of its initial goals. However, the end goal of African unification for socio-economic prosperity for African people has remained elusive. Today, in the twilight of the hydrocarbon-fueled industrial revolution, the fundamental challenge of our era is resource distribution, or more to the point, redistribution. Development must take a different direction. Perhaps the continent of Africa, which has gone the least down the path of industrial development, will fare better in the new ecological economy that is most likely to emerge.

The theoretical background for this paper is Nkrumaism, the set of principles elaborated by Kwame Nkrumah. I also employ world-systems theory, established by Immanuel Wallerstein (1974), and incorporate the pioneering critical work of Andre Gunder Frank (1979), whose theorization of dependency in many ways laid the groundwork; and the work of Cheikh Anta Diop (1978, 1991), premiere African sociologist and theorist of the cultural unity of black Africa. First, I review the Pan-African approach to nation building and situate its strategies within the larger analytical framework of world-systems theory, after which I discuss the findings from the vibrant contemporary transnantionalism paradigm and their relevance to analysis of Pan-African economic development. I then present a quantitative test of the basic thesis of brain circulation. Discussion centers on the implications of brain-circulation research for Pan-African development goals, given the environmental and resource situation that we are entering.

PAN-AFRICANISM AND WORLD-SYSTEMS THEORY

In response to European enslavement and dispersal of millions of people from Africa and subsequent colonization and balkanization of Africa—Africans in the diaspora the Caribbean and the United States—began to articulate the overarching need to liberate the continent of Africa from colonialism and unite the continent in an effective size nation, reuniting all the peoples to overcome their histories of dispersion. Pan-Africanism relies both on an imagined community and the material self-interest of African people worldwide. In terms of the latter aspect, it is a response to what is known as the "Maafa," or the holocaust on Africa, whereby over 15 million of its people where taken as laborers over a 350-year period and scattered worldwide.[1] Pan-Africanism reflects retention of this history in the consciousness of descendants, who constitute "lost" people with a quest to be "found."

Strategically, Pan-Africanists have sought to (1) enhance the cultural interaction among African people, (2) support and demand the decolonalization of Africa politically, (3) bring about the political unification and development of a centralized, militarily defensible nation-state, and (4) increase economic integration. All these aspects were taken to their greatest development by the Universal Negro Improvement Association (U.N.I.A.), led by Marcus Garvey, which came to have approximately 6 million members in over 900 chapters in 41 different nations at its height in the early 1920s (Garvey 1970; Martin 1976). The Garveyites were characterized by their slogan: "Africa for the Africans." As Garvey explains: "We are determined to solve our own problem, by redeeming our Motherland Africa from the hands of alien exploiters and found there a government, a nation of our own, strong enough to lend protection to the members of our race scattered all over the world, and to compel the respect of the nations and races of the earth" (1980: 52). The conceptual framework, including the term Pan-Africanism, was articulated during the five Pan-African Congresses held in Europe, 1919

[1] Estimates of the numbers of people who where impacted by the *Maafa* vary, and include figures for the number who died in route and the number who were transported alive to the Americas. Generally, the number of persons lost is considered to be one to two hundred percent of those who survived.

through 1945, led by W.E.B. DuBois, from the United States; and Kwame Nkrumah, from Ghana.[2] To some extent, the theoretical and political high point of the movement was established through the leadership of Dr. Kwame Nkrumah, who, in 1957, became President of newly independent Ghana, the first black African nation to be liberated from colonialism. Nkrumah led the African unification movement, leading to the formation of the Organization of African Unity (OAU) in 1963. From the earliest support in the African-American community for the defense of Ethiopia from Italian incursion and the outcry against the practices of the European countries in the Congo "Free State," to the concerted boycott of South Africa, an active decolonization movement has existed, leading to successful implementation of the second principle of Pan-Africanism: the liberation of Africa from colonialism.

The third goal of the Pan-African project has been the total unification of Africa. Without this, in the prophetic words of the great sociologist, Cheikh Anta Diop, written in 1960, Africa will "be made up of a proliferation of little dictator-ridden countries without organic ties one to another, ephemeral, afflicted with chronic weakness, governed by terror with the help of outsized police forces, but under the economic domination by foreign countries, pulling strings through the mere presence of an embassy" (1978: 15). Pan-Africanists argue that the colonially administered territories in Africa were broken up into small, independent countries that served to prevent them from having the critical mass of population to effectively develop a skilled class, amass capital, industrialize, and become strong states capable of self-defense and self-determination. This is consistent with world-systems theory analytical frameworks for explaining how nation-state development led to the emergence of industrialized or core countries, and periphery underdeveloped countries. Small nations that have been successful have relied upon their commercial and maritime superiority to carve out a sufficient market share to amass surplus value and industrialize. Those countries that industrialized participated in production of cheap goods under competitive conditions, and scarce goods, such as capital goods (e.g., machinery), that could be sold according to their dictates in a "seller's market, under semi-monopoly conditions for high profits. Countries that did not enter into the profitability of mass production, either through large secure internal markets (countries with large populations) or international commercial domination, generally failed to achieve self-determination and

[2] The first conference on Pan-Africanism was actually held in 1901, where the term was coined by Henry Sylvester-Williams (from Trinidad).

were incorporated into the capitalist system as periphery countries—areas colonized for exploitation of resources to fulfill the core countries' market needs.

The modern European world-system, which began its rise to hegemony in the 1550s, is unique because its continued success is based on the use of state power to dominate markets, creating economic conditions of dependency, and in this manner economically incorporating various regions of the world rather than relying on permanent political administration in the manner of previous empires. Economic dependence includes both the dependence of the post-colonial state (governing elite, bureaucracy, and military) on "aid," and the dependence of the private commercial elite on employment in and sales of raw materials to large multinational conglomerates whose remuneration for management makes possible world-class lifestyles. The combination of nations with relatively small populations and leadership that is "turned outward" and lacks indigenous self-integrity dooms Africa currently to impoverishment. For, even if the production activities of a country are barely productive of surplus, if the laboring population is large enough, and the elite has cultural integrity, this surplus can be centralized through private processes of expropriation (capitalist-led) or by the state—dictatorially or democratically—but with the similar economic result of amassing capital to finance development of infrastructure and key industries, such as steel, communications, and transportation, that are critical to the development of a productive base.

Countries that are too small, even with good leadership, generally cannot carry out this process internally, effectively, or independently. One alternative is that they may serve as an entrepot to a larger market for raw materials and industrial goods sales, as in the manner of Singapore to Malaysia or Hong Kong to China. In Africa today, South Africa seems to desire to serve that function; however, its remote location, lack of strategic placement vis-à-vis other political goals of the core powers (unlike the Asian countries which were well situated to carry out economic transactions for the American needs in the Korean and Vietnam wars, and the Cold War, etc.), and other unfavorable factors seem to make this path tenuous (Patterson 1997). Hence principle three of Pan-Africanism is the need for the unification of Africa.

The fourth principle of Pan-Africanism as a theoretical perspective is the "mass line" or recognition of the issue of class struggle. Commonly, Pan-Africanists focus on the overall outcomes for whole communities, which is consistent with the African ontological stance that the individual does not exist outside of community: the primacy of the collective over the individual. However, the nature of these communities with regard to class divisions is highly debated, basically with the Afrocentric wing being most critical of the class struggle paradigm, and the Nkrumaist school being most adamant about its relevance. Kwame Nkrumah firmly enshrined the importance of improving the conditions of the working people—workers and peasants—as a goal of Pan-Africanism at the Fifth Pan-African Congress in Manchester, England, 1945. While only a few Pan-Africanists, such as Walter Rodney (1982), begin their class analysis with pre-colonial Africa, many more view serious class divisions as an outcome of exploitative social relations, primarily developing during the slave trade and colonialism. During colonialism, one method of rule was to manipulate ruling elites through treaties, debt peonage, appointing and firing chiefs, and through other manipulative means to create puppet or comprador "traditional" elites. As Mahmood Mamdani (1996) so aptly illustrates, much of what we may consider African tradition is of recent origin in the distorting repression and manipulation carried out to secure indirect rule during colonialism. Further, exploitative forces that were previously present in Africa, such as connection to the spread of commercialism and labor exploitation under Islam, were acerbated by imperialism. The practices of favoring particular ethnic groups and co-opting of them into ruling positions in the colonial administration further hardened class structures inherited at the time of independence. Breaking these administrative ties and status structures proved impossible for many societies that entered firmly into the grip of neocolonialism.

The state administrators and the business elite, along with the colonial-created traditional elite, who rely objectively on allegiance to the core imperialist nation-states for their status and survival, constitute the comprador bourgeoisie, the basis of neocolonialism as elaborated by Kwame Nkrumah in 1966 (Nkrumah 1966; 1970). Their interests came to lie in the continued exploitation of the resources and people of their countries, rather than with the people in their quest to retain profits and redistribute social surplus for use in education and health care for all. The particular circumstances of African countries, whereby their nationals lost ownership over their lands and mineral resources, meant that they did not amass capital, as under capitalism the profit goes primarily to the owners (investors). Africans in Sub-Saharan Africa became unable to transform their societies, and instead, the leadership classes tend to take the lead in repressing the people and making sure these conditions that are conducive to Western exploitation of African resources continue. It is for this reason that Pan-Africanists have tended to recognize the conditions for a bitter class struggle to exist.

This issue of class is particularly complicated when the global scope of Pan-Africanism is considered, but the situation is much the same.

Historically, there emerged an axial division of the world into white and black, which replaced Christian and non-Christian, and a whole system of racial formations and ethnic hierarchies, regulated by different states so that status groups were ultimately defined. Different methods of labor control corresponding to different levels of responsibility for organizing capitalist accumulation processes—variegated methods of labor control—evolved, ranging from physical coercion to incentives based on differential quality of lifestyle. As a result, a large pool of ultra-exploitable labor became definable, and a middle-pool of privileged, supervisory, and conceptual labor was also formed, wedded more or less to the system, while an exclusive ownership elite was maintained (Wallerstein 1974).

Africans in America fought for political rights and an end to economic exploitation as a group in an underprivileged social category, and achieved a degree of political freedom at much the same time as Africans in Africa, primarily from about 1957 to 1970. The African/black spearheaded civil rights struggle helped strip racial theories of superiority of their hegemony, and a small portion of Africans (African Americans) entered into this middle-pool of labor, formerly reserved for "whites."[3] The competition to lower labor costs and to eliminate labor altogether through mechanization, enabled by information technology advances, has led to new patterns of globalized production, and new needs for middle-level labor in the United States and other core countries. The struggle to expand markets for these goods has led to the relentless promotion of consumerism, the systematic increase of wants. Workers in relatively privileged positions are the primary consuming classes, and they are disciplined primarily by indebtedness and manipulation/creation of wants; hence, they have a very high standard of material comforts and amenities.

However, very few African Americans have entered into the capitalist ruling class despite shifts in the racial/ethnic division of labor, because the ruling capitalist class is maintained through inheritance organized in the institution of private property and by endogenous (racist) marriage patterns (Hewitt 2002). While a few individual Africans amass considerable wealth stakes, they rarely are incorporated into the transnational capitalist ownership class, the "haute finance," to use Karl Polanyi's term (Polanyi 1957), and therefore remain dominated associates, members of the comprador class, as in Africa. However, a portion of these are actually petty-bourgeois owner/operators within the small business sector and

[3] Today, gross inequality is generally legitimated by pointing to differences in "intelligence" and "educational achievement," social traits that are the *outcomes* of differential access to resources, not really the *causes*, as elaborated by social reproduction theory (MacLeod 1987).

are less tied to the corporate structure and interests, depending upon their markets and clients. While most African people throughout the world occupy positions where hunger/indigence is the method of social control, about 2-5 percent now are primarily controlled through the materialism system of incentives (formerly reserved for Europeans), and a large portion of those are African Americans in the United States. As in Africa, their interests tend to be connected to the interests of the white ruling class rather than the needs of the majority of African/black people. They also lack integrity with respect to the needs of the majority of African/black people, over 90 percent of whom are part of the working class, either its highly exploited or more privileged wings, with a large number in the under-class or surplus-labor category, including those incarcerated.[4]

Essentially, allegiance to this consumerist lifestyle has made identification with impoverished Africa relatively unappealing for skilled African Americans. However, even those African Americans who occupy relatively privileged material positions suffer from the social stigma of inferiority still attached to Africa and Africans; hence a segment of them, as with African elites, have the potential to adhere to an alternative countervailing "imagined community" related to Africa. Africans in the Diaspora are always ambivalent about loyalty to nationalisms that are part of the racist nation-state projects that define them as subordinate, and may pursue other forms of nationalism, including Pan-Africanist transnationalism. One of the clearest expressions of this phenomenon is the lifework and thought of Kwame Ture (Stokely Carmichael), which is reflective of the black power movement ideology (Hewitt 2004). Identification with Africa, like ethnic identities, is fueled by cultural and historical awareness. It is from the bearers of this identification that Pan-African leadership dedicated to strategies of unification has emerged. The promotion of awareness of the cultural unity of African people, including the integration of traditional, Christian, and Islamic ethical traditions and cultural systems, is thus a first principle of Pan-Africanism.

PAN-AFRICANISM AND TRANSNATIONALISM

Transnationalism is a conceptual framework for understanding identity formation when individuals (1) occupy two or more "nationalities" at once, based on a view of the migrant as "transmigrant"; (2) are part of a social system whose networks are based in two or more nation-states;

[4] These proportions may shift if full account of the informal sector of African people making a living "off the books" were counted in the "petty-bourgeois" sector proportion.

and (3) maintain activities, identities, and statuses in several locations (Glick-Schiller et al. 1992: 15). Work in this tradition focuses on providing an adequate framework of understanding transnationalism as an identity-forming phenomenon: "the study of the complex mix of social relations and activities across border that create, shape and potentially transform their identities, statuses and citizenships" (Glick-Schiller et al. 1992: 14). Glick-Schiller et al. also argue that the constant back and forth flow of people, seen initially in the study of Caribbean immigration, could not be captured in the standard categories of migration as either permanent migrants, return migrants, sojourners, or some other. This perspective embodies not only an analysis of the immigrants, but also a reconsideration of the nation-state, both the receiver and sending states, and their bounded identity politics. They define mechanisms of transnationalism, including the role of remittances in maintaining family ties; the importance of home associations; and the development of systems of legalized exchanges, structured and officially sanctioned by the state. In respect to labor contracting, this state involvement is not new, as initial Asian migration to the United States often involved labor recruitment, and was important in the case of Mexico as well. It may be more a question of new tailoring of facilitation to take advantage of new opportunities, such as with the H-1B visa program.[5] Transnationalism research shines a light on the global mobile labor force, a central aspect of life for Africans within the world-system.

Finally, understanding transnationalism involves investigating the ideological work that such border spanning identity structures entail. Particularly relevant is their questioning of "how transmigrants use their social relationships and their varying and multiple identities generated from their simultaneous positioning in several social locations both to accommodate to and resist the difficult circumstances and the dominant ideologies they encounter in their transnational fields" (Glick-Schiller et al. 1992: 216). Issues of class, social status, and consumerism are also discussed. Glick-Schiller and colleagues argue that dominant classes at home and abroad construct hegemonic conceptualizations for control much like nation-state construction and suggest that "we must ask whether transmigrants will continue to participate in nationalist constructions that contribute to the hegemony of the dominant classes in each nation state as they live lives that span national borders" (p. 223).

---

[5] These visas are based on the need to fill gaps in the U.S. workforce in particular skill areas.

As an ideological conception, Pan-Africanism may be viewed as one of the earliest articulations of a transnationalism strategy. Most of the premier leadership was made up of transnationals for a significant portion of their active movement careers, including Marcus Garvey (from Jamaica), Nkrumah (to the U.S. and back to Ghana); and Kwame Ture (Stokely Carmichael, from Trinidad). To some extent, Pan-Africanism represents a transnational solution to the problems faced by Africans. The thought of Kwame Ture is a good example. Ture is very explicit about the importance of taking a critical stance vis-à-vis the "American" identity group project of nationalism. He stresses that European colonialists redefined themselves as "Americans" to create an implicitly autochthonous myth of origin. This national identity formation is both racist and exclusionary, of both Native Americans and Africans. Ture calls for African heritage people in the Americas to take a critical distance from this project, reconstruct an identity as African, and to eschew "American" nation-state identification and its relegation of them to a low position in the social stratification system. By developing their identity as African, they open new options for access to resources and possibilities of autonomous development in conjunction with African liberation. The importance of readjusting the historical vision to include the approximately 5,000 years of African-recorded history rather than the 500-year framework expedient for the "American" historical project is a staple project of Pan-Africanism, which is expressed consistently. This corresponds to the emphasis Schiller et al. ascribe to homelands developing a conducive mindset regarding transmigrant communities.

Clearly the normative system of the hegemonic society continues to have a hold on the psychic of the African student/intelligentsia; however, as Nkrumah posited, through positive action—the conscious increasing of messages positive to identification as African—the balance of consciousness of the ruling class initiate may be swung in favor of Africa. Pan-Africanism is thus a form of nationalism where the "nation" is writ large—the continent of Africa and all its scattered people—in comparison to nationalisms of current neocolonial defined states, which are considered micronationalism. As pointed out by transnationalism studies, nationalism has been the primary tool of forming the solidarity necessary for power—in the form of the state. It is propagated primarily through history education and the news media. It is further grounded in entertainment media as popular culture. However, culture can be the graveyard of imperialism as slavery, colonialism, imperialism, and internal colonialism have not been able to transform the indigenous culture of the masses of a people to an extent that they do not respond to the aesthetics and arts of their own members above others; hence, they retain cultural integrity. And as Amilcal Cabral (1973) clarifies, it is in the culture of the oppressed that the reservoir for alternative conceptions continues to simmer and have the potential to periodically blossom into complete oppositional culture. Thus, the elite of African origin, both from enslavement and more recent migrations, has a dualism, as described by W.E.B. DuBois, that cannot be expiated because they cannot be fully assimilated into the ruling class, and that kernel of African identity remains ready to be activated by their relative deprivation.

The African population, therefore, is always potentially rebellious—this was recognized in the work of popular Harvard University and Manhattan Institute social scientists Stephen Thernstrom and Abigail Thernstrom (1997), who lament that despite the social advances and well-being of the black middle-class, they never settle down and accept their position, and in fact, they are the most vocal in pro-black ideological and political stances. Can this kernel of African identity be the basis of a form of transnationalism nurturing the development of brain circulation?

BRAIN CIRCULATION

The brain-circulation perspective was articulated by Rubin Patterson (2005) in response to the tradition of research around the concept of brain drain. Brain circulation, as theorized by Patterson (2005), refers to a set of purposive policies and investments by a developing nation to increase and enhance development of its Diaspora emigrant communities in core countries that maximize their ability to, in turn, channel financial, human, and organizational capital back into their homeland's development. These policies have tended to focus on development within the information technology industry in the past. Today, the focus of the future, I would argue, should be ecologically sustainable development and the related industries of organic and nutraceutical products.

It is well documented that large numbers of skilled people from African countries emigrate from the continent, leaving behind societies further devoid of the technological and organizational know-how to be utilized in development. Many policies have emanated from concerned entities that enforce return home for African students educated abroad. While these policies are well-intended, they may be misguided. Brain circulation as a concept refers to the political and economic strategies successfully utilized by Asian countries primarily and, now, increasingly by others, including Mexico, to amass capital—financial, human, and organizational—through tapping into its circulation streams and processes and redirecting them into ownership within their ascriptive nation-states, their homelands. Brain circulation relies on careful grooming of the transnational migrant community to gain access to the elite rulers' training ground and to select integrity—maintenance of allegiance to homeland identities rather than complete entry into comprador relationships with the core society.

Empirical evidence is emerging in development studies that show that countries registering more rapid growth often have the largest emigrant Diaspora communities in core countries. These diasporas are formed where relatively large numbers of a country's immigrant population reside in a scientifically advanced core country (Patterson 2005). Patterson uses the South Koreans as an example. They sent large numbers of youth to study in the United States; supported their English language acquisition; supported their entry into information technology industry; went so far as establishing banking branches in California to support their business emergence; held annual conferences in Korea to keep them networked into the advancement strategies of their homeland; and ultimately this homeland became the recipient of overseas branches and investment of the firms in which these transnationals, over time, achieved managerial and technical ascendancy. The transnational migrants also started their own firms, and sold services to or became acquisitions of multinationals, carving out niches in the transnational capitalist accumulation process. At one point, Patterson (2005) asserts that up to 30 percent of the start-up firms in the information technology industry in Silicon Valley, California, were owned by Asian nationals. The strategically directed, critical mass of nationals from a particular country can give that country a comparative advantage in competing within that focal industry in the global system. Similar descriptions apply to East Indians and the software industry, or more currently, to Mexico and the garment and pharmaceutical industries.

It has been found that large Diasporas are a positive source of remittances and may be a source of other types of investments (Gordon 1998). Alejandro Portes (1995) has presented the case that increased investment by a core country, such as the United States, in a third world nation to employ its labor force creates a culture transfer in the process that provides the recipient nationals with a useful "cultural bridge" to understanding America, thus allowing them to figure out how to migrate and navigate the American landscape with increasing efficacy. Overseas investment leads to migration. The question here posed is whether the inverse is true: acculturation of large numbers of emigrants from a nation in American (or other core country's) industry provides a cultural bridge for American capital to migrate over to their homeland. Brain-circulation theory posits that this reverse circulation is an important factor in development. If so, the brain-circulation research paradigm—to elucidate the specific political and social mechanisms utilized by newly developing home countries to strengthen the purposeful economic brain-circulation with core countries—could be very useful in practically orienting Pan-African policies for economic redevelopment of Africa.

TESTING BRAIN CIRCULATION

The basic requirements for brain circulation are (1) a large transnational community with focused assistance to help it attain advanced training in a high value-added rising industry; and (2) maintenance of identification with the homeland through instilling knowledge of its history, and through promotion of cultural events and interaction. If we consider only the most broad outline of what is proposed, there should be a relationship between the size of a particular transnational Diaspora and the amount of financial, human and organizational capital invested in the group's homeland. In the estimation of these factors for analysis, the cumulative amount of U.S. Direct Investment Abroad (DIA) to particular countries was used to proxy capital investment. Direct investment abroad is significant because it generally reflects investment in projects where the foreign investor provides the majority of the investment for a business or enterprise, and not just loans. Such investments involve a long-term relationship where capital and talent are often circulated between the enterprise in the developing country and the core country to which it is connected. Data on DIA was obtained from the U.S. Department of Commerce (2005). As a measure of the extensiveness of the transmigrant community, the number of permanent resident visas awarded to the nationals of the developing country over the previous 15-year period was used. Data were available from the Yearbook of Immigration Statistics for 231 national entities.[6] Since transnational processes are relatively recent (theorized significantly circa 1990), this should be a period when the effect of their presence would be visible. However, the precise amount of lag that is to be expected between the build-up of the transnational core community and the redirection of capital resources to the homeland is a matter for investigation. The model for predicting DIA utilized in the analysis reported here is exploratory. In addition to the factor of permanent resident visas granted, measures of important mineral enterprises

[6] During the period some national entities changed configuration, such as the division of the Soviet Union into multiple countries; hence some entities do not maintain "country" status across all the years.

(to control for unusual amounts of DIA), a measure of political instability (war-torn) to control for inhospitable investment conditions, and a measure of the flow of refugees (asylum) to control for migrant flows with precipitous causes, were employed. Utilizing DIA as the dependent variable and permanent resident visas granted as the independent variable, a regression analysis was done with 231 cases.

The measure for number of immigrants was strongly significant ($t < .001$) and remained so over several permutations; the model was significant ($F = .05$ level), though it was not very strongly explanatory ($R^2 = .036$) (see Table 3). Further analysis of the modeling of DIA will be necessary to fully measure the effects of the presence of a sizeable transnational community on DIA. Preliminary quantitative analysis lends support to the brain-circulation thesis.

Results from the regression analysis give support to a direct correlation between migration flows creating immigrant communities in the United States and levels of investment in their home country. However, in order to be directly supportive of the brain-circulation paradigm, the two other factors would need to be measured, particularly the presence of a purposeful set of policies and targeted industries by the sending nations and their transnationals. This data would also help establish the time frame for the lag, the period of build-up of brain-circulation activities before the resulting investment becomes significant. There are also many factors related to the amount of U.S. direct investment in a country, and unspecified factors may account for both immigrant community build-up and DIA. Again, the exact relationship must be studied. The regression analysis performed suggests that U.S. direct investment abroad is related to transnational community development in the United States. Data on the policy and industrial focus of sending nations and their transnational communities would greatly improve our ability to model and test whether and how the brain-circulation model as stipulated is operative.

AFRICAN DIASPORA IMMIGRATION AND BRAIN CIRCULATION

For brain-circulation strategies and policies to be effectively employed, the first prerequisite is that a significant migrant community can be established in a core country. African people from the continent and the Caribbean constitute a relatively small proportion of the immigrants to the United States, but potentially significant overall. In the 15 years, 1989 through 2004, 15.5 million immigrants from 231 nations received permanent resident status in the United States, including 675,665 immigrants from 57 countries listed in the African Region.[7] However, only one African nation, Nigeria, figures among the top 30 sending nations (see Table 1 and Table 2). These African immigrants constituted 4.4 percent of all immigrants. There were 1,554,747 immigrants from 23 Caribbean nations (who are primarily of African heritage), or 10 percent (U.S. Department of Homeland Security 2005). Thus, approximately 14 percent of immigrants would predominantly have African heritage and form the pool of potential Pan-African adherents. In addition, a portion of the individuals, from South and Central America—particularly such nations as Belize and Guyana, and secondarily, Brazil or Columbia—identify with African heritage, and may identify, immediately or over time, with the Pan-African project.

Table 1

African and African Diaspora Countries Among the Top 100 Sending Countries to the United States (Legal Permanent Residency)

Country	Immigration 1989-2004	Immigration 2005
1. Haiti	289,447	14,529
2. Jamaica	281,164	18,346
3. Guyana	127,458	9,318
4. Nigeria	115,048	9,374
5. Trinidad	97,363	6,568
6. Ethiopia	84,580	8,237
7. Egypt	74,480	5,522
8. Ghana	60,180	5,328
9. South Africa	40,106	3,370
10. Morocco	37,859	4,128
11. Somalia	34,694	3,929
12. Kenya	30,477	5,323
13. Liberia	28,860	2,745
14. Sudan	22,873	3,211
15. Sierra Leone	20,729	1,596
16. Belize	18,579	876
17. Barbados	15,702	846
18. Cape Verde	14,720	1,227
19. Grenada	12,062	840

Yearbook of Immigration Statistics

[7] The U.S. immigration data for Africa include immigration recorded from "French Southern and Antarctic Lands," St. Helena, and Western Sahara, entities that are generally not enumerated among the 54 African states.

Table 2

Immigration to the United States: Top Sending Countries (Legal Permanent Residency)

Country	Immigration 1989-2004	Immigration 2005
1. Mexico	4,052,638	175,364
2. Philippines	834,029	57,827
3. India	707,029	70,116
4. China, Peoples Rep.	698,893	51,156
5. Vietnam	630,464	31,514
6. Dominican Republic	510,471	30,492
7. El Salvador	475,976	29,795
8. Korea	311,887	19,766
9. Haiti	289,447	13,998
10. Cuba	287,319	20,488
11. Jamaica	281,164	14,414
12. Poland	254,590	14,250
13. Colombia	239,427	18,678
14. Canada	234,991	15,567
15. United Kingdom	225,228	15,915
16. Guatemala	216,667	17,999
17. Ukraine	208,810	13,655
18. Iran	200,028	10,434
19. Russia	196,586	13,358
20. Pakistan	194,029	12,086
21. Peru	175,980	11,781
22. Taiwan	173,393	8,961
23. Nicaragua	157,025	4,000
24. Soviet Union	147,727	929
25. Ecuador	132,423	8,611
26. Guyana	127,458	6,329
27. Hong Kong	115,119	3,951
28. Nigeria	115,048	9,374
29. Honduras	109,623	5,505
30. Bosnia-Herzegovina	104,862	10,552

Yearbook of Immigration Statistics 2005

In the short-run, such Pan-African identification has tended not to be the case. The global dominance of the Anglo sociocultural formation—particularly the United States—is increasingly diffusing to Latino American cultural zones;[8] however, in many sending nations, African identity is

[8] In Mexico the leaders of the Afro-Mexican population seek to expand the government recognition of ethnic groups as communities based on indigenous heritage, to include their community based on racial heritage, and among other developments in Brazil, the University of Zumbi, considered the first black heritage tertiary institution, was recently founded.

not valorized. As noted regarding the transmigrant, while the dominant Anglo-American ideology assigns the identity "black" to African heritage immigrants, assimilation to the "under" race may be resisted by immigrants through denying or repudiating black identity. The objective challenges facing the African heritage population in America makes identification as black problematic; however, it appears that alternative identities—such as Latino, immigrant, other religious-based ethnicities, such as Muslim—are often less supported after the first generation. Within one generation, many have become aware of the implicit cap on advancement maintained by lack of interracial marriage and racist oppression and exclusion, particularly of African male youth in the school systems. So assimilation to African-American status, particularly for immigrants from the African continent, is the anticipated intergenerational outcome, with identification with Africa retained, but problematic.

Early on, Malcolm X sought to overcome these divisions as he moved from being a spokesman for the Nation of Islam to founding the Organization of Afro-American Unity (OAAU), whose strategy was to unite African people in the Caribbean and in Central, South, and North America in one organization, with the goal of being accepted into the Organization of African Unity (OAU) and representing the Western hemisphere (Breitman 1970). In 1968, the FBI in one of its most infamous memos of the COINTELPRO Program, listed Malcolm X and Stokely Carmichael, along with Martin Luther King, as possible "black Messiahs" (although Malcolm X was dead), displaying the importance that these Pan-African strategists held in the eyes of the FBI (Garrow 1983: 187). It remains an interesting research question to see what identities individuals who are capable of taking on multiple master statuses will assimilate.

The most important sending nations from Africa are Nigeria, Ethiopia, Egypt, Ghana, South Africa, Morocco, Somalia, Kenya, Liberia, Sudan, Sierre Leone, and Cape Verde (Table 1). By far the largest sending countries in the African Diaspora are Haiti and Jamaica, followed by Guyana and Trinidad. If sheer numbers are to be the criteria for development of brain circulation within Africa, then Nigeria stands out. Interestingly, identification with the cultural heritage of West Africa tends to be stronger among African Americans, maybe in part because of the prevalence of their transnational community here or because proximity and English language have led to more interaction. The large migrant group from Ethiopia is of more recent origin, and having been initiated primarily as a refugee flow, only recently seems to be gradually accepting social integration as the future for the majority. Egypt and Morocco are populated primarily by Arabs and people of middle-eastern heritage; hence, a brain-circulation strategy resting on common historic and cultural heritage would not likely be appropriate. Liberia and Sierre Leone have the uniquely compelling factor that they have been the subject of African repatriation efforts in the past, efforts which led to many failed social outcomes, including recently, a bitter endemic civil war and breakdown of order. It may be that more effort to build a successful nation embodying Pan-Africanism is owed to them than anywhere else.

Among Pan-Africanists, there is increasing discussion of the "new" African Diasporas forming in Europe. In some ways these Diasporas correspond more to the core assumptions of the transnationalism model as currently elaborated. The case of the United States is complicated by the long-term residence of the African population now identified as African-American (Patterson 2005). A Pan-African brain-circulation practice for Africans must rely on increasing stimulation to that kernel of Africanness—perhaps through presenting positive aspects of African culture; networking and keeping them informed of the scientific developments among Africans; providing alternative African-centered histories, myths, and super-heroes for primary socialization; making travel and direct contact possible; and, for the social scientist, explicating the cultural unity of black Africa, including all its "lost and found tribes" in the West, Europe, and Asia, as they were remonstrated to do by Diop (1978) and Chancellor Williams (1995).

Table 3

Coefficients from OLS Regression of Direct Investment Abroad on Cumulative Permanent Resident Visas Granted, 1989-2004

Independent Variable	Coefficient
immtotal	.01875* (.007)
refugees	7832.5 (7542.8)
wartorn	−3816.9 (5533)
constant	−7598.6
R^2	.036
df	231

* $p < .01$
Standard error in parentheses.

DISCUSSION

The African-American community can do more to welcome and help Africans to migrate to the United States. Generally, the African-American community has remained very silent as the politicking for immigrant preferences and opportunities are granted. As a group, African Americans have tended to be defined in relation to the nativist sector, as they worried about foreigners taking their jobs. Rather than reinforce this concern, analysts and the media should focus attention on the need to provide opportunity to African people. Just as other groups, such as Mexicans, Cubans, and Russians, unite in a dedicated way to bring their historic co-nationalists here, so too could African-Americans. Often it is stated as a foregone conclusion that the African (black) community as a proportion of the United States' population will significantly decrease in this century. This is not necessarily so if the 14 percent of immigrants who are black are understood to be an augmentation of the African-American community. By taking a proactive role, African-Americans could not only assure the continued political strength of their community, but could reach out to their ancestral homeland to rejuvenate and build a stronger African-American community here. Many African and Caribbean individuals with top accomplishments and high drive, discipline, and motivation seek to emigrate. Often these immigrants marry within the African-American community and thus become a net asset. Strategically focused, these African immigrants and their Africa-conscious supporters could also make a major contribution back to Africa.

Again, brain circulation does not require the assumption that Africans who come as students or trained technical personnel must return within a few years to their country of birth. Rather, the brain-circulation paradigm relies on their coming and staying a significant amount of time, such that they become integrated culturally with both places and thus become transnationals. When they have peaked in their careers and have control over significant savings, organizational influence, technical connections and expertise, and access to markets, they can then engineer transfer of production units to their homeland with the help of the African and African-American community.

It is also anticipated that, based on research to identify the best practices of promoting brain circulation, such policies and strategies should include promoting cultural transfers so that the African/African-American community develops and retains a strong identification with the African homeland. Living together in the United States will lead to the development of effective cultural bridges, whereby African-sending societies will become aware of the prerequisites and conditions required by African Americans considering immigrating to Africa or working for extended terms in Africa. Developing effective filial identity and relations between the nationals of an African country desirous of becoming a major sender and African-Americans may be a focal area for policy development by African states. For instance, currently, Ghana has taken steps to make it possible for Africans in the Diapora, including the United States, to gain dual citizenship in Ghana. Liberia has struggled to retain its constitutional provision granting Africans in the Americas rights to citizenship despite some challenges to it. This state level is very important, but beyond it, networking events and practices could be nurtured to facilitate strong purposeful mutual identification.

The success of brain circulation is also based on selecting new emerging industries with vast opportunity for growth. The nutraceutical industry (nutrition, herbal healing, and organic foods), the organic engineered materials, and alternative energy industries seem to offer good starting points. Africa and the Caribbean have comparative advantage in the year-round production of important plants and trees. Most of the medicines and healing practices we know today came from observing the traditional herbal knowledge of indigenous peoples. Through promotion of ethnobotany (the study of the ethnic-based knowledge of uses of plants), African nations could be among the leading developers of new treatments and health-sustaining practices. Most significantly, when and if African people become truly aware of the wealth of natural products at their fingertips that they may cultivate, and have cultivated or gathered for centuries, then they will know that a high level of self-sufficiency and prosperity is possible. While debatable in America, Booker T. Washington's comments at the Atlanta Expo in 1895 are possibly apropos for Africans in Africa: "cast down your bucket where you are."

African dependency and impoverishment rely on the mystification of things "Western." Today, many of these commodities are exposed as not being very useful and harmful to our well-being. Production of crops using high energy input methods is destroying soil and water balance, and the use of chemicals, antibiotics, and hormones to enhance production are creating health crises. At this time, when the hydrocarbon (oil and gas) driven industrial economy is being exposed as the way of life most likely to destroy the environment for human life on earth, a new door into what our human condition can be is opening even while this one is being closed (oil and gas depletion). Hydrocarbon depletion is progressing ever more rapidly as supplies and new finds dwindle and new demand grows. Soon prices will be beyond the reach of most people. A myriad of mass-produced products relying on oil by-products or energy—from food to plastics to refrigeration and transportation—will also become increasingly unavailable.[9] The way forward is very likely partially the way back: back to relying more on living in harmony with nature, balancing consumption with replenishing processes. While the West looked down upon the South as the stagnant land of tradition, belittled their lack of "progress," it may yet become clear that what the West was engaging in was over-consumption and that the conservative use and low abuse of nature characteristic of traditional societies is exactly the steady-state economic order, for good reason, which carried humanity for over 250,000 years. Indeed, it is in the grasp of Africans from Africa in dialogue with the Africans in the West to carry out a process of *sankofa* ("looking back that you may see the way forward"), and prepare for the over-consumption party's end. As Bob Marley says, it was the machine that enslaved us.[10]

Finally, a note of caution. The second of the factors that can be seen as promoting effective brain circulation is a focus on immigration of highly educated or skilled individuals. Education policy must take care to provide knowledge of a flexible and practical character to all citizens to reproduce basic societal needs. Increasingly this should focus on valorizing sustainable practices already among the people to achieve sufficiency. Then along with this basic education can come opportunities and requests to the youth to cultivate their talents in particular areas identified as key to the brain-circulation project, with the understanding that they will emigrate. More precisely, these youth will live transnational lives, making choices about moving as part of the multinational development network benefiting their homeland. On both sides of the Atlantic, careful consideration must be given to the prerequisites of advancing the nutraceutical, engineered materials, and sustainable technologies industries. With hard work, such efforts will come easily.

Another circumspection with regard to this program that bears discussion is that Pan-Africanism can be conceived as tantamount to an imagined community with a racialist dimension. This is intuitively unsatisfactory. However, this dimension becomes less prominent if one imagines the community as transnational and global. Revalorizaton of Africa is something of a historic duty: central to African culture is the prominence accorded the understanding that the individual is the present-moment link in a long intergenerational lineage. Within African cosmology,

---

[9] One of the earliest, most cogent and prescient analyses of this impending reality was given in 1960 by Cheikh Anta Diop (1974).

[10] Bob Marley (1973) "Catch A Fire."

links to the past (which are factual) serve to stabilize actions in the present, even more so than visions of the future (which are speculative). To some extent, seeking to realize the past is a quest to maximize the familial health of the social group; it assumes that there were successes and positive patterns to life historically which should be maintained and considered as new solutions to present challenges are brought about.

Solutions for African people in no way presuppose exclusivity. Rather, African people are heir to a unique set of problems, partially rooted in their cultural adaptations (and in response to their enforced status as the quintessential global capitalist labor force), which Pan-Africanism and revalorization of African culture seek to ameliorate. It is a process of rediscovery and criticism, embracing the positive and tabooing the negative. To wish the project of Pan-Africanism well, and yet not be African, is tantamount to wishing one's neighbor well. And it is my firm belief that a valorized Africa and African people will have a positive impact on deracializing and equalizing the world and all people. Racial purity is in no way implied. Anyone who ascribes to African heritage, even primarily culturally, is and can be part of the revalorization process. It is a question of identity. For instance, the Cuban people have decided that they as a whole are an Afro-Cuban people, reflecting their desire to affirm their African heritage vocally and counter-hegemonically. At the extreme, it is no longer debated that all the world's people are of African ancestry, and hence share, to some greater or lesser degree, in the knowledge, beliefs, and social principles invented in humanity's long development there. Here it is argued that the material preconditions for a revalorization of Africa and African people can proceed strategically through the empowerment of nodal African lands and peoples with brain circulation.

There are many other strategic issues and contradictions. As many have argued, identity today is multidimensional for increasing numbers of people, and identities, such as historic origin, cannot be taken for granted as dominant master identities. The historic ties of Africans comprising the African-American population are differentially tied to areas of Africa. Most researchers locate the major sending area as West Africa, although large numbers of inland peoples, such as those from the Congo, were kidnapped and taken to the coast. Another passageway into slavery were some cities on the east coast, but apparently much less so. More importantly, the east coast of Africa, particularly the northeast, is subject to strong Islamic influence, which has tended to neutralize any identification as African. Therefore, although much of the population is autochthonous to the area, unlike regions of North Africa, their identity is religiously defined as Muslim. This complexity is not unacknowledged by Pan-Africanists—Nkrumah called for the integration of the three spiritual traditions as mentioned above—however, an added dimension of complexity arises when Pan-Africanism is based on the "imagined community," as it is in the Diaspora, rather than on geographical proximity, which is objective and inescapable.

It has been hotly debated whether to accept regional integration as a prelude to continental integration, or whether it is another capitulation that will seal Africa into a diminished future (Wallerstein 1969). While continental integration is the dominant goal, there seem to be several cogent arguments for proceeding strategically to support regional Pan-African initiatives. An all-encompassing approach is theoretically satisfying; however, a more targeted approach that focuses on development of enclaves of Pan-African activity may be more efficacious and is consistent with the project of brain circulation. Research on brain circulation has shown that nurturing a large concentrated immigrant enclave in a core country with a committed homeland state is a factor in developing capacity for transferring capital back to home countries. This commitment to a unified Africa, beginning within regions, could be displayed as a principle of practice. These countries could be enjoined to serve as the center of regional integrated projects, or better, the project could always proceed involving two or more nations (Nigeria, Togo, Benin, and Ghana, or Sierre Leone, Liberia, etc.). For instance, a scholarship fund, a research project, or a study abroad program should involve at least two "nation states" and its integrated operation across border becomes a laboratory for tailoring full social integration.

Another factor to consider in the development of the imagined community is the movement toward using genetic testing to identify areas of Africa where it is more likely that forebears of Africans who are part of the African-American population came from. Focusing attention on particular ethnic groups in particular countries seems to spur a sense of responsibility and dedication among newly found "lost" descendants. Additional research into whether and to what extent transnational activities are enhanced among individuals who have acquired this information would be an interesting quest. While Pan-Africanism has hitherto relied primarily on the lack of specific ethnic identification to create a mindset favoring overall unity, it may be that some increased self-interested drive may assist in the development of nodal brain-circulation entrepots as it tends to play a part in development.

CONCLUSION

This is a propitious time for beginning a process of brain circulation to fulfill the Pan-African goal of a prosperous Africa capable of assisting in the well-being of African people worldwide because the modernity project is about to change dramatically and looking back is needed as well as looking forward. Truly, there may only be a rather small window of opportunity to build these transnational ties because air travel may have reached its greatest affordability in the 1990s and is likely to subsequently return to a communication resource primarily for the elite. Establishment of large streams of African immigrants to the United States now will surely bring benefits to the African-American community in the future, and in turn, the African/African-American community in the United States can bring great benefits to African homelands. Preliminary evidence based on a quantitative test for relationship between large immigrant populations and direct foreign investment supports the brain-circulation thesis that a connection exists. Additional research to improve modeling of the factors responsible for the different levels of direct foreign investment would be very useful. Case studies of nations that are successfully employing policies and strategies to promote brain circulation, such as India, South Korea, and China, would also be helpful. Investigation into identity formation among African Americans, African and African Diaspora immigrants to the United States and their potential to engage in collaborative cultural, political, and economic activities would lay the groundwork for planning new brain-circulation efforts. Caribbean heritage communities (such as Haiti) in the United States have pioneered some of these practices as the transnationalism paradigm has highlighted. By helping them, the Pan-African movement would likely gain some valuable skills. Brain circulation, coupled with an environmentally sustaining "return to the land," should reconnect the generations and offer the wisdom of the elders to the youth, self-sufficiency to the people, and global opportunities to the talented.

REFERENCES

Bixler, Mark. 2006. "Immigrants today less likely to sever roots." *Atlanta Journal Constitution*, April 4, A5.

Breitman, George. 1970. *By Any Means Necessary, Speeches, Interviews and a Letter by Malcolm X.* New York: Pathfinder Press.

Cabral, Amilcar. 1973. *Return to the Source, Selected Speeches by Amilcar Cabral.* New York: Monthly Review Press.

Cox, Oliver C. 1970. *Caste, Class, and Race.* New York: Monthly Review Press.

Diop, Cheikh Anta. 1978. *Black Africa: The Economic and Cultural Basis for a Federated State.* Westport, Conn.: Lawrence Hill & Company.

——. 1991. *Civilization or Barbarism, An Authentic Anthropology.* New York: Lawerence Hill Books.

Frank, Andre Gunder. 1979. *Dependent Accumulation and Underdevelopment.* New York: Monthly Review Press.
Gammage, Sarah. 2004. "Exercising Exit, Voice and Loyalty: A Gender Perspective on Transnationalism in Haiti." *Development and Change* 35:743-771.
Garrow, David J. 1983. *The FBI and Martin Luther King, Jr.* New York: Penguin Books.
Garvey, Amy Jacques. 1970. *Garvey and Garveyism.* New York: Collier Books.
——, ed. 1980. *Philosophy and Opinions of Marcus Garvey.* New York: Atheneum.
Glick Schiller, Nina, Linda Basch, and Cristina Blanc-Szanton. 1992. "Transnationalism: A New Analytic Framework for Understanding Migration," Pp. 1-24 in *Towards a Transnational Perspective on Migration: Race, Class, Ethnicity, and Nationalism Reconsidered,* edited by Nina Glick Schiller, Linda Basch, and Cristina Blanc-Szanton. New York: Annals of the New York Academy of Science.
Gordon, April. 1998. "The New Diaspora: African Immigration to the United States." *Journal of Third World Studies.* 15:79-100.
Henry, Sheila. 1999. Ethnic identity, nationalism, and international stratification: the case of the African American." *Journal of Black Studies* XXIX:439-54.
Hewitt, Cynthia Lucas. 2002. "Racial accumulation on a world-scale, racial inequality and employment." *Review* XXV:137-71.
Nkrumah, Kwame. 1966. *Neo-colonialism: The Last Stage of Imperialism.* New York: International Publishers.
——. 1972. *Class Struggle in Africa.* New York: International Publishers.
Lowney, John. 2000. "Haiti and Black Transnationalism: Remapping the Migrant Geography of *Home to Harlem.*" *African American Review* 34:413-429.
MacLeod, Jay. 1987. *Ain't No Makin' It.* Boulder Colorado: Westview Press.
Mamdani, Mahmood. 1996. *Citizen and Subject.* Princeton: Princeton University Press.
Patterson, Rubin. 1997. *Foreign Aid After the Cold War.* Trenton, N.J.: Africa World Press.
——. 2005. "U.S. Diasporas and Their Impacts on Homeland Technological and Socio-economic Development: How Does Sub-Sahara Africa Compare?" *Perspectives on Global Development and Technology* 4:83-123.
Polanyi, Karl. 1957. *The Great Transformation.* Boston: Beacon.
Portes, Alejandro. 1995. "Economic Sociology and the Sociology of Immigration: A Conceptual Overview." Pp. 1-41 in *The Economic Sociology of Immigration,* edited by Alejandro Portes. New York: Russell Sage.
Rodney, Walter. 1982. *How Europe Underdeveloped Africa.* Washington, D.C.: Howard University Press.
Szanton Blanc, Cristina, Linda Basch, and Nina Glick Schiller. 1995. "Transnationalism, Nation-States, and Culture." *Current Anthropology.* 36:683-686.
Thernstrom, Stephen, and Abigail Thernstrom. 1997. *America in Black and White: One Nation, Indivisible.* New York: Simon & Schuster.
United States Department of Commerce. 2005. *U.S. Direct Investment Abroad: Trends and Current Issues.* Retrieved July 15, 2006 (http://www.fas.org/sgp/crs/misc/RS21118.pdf).
U.S. Department of Homeland Security. 2005. *The Yearbook of Immigration Statistics.* Washington, D.C.
Wallerstein, Immanuel. 1969. *Africa: The Politics of African Unity.* New York: Vintage Books.
——. 1974. *The Modern World-System.* New York: Academic Press.
Williams, Chancellor. 1995. *The Destruction of Black Civilization.* Chicago: Third World Press.

2. Diaspora Remittances and the Financing of Basic Social Services and Infrastructure in Francophone Africa South of the Sahara

Fondo Sikod and Gérard Tchouassi**

Abstract

Migration is a human phenomenon that has intensified during the past several decades, reflecting the dynamics of societies and upholding the fact of its being an eternal human phenomenon. Remittances are a form of showing the attachment the migrant has with the country of origin, and one of the most visible and beneficial aspects of how international migration is reshaping the countries of origin. The hypothesis investigated by this study is that diaspora remittances to Francophone Africa south of the Sahara contribute to finance basic social services and infrastructures. A descriptive approach, based on literature review and secondary data shows how the contribution of diaspora remittances is filling the gap in the provision of social services that official sources cannot fill.

1. INTRODUCTION

Migration is a human phenomenon that has intensified during the past couple of decades, reflecting the dynamics of societies and upholding the fact of its being an eternal human phenomenon. Perhaps, the most important causes of migration are the inequalities in the living conditions of people in various societies, the conflicts, and the need to survive. While large numbers of people have been displaced as a result of conflicts, an even larger number have moved to search for better living conditions. Natural phenomena such as earthquakes, hurricanes, and droughts force people to emigrate. When people in rural, less developed areas and

* University of Yaounde ll, Department of Economics, Cameroon.
Email: fsikod2002@yahoo.com

societies learn to appreciate and consume goods they cannot produce, they emigrate to where they can procure such goods through selling their labor or carrying out other types of activities. Economic downturns may also encourage workers to migrate abroad and thereby begin to transfer funds to families left behind.

All those who have migrated and settled in various countries all over the world are those we are referring to, in this paper, as the diaspora. The term diaspora is of recent usage in the social sciences (Bruneau 1995; Hovanessian 1998). Before 1980 very little work considered this notion. It was generally associated with the Jews. It is used here to mean the migratory phenomenon characterized by the dispersion of populations from a country in many receiving countries. Remittances are a form of showing the attachment migrants have with their respective countries of origin.

Remittances are one of the most visible, as well as beneficial, aspects of how international migration is reshaping the countries of origin. In a variety of settings, remittances are quietly transforming these societies and regions and are the most manifest example of self-help available to poor households in the global arena. Their role is particularly important in augmenting private consumption and alleviating transient poverty in receiving countries. Remittances emanating from migration are contributing in a growing way to globalizing the world. A typical example is in the area of information and communications technology. In most parts of rural Africa today, mobile telephone sets are becoming more and more popular, as migrants, especially in Europe and North America, want to keep in touch with relatives and friends back in the countries of origin. These telephone sets are generally supplied and maintained by the migrants in the diaspora. Internet services are becoming popular especially in the urban areas, as people try to stay in touch with sons, daughters, relatives, friends, and others, all being paid for by remittances.

An International Monetary Fund (IMF) report (2001) has indicated that migrant remittances are increasingly becoming a more constant source of income to most developing countries, with a doubling of annual remittances between 1988 and 1999. Sander (2003) also reported that remittances have proven to be the most stable flow compared to official development assistance (ODA) and to private capital flows. In effect, the brain drain resulting from migration is not necessarily negative as has been perceived in some circles, since it provides incentive for individuals and households to make great efforts to obtain a good education. Expatriate nationals therefore serve as important links for financial remittances as well as for trade and technology transmission.

In 2004, remittances totaled some US$126 billion. Salimano (2003) notes that remittance flows have concentrated in a group of developing countries, specifically in Latin America and the Caribbean, where in 2002 remittances totaled US$25 billion. This was followed by South Asia with US$16 billion and the Middle East and North Africa (MENA) with US$14 billion. Sub-Saharan Africa had the lowest level of remittances, amounting to US$4 billion.

Whereas remittances are less affected by economic downturns, on the contrary, they are known to rise during periods of downturn or crisis. It is general knowledge in Cameroon, for example, that families with migrant workers, particularly those in developed countries, are able to withstand shocks to income, even if this relationship has not been tested empirically. Migrant worker remittances have been a form of insurance to many Africans, particularly in times of macro-economic shocks. The importance of migrant worker remittances in Francophone Africa south of the Sahara is evidenced by the proliferation of money transfer institutions (both formal and informal) and the growth in the volume of migrant remittances to these countries. It has been argued that migrant remittances are becoming a potential source of external finance and its magnitude has exceeded the amount of ODA in some developing countries (see Table 4 below).

One benefit expected from labor emigration was that migrants would be bringing an impetus to investments, a transfer of technology and machinery, and new enterprises. Thus, Russell et al. (1990) found in their study that "once subsistence needs are satisfied, migrants do use remittances for investment purposes including education, livestock, farming, and small-scale enterprise." In this paper, we try to look into these benefits in some Francophone African countries south of the Sahara.

2. METHODOLOGY

The hypothesis to be investigated by this work is that diaspora remittances to Francophone Africa south of the Sahara contribute to financing basic social services and infrastructures. This paper uses the descriptive approach, based on literature review and secondary data to determine the contribution of diaspora remittances to the development of basic social services. The study draws on secondary material along with inputs from informants on socioeconomic and commercial initiatives relating to remittances. Also, this study examines remittance flows related to other sources of financing and macroeconomic indicators, the use and developmental effects of remittances, and the use of the financing of basic social infrastructure and services. Eight French-speaking countries in Sub-Sahara Africa, all former colonies of France are included in this paper. These countries are Benin, Burkina Faso, Cameroon, Cote d'Ivoire, Mali, Niger, Senegal and, Togo. All these countries are very poor and heavily indebted. They are all under the Bretton Woods Heavily Indebted Poor Countries (HIPC) initiative. The countries continue to have special relations with France, and so understandably, most of the migrants from these countries go to France. The paper is divided into four parts: the introduction; methodology; discussion; and conclusions, lessons learned, and recommendations.

3. DISCUSSIONS

3.1 *Diaspora Remittances*

Remittances are usually viewed as private financial aid that flow directly into households, and the fact that they tend to be counter-cyclical seems to suggest that, very often, they serve as an important source of both income and consumption-smoothing strategies for vulnerable poor as well as non-poor households. Similarly, the literature analyzing the impact of remittance flows shows that these flows are beneficial at all levels, namely, the individual, household, local community, and national levels and suggest that if well managed, they can help reduce poverty at these four levels.

Buch and Kuckulenz (2004) report that worker remittances constitute an increasingly important mechanism for the transfer of resources from developed to developing countries and that remittances are the second-largest source, behind foreign direct investment (FDI), of external funding for developing countries. The economic impact of remittances has been considered beneficial at both the micro- and macro-levels, at least in the short term and there is increasing evidence that remittances from abroad are crucial to the survival of communities in many developing countries (Quartey and Blankson 2003). A much more important and recent consumption-smoothing mechanism is the sharing of risk among people within an economy or across countries through private transfers.

Table 1 gives an idea of the magnitude and growth path of remittances from 1970 to 2004. The growth of remittances can be seen as manifestation of the attachment migrants have with their country of origin.

Table 2 shows the official flow of transfers of money from the diaspora. More than 60 percent of this flow goes to developing countries. These figures could be double if one includes the unofficial transfers[1]

---

[1] Formal money transfers are offered mostly by banks with account-to-account transfers, such as through SWIFT and money transfer operators, such as Western Union or Money Gram, and their agents. A range of informal systems exist, which include the migrants carrying money themselves or sending it with relatives or friends. There are also a number of informal services, typically operating as a side business to an import-export operation, retail shop, or currency dealership. Most of them operate on the basis of no or very little paper or electronic documentation. The transaction is communicated by phone, fax, or email to the counterpart who will be paying out the money.

Table 1

Diaspora Transfers, 1970–2004

Year	Amount Transferred (Billions US$)
1970	2
2001	72.3
2002	88
2003	100
2004	126

Source: Authors' calculations based on data from Tchouassi (2005).

Table 2

Diaspora Transfers by Regions in Billions of US$

Region	Transfers received (2004 estimates)
East Asia and the Pacific	20.3
Europe and Central Asia	12.9
Latin America and the Caribbean	36.9
Middle East and North Africa	17.0
South Asia	32.7
Sub-Sahara Africa	6.1
Low and Middle Income countries	125.9

Source: Authors' calculations based on data from Ketkar S. and Ratha D. (2005).

(tourists, travelers, mail, etc.). Already, money transferred from the diaspora is second behind FDI in terms of capital flows to developing countries: it surpasses public development aid (Wimaladharma et al. 2004) (Table 4). Latin America and the Caribbean top the distribution list and are closely followed by South Asia. Sub-Sahara Africa comes last with nearly 5% of the remittances. The United States and Saudi Arabia are the leading countries making it possible for migrants to remit part of their earnings. Although comparative statistics are not available, France is the leading source of remittances for the countries of focus in this paper. This is understandable. France has had colonial ties with these countries for many years, and continues to be the country of preference and destination for most emigrants from Francophone African countries. Also, the currency used in these countries is linked directly to the currency used in France (European Union currency).

These contributions add up to an appreciable source of financing. Dembélé Moussa (2001) found that in some of these countries, the remittances of their emigrants in France were comparable to the development

Table 3

Official Yearly Money Transfers to Some SSA (Millions of US$)

Country	1980	1985	1990	1995	1999
Benin	77.0	38.1	88.8	92.4	72.8
Burkina Faso	150.3	125.9	139.7	88.7	66.7
Cameroon	11.0	46.7	60.6	28.2	–
Côte d'Ivoire	–	–	40.4	151.1	137.7
Mali	59.4	67.0	106.9	112.1	83.8
Niger	5.9	2.1	13.1	6.3	7.2
Senegal	74.8	55.1	90.8	86.5	92.8
Togo	9.9	15.4	26.9	15.0	0.0
Total	428.4	370.3	629.2	684.3	529.5

Source: Authors' calculations based on data from IMF Statistics on Balance of Payments (1997), OIM (2002), and Tchouassi (2004b).

aid of the host country to their country. In 1990, remittances by Senegalese in the diaspora were US$132 million, while French aid to Senegal was US$250 million. In Mali, remittances by Malians in France were US$25 million, while French aid to Mali was US$93 million. For Côte-d'Ivoire, it was US$21 million, while French aid was US$305 million (Condamines 1993). These contributions also compare favorably with the balance of payments accounts of some countries. Thus, for Senegal, for example, the remittances of its immigrants in France were equal to earnings from the exports of groundnuts, the main export commodity of the country. In many localities in many African countries, remittances from the diaspora make up the only source of income for some individuals and families that stay behind (Dembélé Moussa 2001). Table 3 shows the remittances to the countries in this study.

In Africa, like all over the world, the main source of information on the transfer of money from the diaspora is the statistics on the balance of payments published by the IMF and the World Bank. These statistics are not accurate for many African countries, given the number of visits to the counters of Western Union and other money transfer agencies that operate even on holidays. Also, the difficulties of keeping statistics in African countries, especially Francophone African countries, make it particularly difficult to have accurate information.

3.2 *Inventory of Mechanisms for Financing Basic Social Services and Infrastructures*

While in the developed world, the supply of basic services is taken for granted, it is not the same thing in the developing world, and yet these services are fundamental to any development efforts. Table 5 shows the pathetic situation with selected basic social services.

Table 4

Diaspora Funds Compared to Other Sources of Development Funds

Sources of Financing	1990	1995 Amount in Billions US$	2004
FDI	20	105	165
ODA	50	59	69
Diaspora Funds	30	51	126

Source: Authors' calculations based on data from Ketkar S. and Ratha D. (2005).

Table 5

Some Basic Social Indicators for 2002

Country	Poverty/Under US$1/day	Access to Health Facilities*	Access to Drinking Water*	Literacy Rate*
Benin	N/A	32	68	40
Burkina Faso	45	12	15	N/A
Cameroon	17	48	63	67
Côte d'Ivoire	11	40	84	46
Mali	72	45	48	23
Niger	61	12	46	17
Senegal	22	52	72	39
Togo	N/A	34	51	60

Source: Calculated by authors from African Development Indicators by the World Bank (2005).
* Figures in cells are in percentages of the total population. Blank cells mean the information was not available.

In this section we look at the inventory of all the mechanisms for financing basic social services and infrastructures in Francophone Sub-Sahara Africa. These include government, multilateral, bilateral, and private—formal and informal. These basic social services and infrastructure concern housing, improvement of living conditions, markets, access to potable water, electricity, health facilities, education, and communications infrastructure (roads, telephone, etc.). Two major levels have been identified: national and bilateral or multilateral financing. As former French colonies, the same structures are found in all the countries.

At the national level, financing for social services and infrastructure comes from the public investment budget, through various Ministries, the inter-communal equipment fund (known by its French acronym as FEICOM), the Housing Credit Fund, banks, rotating savings and credit associations (ROSCAs), private individuals, and other national organizations (Tchouassi 2004a).

Projects financed by public budget covers the national territory. These projects cover all the areas mentioned above. But in the execution of these projects, there are usually delays caused by administrative procedures and bottlenecks. These delays increase costs and sometimes prevent the execution of some projects.

At the level of the communities, delays in getting subsidies and tax revenues lead to some projects not being carried out. Subsidies target specific projects in particular communities. The budget allocations are usually small. The public funds destined to finance projects are from communal taxes (Tchouassi 2004a). The Housing Credit Fund and the banks finance mostly housing projects. The Housing Credit Fund finances are funded through a housing tax paid by all salaried workers in both the public and private sectors. This organization gives loans only to those who have contributed to this fund through their taxes. Non-salaried community members are therefore excluded from this channel of operation. Financing through this institution is on a long- and medium-term basis.

Commercial banks generally do not finance urban infrastructures because they are not able to give long-term loans because of the banking policies in the sub-region. Bank deposits are generally for the short to medium-term. However, some commercial banks in Cameroon have special accounts for housing loans, but with very high collateral demands, and are limited to those who maintain a certain minimum deposit with the banks.

There are also microfinance institutions that collect savings, distribute credit, transfer money and micro-insurance (Tchouassi 2001). These financial products are used to finance micro-development projects, including basic social services. In Cameroon, a recent law made it possible for people to create financial cooperatives. This makes it possible for the very small economic operators, who by the size of their activities have been excluded from the formal financial system, to have a vibrant economic activity. Incidentally, a number of these cooperatives have been started by funds from the diaspora. It is also a way of formalizing the informal financial market that is strong and vibrant in the sub-region.

Rotating Savings and Credit Associations (ROSCAs) are informal groupings that mobilize savings to help members. The associations are loose groupings of people (friends, relations) practicing the same activity, or are held together by some particular bond. Contributions begin from as little as 10 cents (US) to over US$1000.00. In Cameroon there exist many variants of ROSCAs, depending on the use of the funds raised. If it is destined for the construction of a house for a member, the group takes charge of all the activities—buying land and constructing the building—so that at the end of the cycle, all members own their own homes. This is, however, a very restrictive ROSCA, with members that are financially viable. Otherwise, in the normal situation, the recipient of the funds uses it to improve on the quality of his/her home. Funds from this source are only on short-term basis and are available to members only. They nevertheless play a developmental role, even if the financing is only for members. Individuals finance the construction of drainage work (sewer, cesspool/sink/draining well, wells, gutter, spring, etc.), and subscriptions to potable water and electricity. In some parts of the urban or semi-urban areas, these extensions of the basic infrastructure are done by individuals or groups of people. This type of solidarity financing is generally limited because members tend to be poor.

Finally, some national associations, like NGOs and church/religious groups, also participate in a limited way in financing basic social services infrastructure. Financing at the level of the neighborhood or district is strategic for access to housing and the many basic social services.

On the international scene, there are bilateral and multilateral financing concerns. Understandably, France is leading in bilateral assistance. Because the countries are poor and heavily indebted, the French Cooperation Service has put in place the social development fund (SDF), which is a mechanism for financing social activities. Areas being financed by this fund include primary and basic education, professional training, primary health care and the fight against endemic diseases and HIV/AIDS, basic infrastructures, territorial management, and management of the environment and natural resources. There are other bilateral aid programs, but they are not as intense as those in France.

On the multilateral front, there are the HIPC funds. Of course, benefiting from these funds requires meeting a lot of conditionalities, one of which is good governance. This appears to be the most intractable conditionality for nearly all the countries, as most leaders in a number of the countries are trying to convert their countries from Republics to Monarchies, with themselves as the Monarchs. Other organizations that work with the Breton Woods institutions include the United Nations Development Programme and other UN agencies, for example, UNESCO and UNICEF.

The European Union has a program, the Decentralized Support Programme for Urban Development (PACDDU), which intervenes in the institutional, investments, and capacity-building aspects. Project proposals are launched in the areas of lodging/housing, infrastructure, equipment, urban management, and various social services. The proposals are initiated by people in local neighborhoods in towns. In the elaboration of the project, PACDDU aids the local populations not only in matching funds, but also in preparing proposals.

In spite of all these sources, financing needs continue to exceed the available public funds. Also, financing from the above sources tends to focus mostly on macro-needs. The issue then becomes one of diversifying sources of funding to finance basic social services in Africa. This is where diaspora remittances come in.

3.3 *Migrant Remittances and the Financing of the Development of Basic Social Services and Infrastructure*

An important question is whether the African diaspora, considered as the sixth region of Africa, can contribute to the development of the continent. In the development model of the four tigers, one of the Asian countries owes its development to its diaspora, which, thanks to massive re-migration to the country of origin, has contributed to its growth. In addition to the Asian tigers, India today is posing a major challenge and competition to the US Silicon Valley, thanks to its diaspora. The African diaspora, qualified and scattered all over the world, could be considered as a lever for the continent. Take the example of African physicians in the diaspora: they save thousands of lives elsewhere, and yet the continent lacks these medical professionals. Unfortunately, the returns resulting from the efforts of these professionals are too inadequate on the continent. They find it rational to sell their services somewhere, and to remit part of their earnings back home. These remittances do contribute to the financing of basic social services in Africa.

Access to basic services (schools, health centers, potable water, irrigation and drainage, improving housing conditions, roads, urban and semi-urban markets, semi-urban electrification, etc.) contributes to the improvement of the conditions of life of the populations in Africa. It stimulates economic and sociocultural activities. The funds targeting these services can be considerable, if one looks at the balance of payments of any country with a large population that has emigrated, or globally at IMF financial statistics.

As mentioned earlier, these figures are only estimates, because they do not take into consideration transfers through informal channels or by tourists. Sometimes these funds are so substantial that they are comparable to imports, exports, public development aid, FDI, and the like (see Table 4). However, the amounts remitted depend on the host country where the immigrants are, the type of activities they do, how long they have been in the host country, without forgetting the monetary policies of the host country regarding taking money out of the country. Some countries have limits as to how much an individual can take or send out of the country a year.

According to the Moroccan Exchange Office, for example, Moroccans residing abroad remitted approximately US$3.1 and 2.8 billion in 2001 and 2002, respectively. This was 9.62% and 7.97% of the GDP in those years. For 2003, the repatriation was US$3.2 billion. On the average, the remittance of the Moroccans in the diaspora represented 43% of exports and 117% of earnings from tourism. Since 1980, remittances by Moroccans in the diaspora, although quite high, have fluctuated following the economic cycles in the international scene and the immigrants who no longer have the same attachment to their home country.

The African diasporans play an important role in the development of their respective countries. Their contributions are most noticeable in the social sector, where social/tribal groups in the diaspora sponsor or finance, in groups or partnerships or individually, certain activities in their home countries. These may include transferring medical equipment, financing the construction of social services, for example, health centers and schools. Individually, many support their families back home in various ways—paying for the education of family members, improving the quality of life for family members, and other relevant means. Some retired parents depend on remittances from their children to support them in retirement.

Most often, Africans in the diaspora organize in a formal way to work in partnership with the compatriots who stay back home to carry out development projects in their areas of origin. New forms of cooperation emerged in the 1990s. These were mostly associations of Africans in the diaspora held together by some commonality. The most known example is the Sahelian migrants in France: the Association of the Diasporans of the Senegal River Valley (Mauritania, Senegal, and Mali). According to the Panos Institute, in the 1990s, there were about 400 associations of diasporans of the Senegal River Valley in France. These partnership and solidarity associations played a major role in the development of their areas of origin (Dewitte 1995; Condamines 1993), and in the financing of basic urban and semi-urban infrastructures. Their interventions have made it possible for some villages and localities to have some basic infrastructures—schools, dispensaries, health centers, silos for storing grain, water, and other necessities.

Another group, the Association of the Senegal River Valley in France, carried out more than 330 development projects in their countries of origin. These projects go from agriculture, health, education, and potable water, to the construction of churches and mosques. For example, the construction of the Touba Hospital in the North Centre of Senegal is the work of the Senegalese diaspora, which has improved on the quality of life for the people of the region.

The migrants in the diaspora also participate in activities in the social economy, such as development of micro-finance, transport, building, lodging, and cooperatives in diverse social sectors (Dembélé Moussa 1999). The social economy is defined as an approach and economic practice based on the principles of ethics of solidarity, responsibility, autonomy, and collective utility regarding the social values and the initiatives of the citizens. In 1996, sociologist Babacar Sall was seduced by the case of Senegalese immigrants in Italy to write that he attended a Senegalese event that had to do with the electrification by the migrants of N'Diaye Tioro, a village located 150 kilometers from Dakar, the capital of Senegal. Examples of these abound in many countries, in addition to health centers, schools, and post offices (Sall 1996).

In Burkina Faso, important remittances from the diaspora serve as the only means of survival for many families—food, education, health care, marriage ceremonies, and financing of micro-economic activities. Although remittances are very important to Mali, the effect of the diaspora is ambiguous. Most of the migrants cited as being expelled from France are said to be from Mali. This has affected remittances, and the financial manna has dropped (Nforgang and Ouattara 2004). Nevertheless, in the Kayes region of Mali where the climate is hostile and not good for either agriculture or animal husbandry, 80% of the inhabitants are rural, but their main resources come from trade. Malian emigrants in France have financed the installation of electricity, costing US$80,000 and the construction of water-holding areas for irrigation for agriculture, sinking of bore holes for drinking water, all the basics that permit the people, both rural and urban, to be food self-sufficient. In the small town of Yélimané, also in Mali, large villas, equipped with telephones and parabolic antennas, have been constructed by the Malians in the diaspora. This village even has a small airstrip that permits people from the diaspora to visit their families.

In Cameroon, many importers no longer transfer money to pay for their imports. Rather, Cameroonians in the diaspora pay for these imports from their savings, and when the merchandise is sold, the repayment is made in Cameroon in the form of putting up a building, making monthly payments to the family in Cameroon, or carrying out some other project the diasporan wants. This approach is usually based on mutual trust and confidence (Tchouassi 2004b). Also, during visits back home in Cameroon, many of these diasporans accept engagements to contribute towards financing various development projects. The Association of Bali people working and studying in the United States, in the late 1990s, bought tons of drugs and sent to the District Hospital in Bali, Cameroon, which had been built but there were no funds to furnish it. This Association also built a modern mortuary, and partially financed the Bali water supply. Diasporans from other parts of Cameroon are learning from this example and are following suite.

Remittances have also served as a form of social insurance for migrants. Hulme et al. (2001), however, suggest that for remittances to serve as a form of premium payment for future risks, these flows should enable households to accumulate assets that reduce vulnerability to financial shocks and to gain access to entitlements such as education and health that contribute to livelihood security and sustainability. This viewpoint is corroborated by Azam and Gubert (2002) in their study on the impact of remittances, using historical and anthropological surveys on recipients in Africa. In particular, they examined the Soninke labor migration and interpret it as a means of diversifying risk in a context of missing insurance and credit markets.

3.4 *Developmental Effects of Remittances*

Migrant remittances also serve as a source of income for savings and investment, and this is confirmed by Taylor (1996). He found that remittances contribute to savings and investments, thereby leading to growth and development of any economy, and this is corroborated by Findley and Sow (1998) in a study on Mali. They report that remittances not only covered basic food and cash needs but also allowed to pay for irrigation in agriculture. The bulk of the impact is a substantial positive effect on the receiving households in terms of an improved standard of living with a knock-on effect for the local economy due to consumption and investment, such as in land, housing, and livestock.

More recently, interest from other perspectives has emerged—both from developmental angles (economic, financial systems, and livelihood aspects) and from concerns with international security. More specifically, these include the developmental contributions of remittances, given the immense and still growing flow of remittances to developing countries. Since the 2001 September 11 bombing attacks on the United States, there have been security concerns about the possibilities of transferring funds to support terrorist attacks. As for African countries, the issue of access and cost of money transfers affecting remittances is very important in their development. This is because remittances do have country-wide or macro impacts. Benefits to the countries vary, depending on the structure of the local economy and related policies and regulations, such as foreign exchange controls. They also vary by both the capacity and the opportunity of the recipients to make productive use of these transfers, such as poverty alleviation.

4. CONCLUSION, LESSONS LEARNED AND RECOMMENDATIONS

The contribution of Francophone Africans in the diaspora to the financing of basic social services is a complex and multiform process. This contribution is done through monetary, non-monetary and diverse forms. The phenomenon that we have just analyzed in this paper is characterized by asymmetries between the center and the periphery in the global system, the center being the developed economies that have hosted migrants and the periphery being the country of origin of the migrants. The process begins with intermediaries and mobility channels or the circulation of human capital, which ends in the remittance of funds. The contribution from the diaspora puts in relations at least two categories of social actors: Homo œconomicus and Homo donator (Assogba 2002).

As efficient as the big international aid structures, the African diaspora, more taken by the realities of the African continent, has to play an important intermediation role in financing the nation's basic and elementary needs. Money from the diaspora today constitutes a privileged resource of financing African development. The African Union has invited the African diaspora to participate in the development of the region and has decided to amend the organization's charter in order to encourage diasporan participation.

Following this survey, it comes out that on the African plan, African Governments through their public investment budgets finance development projects in the social sectors. There are also new products, from microfinance through small loans made, for the population to finance improvements in their living conditions. Informal financial markets are important sources for financing improvements in living conditions of urban dwellers.

On the international level, funds for social development are a mechanism to finance social utility put in place by the French Cooperation Service to take care of social needs within the level of towns. The HIPC initiative makes it possible for countries like Cameroon to concentrate its efforts on putting in place policies and institutions that are the foundations of sustainable development and leads to poverty alleviation.

African states, within the policies of decentralization, continue to play an important role in the development of basic social services and semi-urban infrastructures: by creating basic conditions for acquiring land, by ensuring land rights and the respect of rights of people and associations, by orienting policy toward increasing savings for lodging, and other actions. This is also the way the fight against poverty should go.

In spite of these efforts, there is still a huge gap in terms of resources needed to improve on the provision of basic social services. Concerting with the migrants is very important so that they can be encouraged to mobilize more funds to fill this gap. It is therefore, imperative that perhaps from the opportunities offered by the co-development efforts, concrete modalities be put in place for a real cooperation between the different local development actors. It is a paradox that remittances from the diaspora, which in some countries are greater than public aid to development, be treated as if they do not exist. A restructuring of the financial mechanism ought to lead to putting in place financial networks to facilitate investment of savings from migrants in the development, particularly in the areas of basic social services and infrastructure and the creation of activities that generate income and employment.

The single biggest contribution of remittances is to the welfare and improved livelihood of the receiving household—be it in terms of basic necessities such as food or clothing, or better health and education, or to a smaller extent, in terms of savings or business investments. Remittances also finance some informal lending (financial intermediation). The bulk, an estimated average of 80% of remittances, however, goes to consumption, thereby building human and social capital. Though benefits are concentrated at the individual or household levels, case studies indicate that there are spill-over effects into extended families, and the local economy as well as into community development projects.

The overall tenor is that the benefits of remittances by far outweigh any actual or potential drawbacks. On balance, however, the contribution to welfare, and thereby to reduced poverty levels, is seen as a net positive transfer. Donors have begun to recognize the role of remittances and have become interested primarily in how to facilitate an increase of the flow and use of remittances for developmental benefits. This includes how to facilitate a reduction in transaction cost and better access to formal sector transfer services, as well as how to better integrate and improve access to a broader range of financial services through remittances as an "entry point."

REFERENCES

Armstrong, John A. 1976. "Mobilized and Proletarian Diasporas." *American Political Sciences Review* 70:393-408.

Assogba, Yao. 2002. "Diaspora, Mondialisation et Développement de l'Afrique." *Nouvelles Pratiques Sociales* 1:98-110.

Azam, Jean Paul, and Gubert Flore. 2002. "Those in Kayes: The Impact of Remittances on Their Recipients in Africa." Retrieved August 14, 2006 (http://www.nuff.ox.ac.uk/users/).

Bruneau, Michel. 1995. *Les diasporas*. Montpellier: Reclus.

Buch, M. Claudia, and Kuckulenz Anja. 2004. "Worker Remittances and Capital Flows to Developing Countries." ZEW Discussion Paper, Mannheim, Germany.

Cameroun. 2004. "Document de Stratégie de Réduction de la Pauvreté." MINEFI, Yaoundé: Cameroun.

Condamines, Charles. 1993. "Les Immigrés, Atouts du Développement." *Le Monde Diplomatique* 477, Décembre, p. 25.

Dembélé Moussa, Demba. 1999. "Le Rôle des Emigrés dans le Développement National du Sénégal: Implications Socio-Economiques et Perspectives." Communication au Colloque sur l'Emigration Sénégalaise: Situations et Perspectives, Assemblée Nationale et la Fondation Friedrich Ebert. 10-11 Juillet, Dakar, Sénégal.

——. 2001. "Le Financement du Développement et ses Alternatives: le Rôle des Mouvements Sociaux et Politiques." *Alternatives Sud* 3:229-251.

Dewitte, Philippe. 1995. "Les migrants, coopérants de demain?" *Projet* 241:80-88.

Diatta, Marie Angélique, and Mbow Ndiaga. 1999. "Releasing the Development Potential of Return Migration: The Case of Senegal." *International Migration* 37:243-66.

Dieng, Seydi Ababacar. 2002. "Pratiques et Logiques de l'Epargne Collective Chez les Migrants Maliens et Sénégalais en France." *Afrique et Développement* 1 & 2:144-174.

Findley, Sally E., and Sow Salif. 1998. "From Season to Season: Agriculture, Poverty and Migration in the Senegal River Valley, Mali." Pp. 69-144, in *Emigration Dynamics in Developping Countries*, edited by Reginald Appleyard, Ashgate: Brookfield.

Hovanessian, Martine. 1998. "La Notion de Diaspora. Usage et Champ Sémantique." *Le Journal des Anthropologues* 72:11-30.

Hulme, David, Karen Moore, and Andrew Shepherd. 2001. "Chronic Poverty: Meanings and Analytical Frameworks." CPRC, Working Paper. IDPM, University of Manchester, Manchester.

International Monetary Fund. 2001. Public Information Notice (PIN). Washington D.C. September 21, 2001.

Ketkar, Suhas, and Ratha Dilip. 2005. "Securisation of Future, Remittances Flows: Global Overviews." Inter-American Development Bank, Washington D.C.

Massé, René. 2005. "Financer le Développement de l'Electrification Rurale." Collection Etudes et Travaux, Série en ligne 2, Editions du GRET. Retrieved August 14, 2006 (www.gret.org).

Médam, Alain. 1993. "Diaspora/Diasporas: Archétype et Typologie." *Revues Européennes des Migrations Internationales* 9:59-66.

Meyer, Jean-Baptiste, David Kaplan, and Jorge Charum. 2001. "Nomadisme des Scientifiques et Nouvelle Géopolitique du Savoir." *Revue Internationale des Sciences Sociales* 168:341-354.

Nations Unies. 2002. "Rapport de la Conférence Internationale sur le Financement du Développement." Monterrey au Mexique, 18-22 mars, ONU, New York.

Nforgang, Charles, and Ouattara Souleymane. 2004. "La Marmite de l'Argent des Migrants." *Défis Sud* 62:27-28.

Quartey, Peter, and Blankson Theresa. 2004. "Do Migrant Remittances Minimize the Impact of Macro-volatility on the Poor in Ghana?" Institute of Statistical, Social and Economic Research (ISSER)—University of Ghana, Final Report Submitted to the Global Development Network (GDN), December.

Russell, et al. 1990. "International Migration and Development in Sub-Saharan Africa." World Bank Discussion Papers. World Bank, Washington D.C.

Sall, Babacar. 1996. "Anétatisme et Modes Sociaux de Recours." *Cahier du GEMDEV*, 24:170-176.

Salimano, Andres. 2003. "Remittances by Emigrants: Issues and Evidence". Discussion Paper. WIDER/UNU, Helsinki, Finland.

Sanders, Cerstin. 2003. "Migrant Remittances to Developing Countries." Bannock Consulting. Retrieved June 2003 (www.bannock.co.uk/).

Sheffer, Gabriel. 1986. *Modern Diasporas in International Politics*. London: Croom Helm.

Tamba, Isaac. 2001. *Cameroun: Enjeux et Défis de l'Initiative PPTE*. Yaoundé: Presses Universitaires d'Afrique.

Taylor, J. Edward. 1996. "International Migration and National Development." *Population Index* 2:181-212.

Tchouassi, Gérard. 2001. "Les Produits Financiers et les Comptes Clients dans les Caisses Coopératives d'Epargne et de Crédit du Cameroun." Pp. 342-347 in *Exclusion et liens Financiers: Rapport du Centre Walras*, édité par Jean-Michel Servet et David Vallat. Paris: Economica.

——. 2004a. "Mécanismes et Stratégies de Financement des Actions en Faveur des Individus, des Groupes d'Individus ou des Municipalités Urbaines dans les Domaines Suivants: Logements Urbains, Accès aux Services Urbains de base, Protection des Groupes Vulnérables en Milieu Urbain, Activités Génératrices de Revenus en Milieu Urbain." Environnement, Recherche—Action (ERA), Yaoundé, Cameroun. Document non Publié.

——. 2004b. "Migrations et Envois d'Argent des Migrants en Afrique au Sud du Sahara." *Techniques Financières et Développement* 76:37-46.

——. 2005. "Argent de la Diaspora et Financement des Infrastructures Urbaines de Base en Afrique." Contribution Présentée à la Onzième Assemblée Générale du CODESRIA sur le Thème: Repenser le Développement Africain: au Delà de l'Impasse, les Alternatives. 06-10 décembre, Maputo, Mozambique.

Wets, Johan. 2004. "Réflexions sur la Migration et le Développement." Dialogue EPC-FRB sur la migration. OIM, Genève.

Wimaladharma, Jan, Douglas Pearce, and David Stanton. 2004. "Transferts des Migrants: un Nouveau Financement pour le Développement?" *Techniques Financières et Développement* 76:29-36.

World Bank. 2000. "Preliminary Document on the Enhanced Initiative for Heavily Indebted Poor Countries." The World Bank Document, Washington D.C.

——. 2003. "Global Development Finance." The World Bank Report, Washington D.C.

——. 2005. "Africa Development Indicators." The World Bank, Washington D.C.

3. Globalization, Migration, and the Challenges of Development in Africa

*John Akokpari**

Abstract

The paper argues that, while globalization is a catalyst for international migration, its impact on Africa's development remains polemical. Generally, discussions on the impact of international migration on African development feature two contrasting views. One view, which is gradually gaining currency, points to tangible benefits from migration in the form of migrant remittance, which recent World Bank reports identify as the second largest form of capital flow to developing countries after foreign direct investments (FDI). This view thus sees the impact of international migration on African development as positive. This paper, however, takes a different view and argues that the adverse effects of international migration on Africa, in the form of brain drain—the emigration of Africa's trained professionals—far outweighs the perceived advantages associated with migrant remittances. Consequently, in the aggregate, Africa's development suffers under the weight of international migration. The paper thus suggests the formulation of workable policies by the AU to manage the brain drain. Such policy measures should include a conscious attempt to address the root causes of the so-called "push factors" which instigate the emigration of Africa's brains in the first instance.

INTRODUCTION

The effects of globalization and migration on growth and development in Africa remain issues of considerable debate. Since the rise to dominance of neoliberalism following the demise of communism, the virtues of globalization have been extolled by the leading international financial institutions and Western governments. African states have been encouraged

* University of Cape Town, Political Studies, Cape Town, South Africa. Email: akokpari@humanities.uct.ac.za

to align economic policies and politics with the dominant principles of globalization. These include undertaking programs of liberalization, deregulation, decontrolling, denationalization and devaluation. Politically, countries are to reform governance practices with emphasis on holding regular multiparty elections, respecting the rule of law and human rights and promoting the twin principles of transparency and accountability. A dominant objective of these reforms is to curtail the traditionally large role of the state in the development and creation of an "enabling environment" for the private sector, which is expected to generate and speed up the process of economic growth and ultimately, development. This logic is, however, contradicted by another school of thought that depicts globalization and its trappings as anathematic to Africa's development (Sawyer 1999; Akokpari 2001; Ninsin 2000; Nabudere 2000). This latter school argues that rather than ameliorating, globalization compounds Africa's developmental crisis by worsening its already grave unemployment situation, decapitalizing the continent, and hastening environmental bankruptcy.

Similarly, the impact of international migration on Africa's development is polemical. Much of the discussion on international migration tends to focus on its effects on receiving countries. Advocates of international migration frequently point to remittances from emigrants as tangible contributions to the development of the labor-supplying region. On the other hand, critics see international migration as promoting brain drain from the home country. The controversy is heightened by globalization and the wave of political upheavals in Africa, which provide fresh pretexts and opportunities for international migration (Borowski 1996; Altzinger 1995). Among its effects, globalization widens the gap between affluent and poor countries (UNDP 1997), leading to what Appleyard (1991) calls the "maldistribution" of the world's population—a situation under which a large population of people live in impoverished countries with low living standards. Such a dichotomy has the predictable consequence of spawning migration to prosperous countries (Akokpari 2000). This paper contributes to the immigration-development debate in Africa. Specifically, it examines the implications of migration for Africa's development within the context of globalization. It opines that while migration has become inevitable under globalization, the net cost of the former in terms of brain drain from Africa far exceeds its benefits in the form of migrant remittances. Further, the paper suggests that workable measures are required to manage Africa's brain drain. The paper is segmented into sections, with the next section providing some brief conceptual discussion on development and highlighting the gravity of Africa's developmental crisis. The following sections provide some cursory explanations of globalization and migration, while the subsequent sections examine the effects of international migration on Africa's development. The conclusion summarizes the main arguments.

DEVELOPMENT

Development remains a nebulous term, often used interchangeably with economic growth, progress, reduction in unemployment, and inequality. There is widespread consensus that Sub-Saharan Africa remains precariously under conditions of underdevelopment, confronted by poverty and disease, among other problems. Early ideas about development were informed by the modernization orthodoxy. Rostow's (1960) stage theory depicting societies as passing through distinct phases (the primitive stage, the pre-take-off, take-off, drive to maturity, and the stage of high mass consumption) to development was an example of an attempt to explain development within the context of modernization. The stage of high mass consumption was equated to the developed societies of the North, which represented the ideal to which other societies should aspire. Importantly, the modernization theory depicted free trade as the impetus for the transition from one stage to another; free trade was the engine for growth, although it had long been established that growth could occur without development (Rao 1984). Orthodox thinking therefore perceived development largely in economic terms, with macro-economic indicators such as GDP, GNP, inflation and balance of payments as its main indices. With its intrinsic trickle down effect, free trade was projected as the main catalyst for development. This neoliberal assumption, however, came under telling criticisms in the late 1960s, following the failure of free trade to generate development in Latin America. Import substitution industrialization became the preferred alternative approach among Latin American and a good number of developing countries. The orthodox perception on development nevertheless continued to inform the thinking of development institutions such as the World Bank. In its 1991 World Development Report, the Bank stated emphatically that "the industrial countries of today grew prosperous through trade. No effort should be spared to ensure that developing countries can follow that same path to development" (World Bank 1991: 108).

The rise to salience of environmental protection as a critical component of sustainable development since the 1972 World Development Conference in Stockholm, together with the coming into vogue of notions of human security, have broadened the development discourse beyond economics. Thus, today's ecological and human security concerns have come to constitute part of the mainstream issues in the sustainable development discourse. Similarly, there is a seeming shift in the thinking of the World Bank on development away from its purely neoclassical outlays. In the early 1970s, the leadership of the World Bank argued for the adoption of development policies that benefited entire populations. While this proposal fell short of clearly spelling out new development strategies that benefit all sections of society, the idea nonetheless represented a tacit recognition of the "anti-developmental" effects of the Bank's market-based policies, which have been central to its policy recommendations to developing countries. Such policy prescriptions have benefited the minority capital-owning elements to the exclusion of the majority of the population. Experience with the ubiquitous market-based structural adjustment programs (SAPs) has shown that such development policies have an inherent tendency to spawn and, indeed, exacerbate inequalities (UNDP 1997).

It is against the background of this fundamental weakness in orthodox development thinking that this study adopts Seers' (1972) notion of development, articulated over three decades ago. In explaining development, Seers argued that

> The [central] questions to ask about a country's development are: what has been happening to poverty? . . . to unemployment? [and] to inequality? If all three of these have declined from high levels, then beyond doubt, this has been a period of development for the country concerned. If one or two of these central problems have been growing worse, especially if all three have, it would be strange to call the result 'development' even if per capita income doubled.

This perception captures some of the menacing threats facing Africa, the reduction of which promotes human security. Although poverty, inequalities, and unemployment are only a few of the legion of challenges facing Africa, a reduction of these conditions is a significant step towards mitigating other threats facing the continent, including diseases, conflicts, genocide and environmental decadence. Africa's post-independence attempts to address this galaxy of challenges that have yielded minimal results. In recent years, efforts to address these challenges have been vitiated by pressures from globalization, which in addition to generating economic hurdles for Africa, also accelerates the emigration of the labor force, whose expertise is critical in mitigating these challenges.

THE REALITY OF AFRICA'S DEVELOPMENTAL CRISIS

The huge paradox between Africa's rich endowments and its underdevelopment is well known. Africa remains the poorest inhabited continent on the globe although it is among the most resource-endowed regions in the world. Between 40 and 60 percent of its 800 million people live below the poverty line—earning less than the UN threshold of $1.00 a day. The bulk of Africa's poor are the vulnerable in society—women, children, the aged and the handicapped. Unemployment is highest in Africa compared to other regions and rocking as high as 40 percent in countries like Mozambique, Lesotho, Liberia, and recently Zimbabwe. In many cases, employment wages are barely sufficient to guarantee minimally acceptable standards of living.

These facts are not accidental; they reflect the realities of Africa's poor economic performance. Africa has the lowest economic growth figures in the world. Between 1990 and 1999, for example, GDP growth was a paltry 2.4 percent per annum compared to 5.7 and 3.4 in South Asia, Latin America and in the Caribbean, respectively (World Bank 2001). The situation is worse in Sub-Saharan Africa where overall economic growth plummeted from a high of 5.3 percent in 1997 to 4.3 percent in 2000 (*Africa Recovery* 16[2-3] 2002). There is little to suggest that this has improved since. Inflation rates are high, ranging in double, sometimes triple-digit figures in certain countries. Balance of payment problems are rife, and the asymmetry in economic power relations between Africa and its northern trading partners has condemned the former into a chronic deterioration in terms of trade. This situation is exacerbated by African countries' precarious reliance on single primary products and the inability to diversify their economies. In the last two decades, the comparative advantage previously enjoyed by Africa in the production of primary commodities has been undercut by biotechnology and the production of cheap synthetic raw materials in other parts of the world.

Foreign direct investments (FDI) generally assumed to provide life support to Africa's fragile economies is on the decline. Although this has recently been increasing in certain countries (Angola, South Africa and Mozambique), and regionally in southern Africa, the flow of FDI to Africa has on the aggregate declined from $8.1 billion in 1996 to $6.1 billion in 2000. Although this figure rose to a high of $13.8 billion in 2001, it fell again to $7 billion in 2003 (Harsch 2003a). Similarly, net overseas development assistance (ODA) has plummeted from a high level of $28 billion in 1990 to $16.4 billion in 2000 (Asante 2003). In spite of numerous international trade agreements promising Africa greater access to world markets, its share of world exports remained at 1 percent at the turn of the century although this was 4 percent in 1960. Thus, outside of Antarctica, which has no permanent residents, Africa remains the most marginalized continent in the international political economy. Worse yet, Africa is the region hardest hit by the HIV/AIDS epidemic. Although it has only 10 percent of the world's population, Africa has 63 percent of global AIDS cases. There are currently over 25 million people living with AIDS in Africa with over 9 million already dead as a result (*Africa Renewal* 18[3], October 2004: 6). UNAIDS estimated that at the turn of the century SSA alone had over 12 million AIDS orphans, representing about 95 percent of the world's total figure (*Africa Recovery* 15[3], 2001). Other diseases such malaria and tuberculosis also continue to take a toll on the vulnerable populations in Africa, posing further challenges to development. These seemingly insurmountable challenges are crowned by high incidents of inter- and especially intra-state conflicts and environmental degradation, which cumulatively threaten to undermine Africa's chances of meeting the millennium development goal of reducing poverty by 50 percent by the year 2015. It is in the midst of such a seemingly distressful economic situation that we evaluate the contribution of international migration to Africa's development.

GLOBALIZATION AND MIGRATION

Although currently a common household word, globalization remains a contested concept in terms of its meaning and effects on migration and development in the South. Contemporary conceptualizations of globalization have focused on its visible characteristics. For example, Hettne *et al.* (1992) define globalization as "the vision of a borderless world in which territory has lost all importance and functionalism is predominant." For McGrew (1992), globalization can be seen in two senses: first as "the multiplicity of linkages and interconnections that transcend nation-states and societies, which currently make up the modern world system" and, second, as "a process through which events, decisions, and activities in one part of the world can come to have significant consequences for individuals and communities in quite distant parts of the globe." Giddens (1990) puts this idea more succinctly, describing it as "the intensification of worldwide social relations, which link distant localities in such a way that local happenings are shaped by events occurring many miles away and vice versa." Others see globalization in terms of the re-ordering of social relations at the global level. Thus, Held *et al.* (1999), for example, perceive globalization as a process (or set of processes), "which embodies a transformation of the spatial organization of social relations and transactions—assessed in terms of their extensity, intensity, velocity and impact-generating transcontinental or inter-regional flows and networks of activity." From the above postulations, a set of basic and incontrovertible attributes of globalization can be discerned. These include internationalization (i.e., the intensification of cross border interaction between countries); liberalization (i.e., its emphasis on deregulation of the political and economic spaces); universalization (i.e., its capacity to spread experiences of one region to all corners of the globe); and deterritorialization (i.e. its capacity to undermine the sanctity of state borders) (Scholte 2001). The dynamics of globalization have intricately linked economies and peoples across the globe such that the world has become what is now euphemistically described as a "global village." International migration is a visible feature of globalization and the global village Findlay et al. (1998).

The relation between globalization and migration, particularly the extent to which the former instigates the latter is often indirect and sometimes unobtrusive. Although globalization theoretically established a "global village," which presumes unrestricted movement, there are practical barriers to the mobility of labor across national borders. Potential receiving countries, fearful of overwhelming influxes, have been careful to impose various forms of restrictions in an attempt to admit only immigrants with expertise lacking in the local labor market. Such restrictions are imposed to maximize benefits of migration while minimizing its perverse impacts. Yet, in spite of restrictive immigration policies, international migration is on the increase. For example, the UN estimated in 1990 that about 154 million people were living outside their countries of birth or citizenship. Estimates ten years later in 2000 put this figure at 175 million (Kapur and McHale 2003). In addition to internal causes of migration, also referred to as "push factors"—conditions that provide motivations for emigration—(Roer-Strier and Olshtain-Mann 1999), the logics of globalization catalyze international migration. This occurs for various reasons.

Neoliberal reforms attending globalization have largely worked against Africa and have widened the gap between it and the rest of the world. This has been due to the inability of Africa, for various structural reasons, to take advantage of the opportunities presented by globalization or confront the challenges it poses. Africa therefore loses out. In his famous Reith Lectures on globalization, Giddens (1999) noted that the share of the poorest fifth of the world's population in global income dropped from 2.3 percent to 1.4 percent over the past 15 years. During the same period, the proportion taken by the richest fifth rose from 70 percent to 85 percent. The effects of globalization on Sub-Saharan Africa were even more ominous. Giddens observed that 20 Sub-Saharan African countries now have lower incomes per head than they did 20 years ago. Social and income inequalities have also become even more palpable as many African cities show a glaring contrast between rich and affluent suburbs on the one hand, and poor and dilapidated slums on the other. Environmental degradation is on the increase in the name of free trade, undercutting the source of livelihood for many rural dwellers. One effect of such grotesque asymmetry in the distribution of the gains and pains of globalization is to fuel migration.

As intimated already, globalization creates virtual borders; it undermines state boundaries that have traditionally served as barriers to migration. The decline of old borders is facilitated by the pressure on countries and companies to raise competitiveness seen as critical for state and corporate survival in the contemporary global economy. The desire to be competitive in turn compels countries to attract scarce expertise from outside their borders. The current international trade regime under the World Trade Organization (WTO) and its offshoot, the Multilateral Agreement on Investments (MAI), which compels countries to relax trade restrictions, create an auspicious environment for foreign investments and migration. The freedom of capital and investors to move and relocate in foreign countries has been significantly increased by the prescriptions of these institutions. The simple fact that investors, whether foreign or local, can sue host governments who pursue policies deemed inimical to the free movement of capital, has served to place restraints on the ability of states to mount immigration fences.

Moreover, globalization and the dynamics of the contemporary international economic environment necessitate the formation of regional economic groupings and common markets. Such regional formations are necessary to insulate states from the damaging impact of international competition which is intensified by globalization. Importantly, in the process of strengthening common markets, regional blocs have moved towards relaxing restrictions on the movement of individuals. Like the European Union (EU), the major regionalist experiments in Africa—the Economic Community of West African States (ECOWAS), the Southern African Development Community (SADC), and the revived East African Community (EAC), all have protocols relating to the free movement of citizens within the community. As a rule, open door policies generally generate migration, particularly so on a continent where there are deeply contrasting levels of development among countries. The stark contrast between prosperous post-Apartheid South Africa and other impoverished Sub-Saharan African countries has presented the former as an attractive destination for migrants from the latter. Thus, South Africa remains the top receiving country in Sub-Saharan Africa (Mattes *et al.* 2000). Thus, common markets and regional groupings, which are responses to globalization, have become important developments in the global migration discourse.

Shrinking formal employment due to the inability of the public sector to expand, coupled with incessant pressure from international creditor institutions on Africa to downsize, have seriously restricted opportunities for public employment. At the same time, the private sector has failed to expand proportionately to absorb labor from the formal sector despite the implementation of excruciatingly painful adjustment policies. The result has been an escalation of unemployment in the region, which has in turn caused a corresponding expansion in the informal sector in Sub-Saharan Africa. One dimension of the informal sector is the growth in informal cross-border trading, which has been facilitated by the artificiality and porosity of African borders. As Muzvidziwa (2000) notes of Zimbabwe, the dire economic adversities generated by long periods of mismanagement and SAP has presented the informal sector and cross-border trading as exit options from poverty. Cross-border traders form an important component of temporal migrants in many African countries.

The pervasiveness of autocratic and military-styled regimes across Africa prior to the democratization wave of the early 1990s has played no mean role in inducing the emigration of political opponents, who were constantly threatened with arrests and detention. In Nigeria, Ghana, and Cameroon, to name just a few, the victims of repression and persecution included academics and professionals who, lacking propitious environments for intellectual and professional activities, migrated to other African countries and destinations beyond the continent. With globalization and democratization, there has occurred a rapid annihilation of autocratic regimes. The last fifteen years has therefore seen the restoration of democratic rule and the respect for human rights in a majority of African countries, albeit at varying degrees. The new democratic dispensation has caused a return home of some political migrants. The demise of apartheid and the institution of majority rule in South Africa have enabled Pretoria to establish diplomatic ties with the outside world. Consequently, restrictions on travels to South Africa imposed by various African governments have been eased, allowing hundreds of migrants to head for the country.

Pellerin (1997) argues that the causes of forced migration and refugee movements in particular must be understood within the broader context of the movement of capital, global economic restructuring, and changes in the social organization of production. Africa's reliance on export agriculture calls for the use of large expanse of land. This is acquired at the expense of small-scale farmers who often fall victims to displacements. This scenario has implication for migration in at least two ways—first, the reduction in the size of arable land for small-scale farming intensifies competition among subsistence farmers and communities, which often lead to conflicts and refugees. Second, displaced and unemployed farmers either move into urban centers in a hopeless search for employment or cross borders into neighboring countries. The pressure to establish large plantations and tea factories, for example, led the Ethiopian government to evict peasant farmers who were then forced to relocate

(Kelbessa 2000). Globalization thus induces migration in various ways. While the impact of globalization on migration remains uncontested, the nature of the relation between the latter and Africa's development continues to generate considerable intellectual debate, an issue we turn to next.

MIGRATION AND AFRICA'S DEVELOPMENT

A cursory discussion of the nature, typologies, and causes of migration is essential in assessing its developmental impact on Africa. The literature discerns four main typologies of migration, namely, intra- and interstate migration; permanent and temporary migration; forced and voluntary migration; and intra- and extra-African migration. Appleyard (1992) breaks these down further into six main categories: (1) permanent settlers with no interest of returning to their original home countries; (2) temporary contract workers who are skilled, semi-skilled or unskilled; (3) temporary professional transients, who are skilled workers that move from one country to another and who are mostly, though not entirely, employees of international or joint-venture companies; (4) illegal or undocumented immigrants; (5) asylum seekers, or those who appeal on grounds of political discrimination and oppression; and (6) refugees, or those who are defined under international conventions such as the UN and OAU, now the AU, conventions relating to the status of refugees. However, the two most relevant for the current discussion are the dichotomies between forced and voluntary migration and between intra- and extra-African migrations. Forced migrants generally refer to people who leave their countries of origin either proactively or reactively in response to conditions beyond their control. Such conditions include political oppression, conflicts, wars, and environmental catastrophes. They are conventionally referred to as refugees (OAU 1969).

Voluntary migrants on the other hand are those who relocate in new areas in their countries or other countries based on discretion rather than uncontrollable factors. This form of migration mostly includes people seeking better economic opportunities outside their original home countries. These are frequently referred to as economic migrants. Although the number of voluntary migrants from African countries is increasing, especially following the deracialization of South Africa, the majority of intra-African migrants are refugees seeking security and peace outside their countries of origin. The UNHCR documents that, while Africa hosted 6 million of the 21.5 million refugees worldwide in 1999, the continent was home to 6.7 million of the global population of 22 million in 2002 (Clover 2002). While some forced migrants return or are voluntarily repatriated back home after the stabilization of conditions that precipitated their initial exit, others acquire permanent residence and citizenship of their host countries.

In addition to globalization, whose impact on migration has remained largely indirect, there are more direct factors spawning immigration in Africa. The causes of voluntary and forced migration in Africa have received enormous attention from scholars. Economic, demographic, political, ethnic conflicts, and cultural factors have been identified as central to the emigration dynamics in Sub-Saharan Africa (Adepuju 1994). Environmental factors, which generate proactive and reactive ecological migrants, have also been identified. Such environmental causes include droughts and floods and human-induced factors such as desertification, pollution, and overexploitation of natural resources. Environmental factors intensify competition for diminishing natural resources that lead to violent conflicts and consequently migration (Timberlake 1991; Obi 1997; Nnoli 1990; Suliman and Omer 1994). Besides the Sahelian droughts of 1973 and 1984, which hit a greater part of Sub-Sahara Africa and caused massive population displacements, conflicts (often resulting from contests over the state and resources, oppression and undemocratic governance) have remained the leading causes of forced migration in recent times in Africa. The UN Secretary-General, Mr. Kofi Annan, warily notes that "in 1996 alone 14 of the 53 countries in Africa were afflicted by armed conflicts, accounting for more than half of all war-related deaths worldwide and resulting in more than 8 million refugees, returnees and displaced persons" (UN 1998).

On the other hand, economic factors have largely served as "push" factors for voluntary migration within and outside Africa. Sluggish growth, stagnation and, in some cases, decline have been marked features of most post-independence African economies. Africa's reliance on single primary products highlights its vulnerability to fluctuations in world prices. The two oil crises of the 1970s along with a crushing debt burden have not helped Africa's economies either. Corruption, self-destructive statist policies, and internal mismanagement all combined to compound economic crisis that caused distortions in Africa's labor market (Itzigsohn 1995). With a slow expansion of the private sector, employment opportunities shrank in Africa and created pressures for migration. Free and heavily subsidized educational systems in many African countries also helped to produce larger numbers of graduates than could be accommodated, increasing the propensity for labor migration (Kapur and McHale 2003:445). Further migratory pressures were exerted by inflation, which constantly eroded the value of real wages. As Stalker (1994) notes, educated professionals whose expertise is marketable beyond their countries are likely to migrate from their locations when they feel inadequately remunerated. Asante-Darko (2002) thus argues that the emigration of Africa's brains is mainly due to the inability of African governments to create, and their tendency to undermine, brain-retaining conditions. Hundreds of professionals and middle-class elements have therefore left their countries for "greener pastures," either in other parts of Africa or beyond the continent, causing a brain drain in their countries of origin. The intensity of economic adversities in Sub-Saharan Africa has in recent years forced unskilled labor to migrate, although most of these use informal routes to their destinations and tend to engage in unskilled jobs (Akokpari 2000).

While internal economic adversities tend to "push" exasperated citizens into migration, the attraction of relatively affluent countries has tended to "pull" them. Relatively opulent countries in Southern Africa, including South Africa, Botswana, Namibia and, to a limited extent, Lesotho, are the leading centers of attraction to Sub-Saharan immigrants (Gay 2000; Mattes et al. 2000; Oucho 2000; Akokpari 2005). South Africa, with its relatively higher economic development, is seen as the "Europe of Africa," to which large numbers of African immigrants—skilled and unskilled—head. Yet, migration to South Africa predated the demise of apartheid in 1994. Historically, migration to South Africa was linked to the process of capital accumulation in the country from the nineteenth century that began with the establishment of white-owned farms, which employed wage labor and led to the migration of indigenous black Africans to the farms (Amin 1972). The pace of capital development and wage labor employment were accelerated with the discovery of precious minerals in South Africa towards the end of the nineteenth century: diamond in 1867 and gold in 1885. This did not only revolutionalize the South African economy, but it also expanded its labor market. With the expansion of the mines, internal labor supply was supplanted by imported labor from neighboring countries such as Lesotho, Malawi, Mozambique, Swaziland, and Zimbabwe. Subsequently, the main supplier countries of Lesotho, Mozambique, and Zimbabwe became known as "labor reserves" (Wilson 1972; Lacey 1981; Matlosa 1996). Migration of skilled and unskilled labor to South Africa intensified after 1994, with large numbers of Africans seeking to work either on permits or as refugees.

Yet, post-apartheid South Africa displays a curious migration paradox in that it simultaneously displays centripetal and centrifugal attributes. While it attracts immigrants, it also repels some of its citizens. Although hundreds of black South Africans who sought refuge in other countries under apartheid have returned home since 1994, the post-apartheid period has seen a phenomenal emigration of the mainly white professionals to Australia, New Zealand, the UK, and the US. By 1997, just three years into black majority rule, South Africa was estimated to have lost 11,225 brains of various professions. Escalating crime, HIV/AIDS, uncertainty, low remunerations and affirmative action are cited as some of the main reasons for the brain drain from South Africa. The influx of immigrants into South Africa, however, outstrips the number emigrating. It is estimated that in 1997 South Africa was home to a colossal 6 million immigrants (Brown *et al.* 2000).

Under incessant economic and intolerable working conditions, skilled labor has found new destinations outside Africa. Professionals from Africa have generally, though not exclusively, found their former colonial powers as preferred destinations. This is because of old historical ties, the shared linguistic similarities, and the ease with which they are assimilated into the host societies. French-speaking African professions tend to head for France, Belgium, Canada, and other French-speaking European countries, while English-speaking professionals tend to prefer the UK, US, Australia, New Zealand, and Canada. Similarly, skilled labor from Portugal's former colonies sees it as a preferred destination. While accurate data on migration is elusive in much of Africa, there is no doubt about the sheer intensity of the brain drain. The UN Economic Commission for Africa (ECA) and the International Organization for Migration (IOM) estimate that 27,000 skilled Africans left the continent for industrialized countries between 1960 and 1975. This figure rose to 40,000 between 1975 and 1984. It is estimated that at least 20,000 skilled Africans have left the continent each year since 1990 (*Africa Recovery* 17[2] 2003). A critical dimension of such extra-African migration pattern is the extent to which it impacts on Africa's development. In the next section, therefore, we first evaluate the effects of intra-African migration, that is the distribution of costs and benefits of immigration on host and home countries, and then turn to the general debate on the impact of the brain drain and migrant remittances on Africa's development.

THE EFFECTS OF MIGRATION ON AFRICA'S DEVELOPMENT—THE UNENDING DEBATE

Arguably, the debate on the impact of migration on development is one of the most heated among social scientists and labor economists. For the host country, the effects of immigration on development are both perverse and positive. Immigration changes the demographic complexion of the population of the host country. It also swells local populations, placing additional strains on the resources and infrastructure of the host economy. Sometimes, immigrants may undermine local systems and cultures. This is often the case where a country has to receive large numbers of refugees. Mutual suspicion and hostilities between host and immigrant communities could lead to tension, xenophobia, and conflict (Kapur and McHale 2003; Akokpari 2002). Host governments require additional resources, which could have been used to promote development, to expand infrastructure in order to accommodate the new arrivals. Similarly, valuable resources have to be expended in mitigating tensions or resolving conflicts between host and migrant communities.

The negative effects of migration on the host country are often neutralized by the positive contribution it makes to development in the host country. Some argue that immigration is an important source of labor that facilitates economic growth and development. The countries losing brains through emigration must of necessity rely on migrant labor force to fill the void. In addition, migration brings scarce expertise to host economies and helps employers to raise the level of efficiency in industries, which is a critical requirement for survival in the globalized and competitive world environment (Papademetrious 1997). The US, Canada, and many of the industrialized countries owe their development partly to the contribution of immigrants. Countries like Lesotho and Botswana, which lack sufficient local human capital, rely heavily on foreign skills (Oucho 2000; Akokpari 2005). Given the Bantu system of education under apartheid and the consequent inability to produce the required number of trained expertise, South Africa has had to rely on foreign skills in certain sectors of the economy. Wocke and Klein (2002) argue that the survival of the South African mining industry, a critical sector for the country's development, is attributable to migrant workers.

The effects of migration on the supplier country or region are equally phenomenal and can either be positive or negative. The debate on the subject remains inconclusive. The discussion on the impact of migration on the supplier country can be broadened to include Africa as a whole, since in terms of extra-continent migration, Africa represents a single supplying region. The positive contributions of migration to development include a reduction in population and, hence, strains on the country's infrastructure. This means resources are "freed" to be used to promote further development. However, the most visible and frequently trumpeted benefit from migration for the home country is migrant remittances. Although the capacity of remittances to impact positively on development cannot be disputed, it is argued that on the balance sheet such positive contributions are counterbalanced by the negative impact of the resultant brain drain on Africa.

Without doubt, remittances have brought some foreign exchange, which in the context of poverty and the exacting economic conditions generated by globalization in Africa, have helped to alleviate, even if temporarily, the plight of governments, communities and families. Examples from a few Sub-Saharan African countries will suffice to underscore the importance of migrant remittances. Until the 1990s, when a large pool of its work force was retrenched from the South African mines, migrant remittances were the second most important source of revenue for the Government of Lesotho after custom duties. By 1976, about a quarter of Lesotho's working population (approximately 100,000) was employed by the South African mining industry. Through a policy of Compulsory Deferred Payments (CDP), a policy that resulted from a bilateral agreement between the governments of Lesotho and South Africa, 60 percent of migrant wages were paid through the Central Bank of Lesotho in Maseru. Lesotho migrant workers in South Africa were thus forced to draw large proportions of their salaries in Maseru. Through interest payments, the CDP became a major source of revenue for the Lesotho government. In 1990, 1991, and 1995, for example, migrant remittances amounted to $148 million, $88 million, and $89 million, respectively (Matlosa 1996). With retrenchments, however, Lesotho's government receipts from migrant remittances have declined. For example, while remittances added a whopping 67 percent to the country's GDP in 1990, the corresponding percentage in 1993 was just 50 percent (Sparreboom and Sparreboom-Burger 1996). Besides serving as a source of revenue for the government, remittances supported extended families. A study in the early 1990s found that each Basotho migrant miner in South Africa supported between 10 and 15 dependents (Coplan and Thoalane 1994).

Other Sub-Saharan African countries rely heavily on migrant remittances as sources of national income. For example, until the massive retrenchments of Mozambican workers in South African mines in the 1990s, migrant remittances accounted for one-third of the country's foreign exchange (de Vletter 1995). Economically destitute Niger also depends quite a lot on the remittances of its migrant workers in Nigeria for revenue (Charlick 1994). However, in 1983 and 1985, Niger suffered a fatal blow when, in response to economic crisis, Nigeria expelled millions of migrant workers from the country. Migrant remittances to Niger consequently plummeted. Remittances to Burkina Faso from its nationals in Ivory Coast have also declined from $110 million in 1994 to $41 million in 2001 as a result of growing xenophobia and conflict in the latter. These have led to the exit of many of the 2.2 million Burkinabe previously working in Ivory Coast (Harsch 2003b: 22). While remittances from migrants in host to home African countries are on the decline, this is on the increase for countries with large numbers of migrants in the diaspora outside Africa. In Ghana, for example, migrant remittances from abroad reached a record high of $2 billion in 2004, exceeding the earnings from cocoa, the country's main export earner by 100 percent.

Thus, Ghanaian president, John Kuffour, was full of praise for Ghanaians in the diaspora for their contribution in rebuilding the country.[1] Similarly, Somaliland, a breakaway province of Somalia and still struggling to attain full international recognition, receives an estimated $500 million a year in remittances from its nationals in the diaspora. This amount is four times more than the annual revenue from its main export, livestock.[2] In 2002, Morocco and Tunisia received $3 billion and $1 billion respectively in remittances from their citizens in the diaspora (World Bank 2004: 241).[3]

On the aggregate, remittances have become the second largest form of capital flow to developing countries after FDI, although some studies, in fact, depict them as leading (Kapur and McHale 2003).[4] In 2001, for example, remittances to developing countries represented 42 percent and 260 percent of FDI and ODA, respectively. In terms of regional distribution, Sub-Saharan Africa received 5 percent of total global remittances with the bulk going to Latin America and the Caribbean (UK Department of International Development 2003). It is, however, believed that the percentage of global remittances to Sub-Saharan Africa could be higher if accurate data existed. Thus, migrant remittances provide a lifeline not only to communities and families, which are enabled to access basic services such as housing, education and health, but also to governments, whose capacities to provide public services are enhanced. The efficient management and use of remittances could help advance the development agenda of African countries.

The true extent to which remittances promote development, however, remains polemical. Scholars writing from a classical economic perspective argue that migrant remittances impact positively on development. This argument is predicated on the thinking that remittances constitute an important source of foreign currency. As the argument goes, foreign currency not only helps to level the balance of payments, but it also helps to settle the import bills of labor-sending countries. Thus, the availability of and access to foreign exchange are critical factors in development (Bliss 1989: 1196-97). Further, remittances provide incentives for the local production of goods and services (Stark 1982). In addition to improving income distribution, remittances also improve the living standards of beneficiaries (Stahl and Arnold 1986; Keely and Tran 1989).

---

[1] www.ghanaweb.com:diasporian news of Wednesday 5 January 2005 (6/1/05).

[2] www.globalization101.org/issue/migration/4.asp (10/1/05).

[3] www.ghanaweb.com: diasporian news of Monday 21 February 2005 (22/2/05).

[4] Also, see a summary of a study done by Dilip Ratha, a World Bank economist, at www.economist.com/finance (15/5/05).

Studies on the impact of remittances on development in various parts of the developing world found this to be positive. In Turkey, for example, remittances helped recipients to set up small businesses, under periods of austerity, which positively affected development (Portes and Guarnizo 1991). Similarly, in the Caribbean basin—Jamaica, the Dominican Republic, Haiti and Guatemala—remittances significantly improved the living conditions of low-income populations (Itzigsohn 1995). And in Mexico (Taylor and Wyatt 1996), Southern Africa (Lucas 1985), and Botswana (Lucas and Stark 1985), the positive impact of remittances on local production activities were confirmed.

However, studies alluding to the positive contribution of remittances hardly tell the whole story. And often, the advantages of remittances for development are overstated. Glytsos (2002) contends that "most of the literature about the impact of remittances on the economies of labor exporting countries looks at the visible side and leaves more or less unexplored the multiple indirect [and negative] effects, thus giving an incomplete picture." Beyond raising the level of national savings, remittances are essentially private transfers that do not directly augment the public budget. Governments have no control over them and do not determine their destination or use. Nor are market forces able to channel remittances to the most productive sectors, or into the most innovative hands to promote development. Rather, the use of remittances is determined entirely by recipients. Studies have shown that a greater proportion of remittances are spent on housing and consumer goods rather than on investments, although it is acknowledged that financing education with remittances is a long-term investment in human capital (Glytsos 2002; Macmillen 1982; Russell 1986).

Indeed, studies have established the potential dangers of remittances to growth and development in the labor-supplying country. Migrant remittances, although an important source of foreign exchange and income, are in reality a risky and a highly unreliable source because of their lack of ontological status. The flow of remittances is contingent on a number of intervening factors, including the continuous labor process and the willingness of migrants to remit, while some host governments place restrictions on how much migrants can remit at a time.[5] These

[5] The South African Reserve Bank, the institution responsible for regulating capital flows in and out of the country, has strict quotas on remittances. There are specific Rand values that can be remitted per year through commercial banks, as well as percentages of known incomes that can be remitted per month through forex bureaus. For example, the maximum monthly remittable amount through Western Union and Money Gram cannot exceed one's monthly income.

factors, along with economic recession and restrictions on immigration by receiving countries may sharply reduce the volume of remittances and cause problems in the balance of payments of the labor-sending countries. In addition to questions of reliability, remittances tend to increase and, in fact, perpetuate the dependence of recipients (Kritz and Keely 1981; Glytsos 2002). Others argue that because remittances tend to increase purchasing power, they fuel inflation. By adding directly to household incomes, remittances change consumption patterns and lead to the demand for more imported goods that often undermine balance of payment. In Egypt and Syria, for example, increased demand for and consumption of imported goods generated by remittances impacted negatively on development (Glytsos 2002).

Remittances also have the capacity to undermine long-term development in the home country in a number of ways. Remitted monies may make governments relax in their bid to adopt long-term economic policies for development. The continuous flow of remittances may, for example, blind labor-sending countries from the urgency to change the structures of the economy to increase competitiveness. Continuous dependence on remittances deprives an economy of diversification and adaptation to changing conditions in the global economy and thus undermines governmental innovation. In the final analysis, critical sections of the economy may suffer. The decline of agriculture in Lesotho in the 1980s was, for example, attributed to the country's heavy reliance on migrant remittances (World Bank 1984).

In recent years huge concerns are being raised about the role of remittances in collapsed and war-raved African states. Collapsed states are viewed by the West either as breeding grounds or havens for terrorists. Since the September 11 attack on the US, and George Bush's declaration of war on global terrorism, Washington in particular has been concerned that remittances to Somalia, which has failed to establish a credible central government since 1991, are destined to help militants and terrorist organizations. Consequently, the US shut down a firm in Mogadishu that dominated the remittance business in Somalia and caused a decline in remittances to the country. However, the exact extent of the impact of the US move is still unclear. Migrant remittances to Somalia are still estimated at between 25 and 40 percent of the country's total GDP (Kapur and McHale 2003: 56). The challenge for the west, which is concerned with contributing to peace and development in Somalia, is how to distinguish between "good" money (remittances destined for genuine development) and "bad" money (that which is used to finance terror). Similar security concerns are valid for imploding states such as Sierra Leone and Liberia, where although remittances may not directly finance American- or Western-targeted terror, they could nevertheless be used to acquire offensive weapons that fuel local conflicts. Thus, remittances, frequently identified as the most important contribution from migration to home governments, are not without dangers to development. On the whole, the advantages generated by migrant remittances are counter-balanced, sometimes completely negated, by the huge cost Africa bears as a result of international migration.

Without doubt, the large volumes of migrant remittances are the direct costs of Africa's huge brain drain. In the midst of the brain drain the health and education sectors are often the hardest hit, leaving home governments with the onerous task of either replacing lost skill or grappling with massive declines in the quality of service delivery in the affected sectors. Here, too, a few examples are germane to illustrate the extent of the brain drain. In Zambia, for example, emigration caused a drastic reduction in the number of doctors from 1,600 to a staggering 400 in the last twenty years. The massive exodus of health workers left critical implications for the health sector, which even under normal situations was struggling to meet the healthcare needs of the population. The IOM estimates that at least 60 percent of doctors trained in Ghana during the 1980s have left the country (*Africa Recovery* 2003). It also estimates that 21,000 Nigerian doctors are working in the US alone, while more doctors from Benin work in France than in their own country.[6] The South African Network of Skills Abroad (SANSA), a coordinating network that keeps in touch with skilled South Africans in the diaspora, confirms that Canada is the leading destination for South African doctors. It estimates that one in every 5 of the 1,530 medical doctors in the Canadian province of Saskatchewan alone received their medical degrees from South Africa. SANSA also estimates that 60 percent of South Africa's expatriate graduates are located in the top 6 destination countries, with Australia, the UK and the US accounting for more than half of them. In 2003/2004, 1,689 and 511 nurses from South Africa and Nigeria respectively joined the British health sector. And by the beginning of 2004, 6,208 and 1,661 doctors from South Africa and Nigeria respectively were registered on the British doctors' roll.[7]

The costs of the emigration of South African doctors are the growing shortages of health workers and the country's reliance on Cuban and expatriate African doctors, which cost the South African government millions of rands annually. South Africa is perhaps better off than other

[6] www.ghanaweb.com/ghanahomepage/newsarchives/printnews.php (28/1/05).

[7] www.ghanaweb.com/GhanaHomePage/NewsArchives/printnews.php?ID=82395 (28/5/05).

Sub-Saharan African countries in that it has the financial strength to recruit from Cuba. Zambia, Nigeria, or Ghana lacks such financial ability to import expatriate doctors. It is estimated that 23,000 African health professionals emigrate every year. A study in 1989 showed that many Basotho health workers, including doctors, dentists, and nurses, were migrating to South Africa (Transformation Resource Center 1989). A great number of the skilled posts left behind had to be filled by migrants. Statistics in mid-2002 showed that of the 109 doctors in the country, 76 were foreigners (Akokpari 2005). Countries like Lesotho and Botswana, which suffer from chronic shortages of manpower, however, have of necessity to rely on skilled migrants (Akokpari 2005; Oucho 2000). It is estimated that poor countries, including those in Africa, spend $500 million a year in the training of health workers (*Africa Recovery* July 2003).

Educational sectors in Africa are other visible victims of the continent's brain drain. Following growing economic adversities, Zambian universities lost more than 200 lecturers during the 10-year period between 1985 and 1995, creating a massive shortage of academic staff. This shortage caused the closure of some academic departments. Nigeria and Ghana also suffered massive losses of academics at the height of their economic adversities in the 1970s and 1980s, which, although in many cases, did not result in departmental closures but nevertheless led to the appointment of underqualified academics as lecturers. In the estimation of the IOM, it would have cost rich nations, the brain-gainers from Africa's skills, $184,000 to train each of the estimated 3 million professionals educated in poor countries now working in the developed world. IOM also estimates that African countries spend around $4 billion to employ about 100,000 non-African expatriates (*Africa Recovery* July 2003). In the reality of migration dynamics, one country's loss is another's gain. Africa's loss of skill through emigration is a gain to the receiving countries in the developed world; while the delivery systems in the health and educational sectors are weakened by the exodus of doctors and academics, those of the receiving countries are strengthened and made efficient by the skills of professionals Africa helped to train. IOM further estimates that it has, on the aggregate, cost Africa $9 billion in lost of human capital since 1997 as a result of skilled emigration. In the face of unattractive working environments at home, the emigration of African professionals may continue unabated. The conjecture of conflicts, instability, insecurity, and low public sector remuneration, along with the ease at which labor moves under globalization is certain to accelerate emigration. IOM, in fact, estimates that one in 10 Africans will work outside their countries by 2015, the year in which Africa is expected to be half its current level of poverty.

Arguably, the negative effects of the brain drain outweigh its perceived benefits, particularly in relation to Africa's quest for poverty reduction and development. Migrant remittance, which as noted already, is the major positive gain from Africa's brain drain, is insufficient to offset the costs of emigration of skilled migrants. In the first place, with the exception of countries like Lesotho and to some extent Mozambique, which have devised ways of managing remittances through their central banks, the flow of remittances to the majority of Sub-Saharan African countries is uncontrolled and well beyond the reach of the state. Although in a few cases beneficiaries of remittances enter into ventures that create few jobs, overseas monies are scarcely invested in long-term projects. In much of rural Africa, these are used on non-investible and unprofitable ventures such as making expensive funeral donations, paying bride prices, and paying for weddings, and for short-term ostentatious life-styles. The contribution of such consumption patterns to national development is thus minimal. The lack of transparency and the ubiquitous corruption characterizing governance systems in Sub-Saharan African countries raise doubts about the state's judicious use of migrant remittances. Remittances neither create doctors, dentists, and nurses for hospitals, nor provide academics for universities. There is a trade-off between migrant remittances and development, as alluded to by the Ghanaian minister for tertiary education, Ms. Elizabeth Ohene in a speech at the 57th Annual New Year School at the University of Ghana on 3 January 2006: "the monies they [migrants] send are certainly most welcome, but we require a critical mass of educated human resource to make the nation what we all wish it to become."[8] Migrant remittances can hardly compensate for the loss of Africa's skills.

While the benefits of migrant remittances are enjoyed by a fortunate few, the cost of emigration and especially brain drain are borne by the nation as a whole. The consequences of the lack of doctors, lecturers, and engineers, for example, are felt not just by recipients, but also by non-recipients of remittances. Resources expended on the training of emigrated skill and on hiring replacement skills are public resources that could have been expended on other equally pressing needs of society. The emigration of skills also means the state is getting little or no returns from its investments in the training of skilled emigrants. This is especially compelling in Africa where, until the imposition of SAPs in the 1980s,

[8] "Brain drain undermines development". http://www.ghanaweb.com/GhanaHomePage/NewsArchive/artikel.php?ID=97018 (3/1/06).

education was heavily subsidized by the state. Clearly, the cost of skilled emigration to Africa is enormous, in financial, human, and developmental terms. The challenge is to devise ways of halting, even reversing, the brain drain in order to retain the vital expertise for development.

MANAGING AFRICA'S SKILL EMIGRATION—PROSPECTS AND PROBLEMS

A few initiatives have been attempted in the past to address Africa's brain drain. One of these is SANSA, a South African network. However, as noted, SANSA does not technically advocate the repatriation of South African skilled emigrants. Rather, it merely seeks to keep in touch with South Africa's skills in the diaspora. Thus, in terms of halting and reversing South Africa's brain drain, SANSA's influence is minimal. Portes and Sensenbrenner (1993) note that immigrants from particular countries continue to exhibit their common identities—what they refer to as "bounded solidarity." This solidarity has led to the formation of hometown and country associations among migrants in the diaspora. These associations hold meetings in which they discuss the affairs of their home countries and the contribution they can make towards development at home. However, these associations hardly encourage the return of their members to the home countries. Nevertheless, in keeping in touch with family and community members in the home country, migrant associations mobilize resources to assist communities at home. These often include, sending to their home communities educational materials ranging from books to computers. The Africast Foundation, a group of Ghanaian expatriates that send refurbished computers in the US to Ghana's educational institutions, is a notable example in this regard.

Repatriation and the physical relocation of expatriates either to their home countries or to another African country has been another approach to the emigration question. The IOM attempted to assist in the repatriation of skilled emigrants back to Africa. Between 1983 and 1999, its leading program on skill repatriation, the Program of Reintegration of Qualified African Nationals, yielded modest results. During the 16-year period, it managed to relocate about 2000 nationals to 11 participating African countries. Repatriation was also attempted by the Kenya-based Research and Development Forum for Science-led Development in Africa (RANDFORUM). In 1999, the Presidential Forum on the Management of Science and Technology, a group of serving and retired African heads of states, requested RANDFORUM to identify and assist African expatriates willing to return to the continent. However, RANDFORUM achieved very little on this front mainly because it lacked regional or continental support; its activities were initiated by a few African countries. On the whole, repatriation and relocation failed to make a significant impact on reversing the brain drain because the projects required huge sums of money (Mutume 2003). Relocating emigrants may demand remunerations and facilities comparable to what they enjoyed in the host country. In Sub-Saharan Africa, where income levels are extremely low and basic research or working infrastructure are either poor or non-existent, repatriation or relocation as programs was destined to fail.

Other challenges to repatriation include problems of immigration. Some African emigrants in the diaspora have emigration status that allows for just one entry. Immigrants with such single-entry permits cannot return to the host country after an exit. This fear may keep some African emigrants more or less permanently in the diaspora. Emigrants on single-entry permits are unlikely to respond to relocation calls, if they are unsure about economic conditions at home. Still others are not inclined to return because of the social tension they are likely to face in home societies. At the same time there is little incentive for many of the labor-receiving countries, especially those in the North and who rely on African skills, to take drastic measures towards repatriating Africans. As these tend to benefit from migrant skills at relatively lower costs, they will rather continue to lure African professionals with better remuneration and service conditions. Reaping where they have not sown, receiving countries have no inclination to seriously support any policies on repatriation. Devastated by HIV/AIDS and needing to retain its health professionals, South Africa is at the forefront of a campaign to establish an international regime to control the exodus of professionals from critical sectors (such as health) from Africa. Although the campaign is supported by certain Northern NGOs, this is unlikely to elicit the immediate support of the leading beneficiaries of Africa's emigrating brains.

A further source of concern is that returnees are often perceived as unpatriotic for leaving the country in the first place. They may be considered strangers in their own communities, which may leave them with a sense of alienation. It might take some time for these individuals to feel integrated into their own societies. Also, the difficult question of finding a job suited to one's expertise may be another discouraging factor for repatriation. While doctors may easily find placements, others like academics may not. For example, the thousands of Ghanaian academics in the diaspora cannot be accommodated by the few universities in the country if they were to return. Remaining in the diaspora, even at the risk of facing xenophobia or taking menial jobs for which a professional is practically underutilised, is a preferred alternative to becoming unemployed at home.

Above all, it has to be noted that migration, whether national or international, does not occur out of the blue. Migration is nearly always a proactive or reactive response to conditions and developments that threaten human peace and security. Even the absence of such conditions does not guarantee the absence of migration. Unfortunately, many of the "push factors" that have spawned emigration still remain. Conflicts, insecurity, low living conditions, and various diseases continue to threaten decent living in Africa. Moreover, notwithstanding the institution of democratic rule, corrupt and oppressive practices are rife in many parts of Africa. The conjuncture of these threatening conditions, while creating powerful disincentives for the voluntary repatriation of skilled emigrants, also incites new waves of emigration.

CONCLUSION

Development has remained a serious challenge for Africa. Globalization places Africa in an ambivalent position where it is threatened with marginalization at the same time that it is being strongly incorporated into the global politico-economic system through the implementation of neoliberal policies. The pressure to displace and replace the state with the market as the engine of development, exemplified in the adoption of SAP, has brought little developmental gains. Migration has thus become an inevitable consequence. These have been made worse by the pressures of which globalization, tends to compound Africa's economic adversities. Against a background of chronic shortage of skills, some African countries have had to rely on migration to meet their skills requirements. For these countries, then, immigration is a positive phenomenon. However, for the majority of African countries, extra-African emigration has proved particularly detrimental, as it has led to a serious brain drain and daunting developmental challenges for home governments. Although skilled emigration has brought in volumes of migrant remittances, which have helped governments and raised the purchasing power of beneficiaries and increased access to services, among other things, this has not been sufficient to offset the overall cost of emigration. As noted, some African governments have had to employ African expatriate doctors or recruit them from outside the continent. This is after they had spent large sums of money training doctors who serve in countries in the North. The continued prevalence of the factors inciting emigration, along with globalization, which facilitates the international movement of capital and labor, means that the challenge from the brain drain is far from over.

The AU and NEPAD consider Africans in the diaspora as a critical constituency in the continent's development. Although the AU has yet to specify clearly how it intends to integrate Africans in the diaspora into its development agenda, it is clear that an inescapable question is how to confront skilled emigration. A first step for the AU is to develop a regional response to the brain drain. This response should include a program in which the AU champions an international campaign to establish a global regime to regulate the emigration of skills from Africa, particularly skills considered immediately vital for national development. This program should be developed in a way that does not compromise the rights of potential migrants. South Africa advocates for the establishment of such a regime and the added voice of the AU could provide stronger and credible justification for such a scheme. This could help Africa maximize benefits from international migration, while minimizing its related costs.

REFERENCES

Adepuju, Aderanti. 1994. Preliminary Analysis of Emigration Dynamics in Sub-Saharan Africa" *International Migration* 32:197-216.

Africa Recovery. (UN Department of Public Information), Various issues.

Africa Renewal. 2004. (UN Department of Public Information) (18), October.

Africa Today. (Denver) March/April 1997.

Akokpari, John. 2000. "Globalization and Migration in Africa" *African Sociological Review* 4:72-92.

——. 2001. "Globalization and the Challenges for the African State." *Nordic Journal of African Studies* 10:188-209.

——. 2002. "International Migration, Xenophobia and the Dilemmas of the South African State." Pp. 221-246 in *South Africa Since 1994: Lessons and Prospects*, edited by Sipho Buthelezi and Elizabeth Le Roux. Pretoria: Africa Institute of South Africa.

——. 2005. "Strangers in a Strange Land: Citizenship and the Immigration Debate in Lesotho." *Development Southern Africa* 22:87-102.

Altzinger, Wilfred. 1995. "How Labor Market Experience of Migrants Differ: Australia and Austria Compared." *International Migration* 33:55-77.

Amin, Samir. 1972. "Underdevelopment and Dependence in Black Africa—Origins and Contemporary Forms." *Journal of Modern African Studies* 10:503-524.

Appleyard, Reginald. 1991. *International Migration: Challenge for the Nineties*. Geneva: IOM.

——. 1992. "International Migration and Development: An Unresolved Relationship." *International Migration* 30:251-266.

Asante, Sam K. 2003. "NEPAD: A Partnership of Unequal Partners." *New African*, (London) June:14-16.

Asante-Darko, Kwaku. 2002. "Pitfalls in the African Brain Drain Discourse." *MOTS PLURIELS* 20, February: 1-10. Retrieved July 14, 2006 (www.arts.uwa.edu.au/Mots-Pluriels/MP2002 kad.html).

Bliss, Christopher J.E. 1989. "Trade and Development." Pp. 1187-1240 in *Handbook of Development Economics V.2*, edited by Hollis Chenery and T.N. Srinivasan. Amsterdam: Elsevier Science Publishers.

Brown, Mercy, David Kaplan, and Jean-Baptiste Meyer. 2000. "The Brain Drain: An Outline of Skilled Emigration From South Africa." *Africa Insight* 30:41-47.

Borowski, Alan. 1996. "Israelis from Thailand and Ghana: Temporary Labour Migration and Illegal Immigration to Israel." Paper presented at a Seminar-Colloquium, Department of Sociology, McGill University, Montreal, Canada.

Charlick, Robert B. 1994. "Niger." Pp. 103-124 In *The Foreign Policies of ECOWAS*, edited by Timothy Shaw and Julius Okolo. London: Macmillan.

Clover, Jenny. 2002. "Situation Report: Refugees and Internally Displaced People's in Africa" Retrieved October 5, 2005 (http:/www.iss.co.za/AF/current/Refugees_IDPs.html.)

Coplan, David, and Thoalane, T. 1994. "Motherless Households, Landless Farms: The Social Implications of Changing Employment Patterns Among Lesotho Migrants." *IDRC Migrant Labor Working Paper*, No. 18.

De Vletter, Fion. 1995. "The Implications of Changing Migration Patterns in Southern Africa." in *Labor Migrancy in Southern Africa: Prospects for Post-Aparthied Transformation*, edited by J. Crush et al. Cape Town: University of Cape Town Labor Unit).

Findlay, Alan M.; F.L.N. Li, and H. Jones. 1998. "A Cultural Economy Perspective on Service Sector Migration in the Global City: The Case of Hong Kong." *International Migration* 36:131-157.

Gay, John. 2000. "Migration Attitudes of Skilled Professionals in Lesotho." *Africa Insight* October: 65-74.

Giddens, Anthony. 1990. *The Consequences of Modernity: Self and Society in the Late Modern Age*. Cambridge: Polity Press.

——. 1999. "Globalization." Reith Lectures Online. Retrieved December 5, 2005 (http://news2.thdo.bbc.co.uk/hi/english/static/events/reith_99/week1/week1).

Glytsos, Nicholas. 2002. "The Role of Migrant Remittances in Development: Evidence from Mediterranean Countries." *International Migration* 40:5-26.

Harsch, Ernest. 2003a. "Foreign Investment on Africa's Agenda." *Africa Recovery* 17:12-13.

——. 2003b. "Ivorian War Sends Regional Shockwaves." *Africa Recovery* 17(2), July.

Hettne, Bjorn, Adreas Inotai, and Osavaldo Sunkel. 1999. *Globalism and the New Regionalism*. London: Macmillan.

Itzigsohn, Jose. 1995. "Migrant Remittances, Labor Markets, and Household Strategies: A Comparative Analysis of Low-Income Household Strategies in the Caribbean Basin." *Social Forces* 74:633-655.

Kapur, Devesh and McHale, John. 2003. "Migration's New Payoff." *Foreign Policy* November/December 139:49-57

Kelbessa, Workineh. 2001. "Globalization and Indigenous Environmental Knowledge in Ethiopia," in *Globalisation, Democracy and Development in Africa: Challenges and Prospects*, edited by Taye Astefa, Severine M. Rugumamu and Abdel Ghaffar Ahmed, Addis Ababa, OSSREA, pp. 275-306.

Keely, Charles B. and Tran, Bao Nga. 1989. "Remittances from labor Migration: Evaluations, Performance and Implications." *International Migration Review* 21:500-525.

Kritz, Mary M. and Keely, Charles B. 1981. "Introduction." Pp. xiii-xxxi in *Global Trends in Migration* Mary M., edited by Kritz, Charles B, Keely and Silvano M Tomasi. Staten Island, New York: Center for Migration.

Lacey, Miriam. 1981. *Working for Boroko: The Origins of Coercive Labor System in South Africa: 1890-1933*. Johannesburg: Ravan Press.

Lucas, Robert E.B. 1985. "Emigration to South Africa's Mines." *American Economic Review* 77:313-330

Lucas, Robert E.B. and Stark, Oded. 1985. "Motivations to Remit: Evidence from Botswana." *Journal of Political Economy* 39:901-918.

Macmillen, Malcolm J. 1982. "The Economic Effects of International Migration: A survey." *Journal of Common Market Studies* 20:245-267.

Matlosa, Khabele. 1996. "The Future of Basotho Migrant Miners in Post-Apartheid South Africa: Rethinking Lesotho's Regional Identity." *Lesotho Law Journal* 9:169-191.

Mattes, Robert; Crush, Jonathan and Richmond, W. 2000. "The Brain Gain and Legal Immigration to Post-Apartheid South Africa." *Africa Insight* October: 21-30.

McGrew, Anthony. 1992. "A Global Society?" Pp. 61-116 in *Modernity and its Futures*, edited by Stuart, Hall; Held, David; and McGrew, Anthony. Oxford: Blackwell.

Muzvidziwa, Victor N. 2001. "Forging New Identities: Globalization, Cross-Border Women Traders and Regional Integration." Pp. 42-59 in *Towards an African Economic Community*, edited by S.K.B. Asante, F.O.L. Nwonwu and V.N. Muzvidziwa. Pretoria: AISA.

Mutume, Gumisai. 2003. "Reversing Africa's Brain Drain." *Africa Recovery*. July: 18-22.

Nabudere, Dan W. 2000. *Globalization and the Post Colonial African State* (Harare: AAPS Books).

Ninsin, Kwame. 2000. "Globalization and the Future of Africa." *AAPS Occasional Paper* 4(1).

Nnoli, Okwudiba. 1990. "Desertification, Refugees and Regional Conflict in West Africa." *Disaster: The Journal of Disaster Studies and Management*, 14: 132-139.
Obi, Cyril. 1997. "Economic Adjustment and the Deepening of Environmental Conflict in Africa." *Lesotho Social Science Review* 3(1) June: 13-29.
Organization for African Unity—OAU. 1969. *Convention Governing the Specific Aspects of Refugee Problems in Africa*, Art. 1, Sec. 2, Addis Ababa.
Oucho, John. 2000. "Skilled Immigrants in Botswana." *Africa Insight* October: 56-64.
Papademetriou, Demetrious G. 1997. "Think Again Migration." *Foreign Policy Online* Winter 1997/1998, Edition 109. Retrieved October 5, 2005. (www.queens.ca/samp.)
Pellerin, Helene. 1997. "New Global Migration Dynamics" Pp. 105-125 in Stephen Gill (ed.) *Globalization, Democratization and Multilateralism* (London: Macmillan).
Portes, Alejandro and Guarnizo, Luis. 1991. "Tropical Capitalist: US Bound Immigration and Small Enterprise Development in the Domincan Republic." Pp. 101-132 in *Migration, Remittances, and Small Business Development in Mexico*, edited by Sergio Diaz-Briquets and Sydney Weintraub. Boulder: Westview Press.
Portes, Alejandro and Sensenbrenner, Julia. 1993. "Embeddedness and Immigration: Notes on the Social Determinants of Economic Action." *American Journal of Sociology* 98:1320-1350.
Rao, Vaman. 1984. "Democracy and Economic Development" *Studies in Comparative International Development* 19(4), Winter: 67-81.
Roer-Strier, Dorit and Olshtain-Mann, Orly. 1999. "To See and Not To Be Seen: Latin American Illegal Foreign Workers in Jerusalem." *International Migration* 37:413-436.
Rostow, Walter. 1960. *The Stages of Economic Growth: A Non-Communist Manifesto* Cambridge, England: Cambridge University Press.
Russell, Stanton S. 1982. "Remittances from International Migration: A Review in Perspective." *World Development* 14:677-696.
Sawyer, Akilagpa. 1999. "Globalization and Social Sciences in Africa." *African Sociological Review* 3:1-19.
Scholte, Jan A. 2001. "The Globalization of World Politics" Pp. 13-32 in *The Globalization of World Politics: An Introduction to International Relations*, edited by John Baylis and Steve Smith. New York: Oxford University Press.
Seers, Dudley. 1972. "The Meaning of Development" Pp. 123-129 in *The Political Economy of Development*, edited by Norman T. Uphoff and Warren F. Ilchman, Berkeley: University of California Press.
Sparreboom, Theo and Sparreboom-Burger, Pete. 1996. "Migrant Worker Remittances in Lesotho: A Review of the Deferred Pay Scheme." *Poverty-Oriented Banking Working Paper No. 16.* Geneva: ILO.
Stahl, Charles and Arnold, Fred. 1986. "Overseas Workers" Remittances in Asian Development." *International Migration Review* 20:899-925.
Stalker, Peter. 1994. *The Work of Strangers: A Survey of International Labor Migration* (Geneva: ILO).
Stark, Oded. 1982. "Research on Rural-to-Urban Migration in LDCs: The Confusion Frontier and Why We Should Pause to Rethink Afresh." *World Development* 10:63-70.
Suliman, Mohamed, and Omer, Ahmed Osman. 1994. "The Environment: A New Dimension in Sudan's Political and Social Landscape." *Africa World Review* November 1993-April 1994: 23-25.
Taylor, J. Edward, and Wyatt, T.J. 1996. "The Shadow Value of Migrant Remittances, Income and Inequality in a Household—farm Economy." *The Journal of Development Studies* 32:899-912.
Timberlake, Lloyd. 1991. *Africa in Crisis: The Cures of Environmental Bankruptcy* London: Earthscan.
Transformation Resource Center—TRC. 1989. "Health Workers Without Jobs." *Work For Justice* (Maseru) 22(10).
UK Department of International Development—DFID. 2003. "Migrant Remittances to Developing Countries—A copping Study: Overview and Introduction to Issues for Pro-Poor Financial Services." London: Bannock Consulting. Unpublished Document.
United Nations—UN. 1998. "Report of the Secretary-General: The Causes of Conflict and the Promotion of Durable Peace and Sustainable Development in Africa in Africa" *Security Council Document* S/1998/318, 13 April 1998.

UNDP. 1997. *Human Development Report 1997* (New York: Oxford University Press).
Wilson, Francis. 1972. *Labor in the South African Gold Mines 1911-1969* (Cambridge: Cambridge University Press).
Wocke, Albert and Klein, Saul. 2002. "The Implications of South Africa's Skills Migration Policy for Country Competitiveness." *Development Southern Africa* 19:441-454.
World Bank. 1984. *Fourth Education Project in the Kingdom of Lesotho* Washington, D.C: World Bank.
——. 1991. *World Development Report.* New York: Oxford University Press.
——. 2001. *World Development Report 2000/2001: Attacking Poverty.* New York: Oxford University Press.
——. 2004. *World Development Indicators.* New York: Oxford University Press.

4. On the Brain Drain of Africans to America: Some Methodological Observations*

*F. Nii-Amoo Dodoo***
*Baffour K. Takyi****
*Jesse R. Mann*****

Abstract

Recurring debates about the impact of the brain drain—the developing world's loss of human capital to more developed countries—has motivated estimation of the magnitude of the phenomenon, most recently by the World Bank. Although frequently cited as a key contributor to Africa's wanting development record, what constitutes the "brain-drain" is not always clearly defined. Today, in the absence of an accounting system, resolution of the definitional and measurement question depends on relative comparisons of measurement variants, which will identify definitional shortcomings by clarifying the merits and demerits of these variants, and thereby suggest corrective imputations. This paper compares the World Bank's approach to a chronological precedent (Dodoo 1997) to clarify the value of variant comparisons. The resultant implications for corrections are also discussed.

BACKGROUND AND PROBLEM STATEMENT

A revival of global interest in the issue of "brain drain" is marked by the World Bank's release of a volume on a phenomenon that has had

* The authors assume equal responsibility for the conceptualization and writing of this paper.

** The Pennsylvania State University, Sociology and Demography, College of Liberal Arts Research Professor, University Park, PA 16802; and Regional Institute for Population Studies, University of Ghana. Email: duf2@psu.edu

*** University of Akron, Sociology and Pan-African Studies, Akron Ohio 44325-1905. Email: btakyi@uakron.edu

**** University of Akron, Sociology, Akron Ohio 44325-1905. Email: jmann@uakron.edu

a presence in the literature for at least a few decades (see Ozden and Schiff 2006). The World Bank's interest in a sense signals a shift in sentiment on the brain drain from a time when it was primarily an issue of contention articulated by developing countries, to the current situation where industrialized countries and global organizations lament the problem. The brain drain, which generally refers to the developing countries loss of human capital to more developed countries, is increasingly recognized as problematic. While poor countries spend sizeable proportions of their gross domestic product to educate their nationals, richer countries lure them away with more lucrative opportunities that are advantageous for the individuals but frequently not for the investing countries. The problem is particularly acute in Sub-Saharan Africa, simultaneously the poorest of global regions and the most educated of immigrant groups in America. With its US Visa Lottery program that confers preferential immigration status to individuals with some higher education and skills, America is increasingly deemed a culprit in this phenomenon. Even though the statistics are not readily available, the International Organization for Migration (IOM) estimates that 20,000 skilled Africans leave every year for jobs in the West. At the same time, according to a BBC report, Africa spends $4 billion a year on recruiting Western expertise.[1]

While it is true that African immigrants are a diverse group, the extant literature also suggests that they include a higher preponderance of educated and skilled professionals such as health workers and other professionals. Sanders (2003), for example, has reported that overseas migrants from Africa typically are more educated than other migrant groups. With respect to America, and using traditional indicators of human capital, Dodoo (1997), Takyi (2002), and Dodoo and Takyi (2002) have clarified that Africans have "'one of, if not the' highest levels of education of all immigrants to America" (Dodoo and Takyi 2002: 914). Also, Carrington and Detragiache (1999) note that the biggest migratory flows from Africa to the United States are from countries such as Egypt, Nigeria, Ghana, and South Africa, with more than 60% of their migrants to America having a tertiary education. Carrington and Detragiache (1999) further conclude that, with the exception of Central America and Mexico, the highest migration rates from developing world countries, including some of the small African countries, were of individuals with a tertiary education.

The question of whether the brain drain confers a net loss particularly to African-sending societies is a vexing one, in that there is no easy

[1] BBC Report on the brain drain. Online at: http://news.bbc.co.uk/1/hi/world/africa/652801.stm.

adjudication of the trade-off between skill and investment losses, on the one hand, and the remittances Africans send home annually. While some commentators view emigration from Africa and other parts of the developing world as a "drain" on skilled manpower that has implications for socioeconomic development in these regions (see, e.g., Stark 2003; World Bank 1995; Bhagwati & Wilson 1989), others argue that these population exchanges between the rich and poor nations are a potential net gain for Africa and other developing regions (see, e.g., Buch, Kuckulenz and Le Manchec 2002). Pointing to remittances and other contributions from African-born residents in America, proponents of the "brain-gain" thesis argue that these transfers are but one example of the sharing of their relative prosperity with family members and friends back in their countries of origin. Indeed, according to the limited data available, remittances constitute a significant proportion of revenue for many developing countries (Saravia & Miranda 2004). Indeed, remittances have become the second largest capital inflow to developing countries behind foreign direct investments (FDI) (see, e.g., Ratha 2003).[2]

Despite the fact that the data on actual remittances to Africa are underreported,[3] some have argued that the amount of money remitted by diasporan Africans unofficially estimated at between $12 and $17 billion per year is larger than the amount of foreign direct investment (FDI) in Africa, and rivals official development assistance grants or loans ($25 billion per year) (see, e.g., Sander and Mainbo 2005). It is difficult to overstate the magnitude of importance of remittances to most African and developing world nations. In some African countries, remittances alone represent as much as 27% of the gross domestic product of those nations. The UN Office of Special Advisor on Africa has reported that the average African immigrant living in a developed nation sends in about $200 per month to his or her family, not insignificant on a continent where per capita GDP is quite low. Further, an anecdotal argument, occasionally heard in diasporan communities that is hard to dismiss, regards how much worse the unemployment problem would be in Africa if the émigrés still lived in their home countries.

---

[2] More importantly, it has been argued elsewhere that unlike FDI, remittances have proved to be more stable than other sources of finance (see Buch and Others 2002).

[3] This is to be expected as informal means of remittances such as those sent through friends and others during visits are not captured by official data that goes through the Banks and money transfer companies such as Western Union.

MEASUREMENT ISSUES AND IMPLICATIONS

Resolution of these significant issues surrounding the brain drain will only be viable if one can accurately capture the true volume of the phenomenon. Yet, while there is a substantial body of theoretical literature on the brain drain (see Bhagwati and Hamada 1974; Bhagwati and Partington 1976; Stark, Helmenstein, and Prskawetz 1997), the scarcity of data imposes significant constraints on empirical measurement and analysis of the concept itself. Indeed, the measurement of brain drain has proven elusive in no small part because of the unavailability of an accounting system for this purpose. Moreover, as Saravia and Miranda (2004) point out, besides the lack of up-to-date data on international migrants as a whole, the definition of "immigrant" varies widely and sufficiently enough to confound attempts to construct or utilize statistical data on this population.

Most recently, in an attempt to redress some of the impediments regarding our understanding of the brain drain, the authors of the World Bank volume took a bold step forward in operationalizing the brain drain as representing the "foreign educated"—or immigrants with at least a bachelor's degree—who entered the US after he or she would have "normally" finished a bachelor's level of schooling (this was designated as age 23 and older). Thus, for example, if a university graduate arrived at the age of 23 or older, then s/he would be considered "foreign educated." A proxy was deemed necessary probably because the US census, like others, does not ask where respondents' education was obtained. Although a proxy measure is the best one can hope for with the data constraints, there are several downsides to this particular characterization of immigrants that beg further consideration, and serve as the backdrop for a paper that questions the measurement approach. These include: assigning a value for the "normal" number of years to degree completion; aggregating bachelors, masters, doctoral, and professional degrees; and non-accounting for any events that occur prior or subsequent to migration. These factors potentially create errors in the calculation of the volume of "brain drain" per the proxy measure.

Working within the confines of the World Bank method, these errors manifest primarily for two distinct groups. The first involves those who did actually receive an education in a foreign country, but are classified as American-educated. These are the individuals who graduated from college with a bachelor's degree earlier than the considered "normal" time and then immediately emigrated to America. For example, if a person graduates from high school at age 17 (which is early for Africa), proceeds to college for four years and receives a bachelor's degree at 21, and then immigrates to the United States, that person would erroneously be classified as American educated. Likewise, if a student graduates from high school at 18 and college at 22, and shortly thereafter emigrates, perhaps to enter a master's program, that person too would be similarly misclassified. These groups would contribute to an understatement of the brain drain.

The second group comprises those who actually receive an education in America, but may be classified as foreign-trained. These might include individuals who arrive in the United States with little to no education, at or above the age of 23, some of whom may later enroll in college and consequently receive degrees. Subsequent censuses will capture them as part of the brain drain, overstating its magnitude. It is not far-fetched to think that, although African immigrants comprise the group with the highest levels of bachelor's degrees in America, the continent is also the least educated of all world regions and with, arguably, the smallest proportion of college graduates. Simultaneously, because the continent is the poorest and has the least educational resources, it probably also has the highest age distribution at each grade level (e.g., the oldest fourth graders will probably be found in Africa). These two factors combine to elevate the likelihood that Africa has the highest proportion of, say, 24-year-old precollege degree migrants who subsequently acquire degrees in the US; indeed, this is consistent with the finding in Dodoo (1997) that 24.8% of African male immigrants, aged 25-64 in 1990, got their degrees in the US, compared to 7.6% of Caribbean immigrants (see Table 1 of Dodoo 1997).

The size of this group is important. If it is equal to the smaller group discussed earlier, then the overall effects will offset each other. However, a 5% sample of the 2000 census reveals that, for those who immigrated between the ages of 24 and 30 years, over 30% went to college within their first five years in America. Additionally, for those who immigrated between the ages of 30-39, over 22% were in college within five years of immigration. All of this suggests an overall overstatement of the African brain drain. It is probably also safe to argue that this overstatement, itself problematic, is not consistent across world regions, and is probably worse for Africa.

Another point of consideration involves those who arrive with a master's or doctoral level of education. Under the World Bank classification, the "normal" amount of time it takes to finish a bachelor's degree is applied to master's and doctoral students. Is it reasonable to think that individuals receiving a master's, doctoral, or professional degree in a foreign country can do so by the age of 22? Instead of applying the 22/23 age cutoff to all levels of schooling, it would be much more realistic to consider that particular age cutoff for only bachelor's degrees, and use progressively higher cutoffs for the more advanced schooling levels (e.g., a 24/25 year cutoff for master's degrees [i.e., Bachelor's cuttoff plus 2 years] and, likewise, a 28/29 cuttoff for those with a PhD or professional degree [i.e., Master's + 4 years]). This might better reflect "normal (cy)" in the length of time it takes to complete the various levels of schooling. This observation is due in large part to the fact that even in the same country, there are some who are 24 that have completed their bachelor's degree, while some of their age-mates have not. In this vein, another way of capturing the brain drain would be to include a measure of whether the immigrant was educated overseas (i.e., in their country of origin or elsewhere) or in the country of residence, say, America. This approach has been used in an earlier study (see Dodoo 1997: 538) on Black immigrants in America.

How different would brain-drain measurements be with the revised age cuttoffs for those with advanced degrees? To answer this question, we used a 5% micro-data sample drawn from the 2000 Census of Housing and Population and applied the same limitations and methods as were used by the World Bank. The World Bank calculations resulted in a brain-drain estimate of 4,384 foreign educated and 1952 American-educated Africans; with the revised cuttoff model there were 3,726 foreign educated and 2,610 American educated. In other words, there was a considerable overstatement of the brain drain; fully 658 people in a sample size of 6,336 were classified as foreign educated, because the 22/23 age split was applied to every educational level. The implication is that, to impute an age for when a person would "normally" complete his or her education, each level of education must be pegged to an appropriate amount of time. Once multiple age cutoffs are imputed, the earlier Dodoo and later World Bank methods yield the same estimates. It is worth noting that even these "corrections" do not address the problems associated with the two misclassified groups discussed earlier. Still, it should be possible to estimate the size of those groups; work continues along these lines. Clearly, without a better accounting system than the census currently presents, variants of the measure can only help us refine our estimates of the brain drain. Relative assessment of the merits and demerits of these variants will, at the very least, help deduce sources of error and provide direction vis-à-vis potential corrections.

CONCLUSION

The brain drain has emerged as a central piece in the ongoing discourse on the socioeconomic developments of developing world nations. For

African countries, like many others, there are continuing debates regarding the pros and cons of the exodus of its skilled professionals. Some posit that the loss of human capital compromises development, still others argue that remittances from the Diaspora comprise a significant boost to the development engines of these developing countries, while at the same time that the outflows attenuate what would have been an even worse degree of unemployment in what are, arguably, slow-growing economies. Adjudication of this debate on the pros and cons of the brain drain hinges on measurement accuracy vis-à-vis the volume of the brain drain.

In this article, we have identified some of the shortcomings in the empirical research on the brain drain, particularly as they relate to the measurement of the concept itself. We argue that, precisely because the lack of an accounting system compromises our measurement, it is imperative that we assess the merits and demerits of various formulations of the phenomenon. Comparing the recent World Bank measure (Ozden and Schiff 2006) to that of a chronological precedent (Dodoo 1997), we demonstrate how relative assessments of measurement variants can forward our understanding of the brain drain. We contend that the approach used by the World Bank most likely overestimates the true magnitude of the problem. In this regard, we call for more refined measures of the concept of the brain drain to sharpen our understanding of the phenomenon.

REFERENCES

Buch, Clauduia M., Anja Kuckulenz, and Marie-Helene Le Manchec. 2002. "Worker Remittances and Capital Flows." Working Paper. Kiel Institute of World Economics. Retrieved: July 15, 2006 (http://www.uni-kiel.de/ifw/pub/kap/2002/kap1130.pdf.)

Carrington, W.J., and Enrica Detragiache. 1999. "How Extensive Is the Brain Drain?" *Finance and Development* 36:46-49.

Dodoo, F. Nii-Amoo. 1997. "Assimilation Differences among Africans in America." *Social Forces* 76:527-546.

Dodoo, F. Nii-Amoo and Baffour K. Takyi. 2002. "Race and Earnings: Magnitude of Difference among American Africans." *Ethnic and Racial Studies* 25:913-941.

Ozden, Caglar and Maurice Schiff, eds. 2006. *International Migration, Remittances and the Brain Drain.* Washington, D.C.: The International Bank for Reconstruction and Development/World Bank (co-published with Palgrave McMillan).

Ratha, Dilip. 2003. "Workers Remittances: An Important and Stable Source of External Development Finance." Pp. 157-176 in *Global Development Finance: Striving for Stability in Development* Finance, edited by World Bank. Washington D.C.: The World Bank.

Sander, Cerstin, and Samuel M. Maimbo. 2003. "Migrant Labor Remittances in Africa: Reducing Obstacles to Developmental Contributions." Africa Region Working Paper Series #64.

Saravia, Nancy G., and Juan Francisco Miranda. 2004. "Plumbing the Brain Drain." *Bulletin of the World Health Organization* 82:608-615.

Stark, Odek. 2003. "How Extensive is the Brain Drain?" *World Development* 32:15-22.
Stark, Odek, C. Helmenstein, & A. Prskawetz. 1998. "Human Capital Depletion, Human Capital Formation, and Migration: A Blessing or a "Curse?" *Economics Letters* 60:363-367.
Takyi, Baffour K. 2002. "The Making of the Second Diaspora: Emigration from Africa to the United States and Its Policy Implications." *Western Journal of Black Studies* 26:32-43.
World Bank. 1995. *World Development Report* 1995. New York: Oxford University Press.

5. Cyberorganizing United States Constituencies for Africa

*Jill M. Humphries**

Abstract

This case study examines how state level constituencies for Africa used advanced communication technology to organize and mobilize state delegations to the National Summit on Africa with the intent of influencing United States foreign policy toward Africa. More specifically, it focuses on the application of information communication technology (ICT) usage as a communication and coordination tool by the National Summit Secretariat. Secondly, it examines the extent to which state delegations used advanced communication technology to complete the relevant task of developing a national policy plan-of-action. I hypothesize that ICTs might assist the National Summit by reducing costs of attracting and maintaining membership and facilitating coordination and communication both horizontally (among membership) and vertically (to policy-makers). Primary data collection methods included administering a survey to state chairs, conducting semi-structured interviews, and reviewing state web-pages and e-groups. Preliminary results indicate that information technology to some extent can reduce coordination problems and barriers to participation; however, other factors, such as computer literacy, access to computers, and the ability to use alternative institutional resources, mediate the effectiveness of information technology usage. Implications for implementing information technology as a more effective tool for collective organizing are explored.

INTRODUCTION

Information communication technologies (ICT) such as electronic mail (e-mail), electronic groups (e-groups), teleconferencing and web-pages are

* Temple University, The Institute for the Study of Race and Social Thought, Philadelphia, Pennsylvania. Email: jhumphries@nyc.rr.com

being used in a variety of ways by different political actors in society. Many scholars argue that the introduction of computer-mediated communication and the Internet has impacted the political landscape and public sphere (McCaughey and Ayers 2003; Wim van de Donk et al. 2004). First, advanced communication technology is altering the ways in which elites and politicians at the national level are conducting business (Seifert and Peterson 2002; Adler 1997). Also, local governments and cities are using the Internet to develop municipal web-sites for contracting purposes, and receiving citizen input and civic networking projects (Seifert and Peterson 2002; Musso et al. 2000; Tsagarousianou et al. 1998). Political activists from an array of specific identity and issue groups are using the Internet as a tool for promoting organizing and mobilizing national and transnational issue groups (Bennett 2004; Stoecker 2004; Van Aelst and Walgrave 2004; Gurak 1997; Wittig 1996). An area where the Internet has particular potential is in transforming societal relations between citizens by facilitating political and grassroots organizing (Elin 2003; Brainard and Siplon 2002; Castells 1997). This study contributes to a growing body of literature that explores the extent to which ICT can assist political and grassroots organizing efforts to access and influence the foreign policy arena.

This study examines the use of advanced communication technology by the National Summit state leadership and considers its potential to improve political and grassroots organizing in this arena. The National Summit on Africa was established as a non-governmental organization designed to coordinate and mobilize African advocates to influence United States foreign policy toward Africa.[1] Specifically, it examines (1) national-state level structure and its impact on state delegate resource mobilization to attend the National Summit on Africa, (2) technology use by the National Summit Secretariat and State Leadership to coordinate organizing efforts, and (3) technology preferences of state delegates.[2]

The first part of this paper briefly discusses the historical context for the National Summit on Africa as an African advocacy initiative and its relationship to U.S. foreign policy toward Africa, given the constraints imposed by the anti-democratic nature of the process and the rationale for such constituency-building initiatives. The second part, examines the relationship between resource mobilization and the potential of advanced

---

[1] I use the terms African advocacy organizations and Africa specific constituencies interchangeably to refer to U.S. state constituencies for Africa.

[2] The National Summit on Africa has evolved into the Africa Society, a Washington based public education organization that has six state affiliates: Arizona, Massachusetts, Georgia, Maryland, Virginia, and Washington, http://www.africasummit.org.

communication technology as an enabling agent for political and grassroots organizing, while the third section examines this issue in the context of the National Summit on Africa's results from the state leadership survey and discusses implications for future grassroots organizing.

THE "NON-DEMOCRATIC" NATURE OF U.S. FOREIGN POLICY

The end of cold war politics (Gordon et al. 1998; Clough 1992), the decline of authoritative leadership (Gordon et al. 1998), and the rise and consolidation of democratic transitions (Walters 2004; Diamond et al. 1999) among African states signal a new period for Africa in global affairs and in particular United States-Africa relations. As a result, U.S. policymakers are faced with the challenge of developing a new policy mandate that is mutually beneficial with the 53 African States in order to address a wide array of transnational issues such as increasing globalization, sustainable development, economic and trade relations, health, and environment and security issues. Previously, U.S. national interests in Africa were defined through a Euro-centric and masculine bias, with a focus on resource extraction and with a priority given to geo-strategic concerns (Horne 1999; Brown 1991). This myopic approach has contributed to the U.S.'s inability to develop a proactive and comprehensive policy toward Africa.

Historically, the process of defining U.S. interests in Africa has been circumscribed by three constraints: racism, gender, and bureaucratic dominance. First, U.S.-Africa relations have been informed and deformed by racism since the inception of this country—from colonial America policies toward Africa that legalized slavery in the mid-1600s, to U.S. support for apartheid South Africa centuries later (Horne 1999; Krenn 1999; Booker 1999). Race as a determinant of foreign policy informed and shaped a "worldview" for much of America's encounters with Africa (Booker, 1999; Krenn, 1999). Spanning over a 200-year period between America's independence and the independence of African states, the U.S. government aligned itself with European colonialism while the majority of American society disowned its African roots. America's tragic role in Liberia's troubled history (from 1820 onwards) and its complicity in King Leopold II's genocide against the people of the Congo Free State (1884-1908) (Hochschild 1999) are but two examples of the salience of race in U.S. policies toward Africa during the nineteenth and twentieth centuries.

The second constraint in redefining U.S. national interests in Africa is gender. Brown (1991) argues that more than any other kind of human activity, politics has historically borne explicitly masculine identity. Studies of women and public policy primarily focus on domestic issues at the exclusion of international affairs while men have historically dominated U.S. foreign affairs. It was not until the 1990s that a mere seven women had served on the House Armed Services Committee and thirteen on the Foreign Affairs Committee. The State Department has had a history of discriminating against minorities and women (Dumbrell 1997).[3] Further studies indicate that women tend to focus more on issues of equality, economic advancement, social justice and peace rather than defense and war (Jeffreys-Jones 1995).[4]

Finally, Schraeder (1991, 1994, 1996) articulates a third constraint: bureaucratic dominance by the national security agencies and career bureaucrats in decision-making and the lack of interagency coordination.[5] The U.S. national interests in Africa continue to be defined through a narrow prism of resource extraction, and geo-strategic terms at the expense of addressing the fundamental issues of democratization, security, and development (Booker 1996). The end result is a fragmented, bureaucratic, and crisis-driven policy process that yields less than optimal results.

It was not until the 1970s as a result of two converging factors—1) increasing congressional participation and 2) grassroots agitation and protests over U.S.-South African investments—that a space was created for citizen input, which ultimately led the United States to begin addressing other issues pertaining to U.S.-Africa relations (Clough 1992). Nevertheless, there is still a pressing need to articulate a "new mode of thinking" about U.S.-Africa relations within the foreign policy arena and American society. This new framework situates U.S.-Africa relations in a broader context of U.S. foreign policy relations with other nations. From this perspective, U.S. national interests are best served by building viable partnerships with African States that support economic and security issues promoting prosperity at home, preventing crises that threaten security or require costly political-military and/or humanitarian interventions, and working with partners to address common political and security concerns, such as international terrorism, drug trafficking, and environmental degradation (Gordon et al. 1998).

The question of organizing domestic constituencies plays an increasingly more important role given that many scholars suggest that new

[3] Polls consistently show blacks to be more 'dovish' than whites.

[4] Women experience different degrees of discrimination depending on how their race and class intersect.

[5] For example, National Security Council, Department of State, Bureau of African Affairs, Central Intelligence Agency, Bureau of Intelligence and Research.

information and communication technologies can transform the policy arena to be more democratic. In the next section, I discuss the link between social movement organizations, advanced communication technology, and political organizing.

RESOURCES AND COMMUNICATION NETWORKS

National-State Level Relations and Resource Mobilization Capacity

I draw from the social movement literature and in particular resource mobilization studies to understand the importance of mobilizing resources to accomplish organizational goals. One important component of political organizing is the ability to mobilize the appropriate type and level of resources, including volunteers and money, to accomplish stated goals (McAdam 1988; Jenkins 1983). Freeman (1979) argues that both intangible and tangible resources are required to support social movements. Intangible assets include things such as human resources and expertise, whereas tangible assets are physical resources such as money and space. Freeman (1979) makes a major distinction between interest group organizations and social movement organizations, arguing that interest group organizations typically have more tangible assets, particularly money, while social movement organizations rely more heavily on human resources, and mobilizing volunteers. Subsequently, social movement theorists argue that there is no free entry into the political system (Williams 1997), but rather citizens experience institutional barriers, such as lack of resources, and racial-, gender-, or class-related constraints to participation (Piven 1979). As such, they argue that it is only through mobilizing protests in social movements that the system will be responsive (Piven 1979).

Moreover, the structure of national and local organizational relations can affect local-level mobilization capacity (McCarthy and Wolfson 1996). Zald (1970) and Young (1989) identify two types of relationships: federations and franchises. Federated structures have autonomous local member organizations that share a common purpose, mission, and history while a franchise model is characterized by less autonomous local organizations with a centralized national coordinating body. Typically, federated structures are under an umbrella national organization that expresses the mission of and provides leadership for the movement. The structure of national and local organizations can affect both the recruitment of volunteers and material resources (Zald 1970). Piven (1979) argues that local activism is dampened as a result of formalization and national level affiliation. In contrast, other studies (e.g. Kleidman 1993) suggest that some formal social movement organizations stimulate activism. National organizations may also affect material resource levels by either providing grants or "seed money" and technical assistance to local affiliates for grassroots mobilization efforts (Kleidman 1993). In turn, some national organizations require membership dues from local organizations (Staggenborg 1991; Oliver 1989).

The Internet as an Organizing Resource

Several scholars suggest that information technologies have the potential to make political organizing and mobilizing efforts more effective by creating "virtual communities" (Wittig and Schmitz 1996). Meeks (1997) argues that "virtual communities" are, "built on the back of e-mail and the Web and tied together with the phosphar asphalt of the Internet. . . ." According to Coombs (1999), the Internet has become an important and cost-effective communications tool for conducting grassroots media campaigns. A well-designed web-site can be used to disseminate information but also to recruit members, raise funds, and engage individuals through feedback mechanisms (Coombs 1999).

E-mail has virtually transformed mass mobilization efforts by increasing access and information dissemination (Gurak 1997; Grossman 1995) and by reducing the time and cost associated with phone-banking and faxing efforts to mobilize supporters. At the drop of a "key stroke" targeted distribution lists, action alerts, and newsletters are sent to hundreds of people and their networks—creating a multiplier effect (Coombs 1999).

Furthermore, the Internet can increase political organizing efficiency by streamlining the planning process, reducing hierarchical relationships among participants, creating more decentralized networks that promote more democratic structures and participation, and the formation of trans-issue-specific networks. The Internet also has the potential to create new linkages between institutions and to affect policy outcomes at the local, national, and international levels (Denning 2001).

In sum, there is reason to believe that the Internet can transform social relations by promoting collective action among disparate groups, different social classes (Wittig and Schmitz 1996), reduce gender bias (Faigley 1992; Siegel 1986) and racial bias (Kang 2000) associated with face-to-face interaction. To the extent that political organizers can use digital technologies to mediate conflicting divergent political views, class conflict, racial and ethnic strife as well as reducing gender discrimination, they can build more viable and lasting multiracial U.S. constituencies and coalitions for Africa. In the next section, I explore the potential and use of high-speed and Broadband technologies in U.S. society and their implication as organizing tools for National Summit delegations.

The Digital Divide and U.S. Society

A concern about the use of digital technologies in this context is related to the gender, social-class, and multiracial character of the political organizing effort. To the extent that African Americans, women, and the new emerging polity of African immigrants can harness information communication technology for political organizing efforts, information and advanced communication technology might increase their effectiveness; but on the other hand, the goal of the National Summit was to engage people and groups (women, Blacks, and grass-roots) who, according to the statistics, have low computer access and are not as technologically advanced.[6, 7] Hence, it is important to consider the possibility that the digital divide might hamper its effectiveness in this arena. Issues of accessibility, usage and distribution of digital technology along race/ethnicity, gender, social classes, and urban/rural dimensions are particularly important for increasing political participation of traditionally disenfranchised individuals.

The successful introduction, implementation, and adoption of information/computer technologies by women and ethnic minorities are contingent upon the institutional environment with which the communications sector operates. To some extent, the "digital divide" still exists for women and some ethnic groups who cannot afford the cost associated with the Internet and expensive online access. Structural barriers such as the lack of access to training and technical information further hinder disadvantaged groups. Additionally, cultural attitudes about technology impede the adoption and implementation of computer and technology. Huyer (1997) also notes that the barriers to ICT adoption are further exacerbated for women and ethnic minorities as a result of their lower economic and educational status (Simms 2006; Hoffman and Novak 1998), lack of training and literacy, concentration in lower-level and entry-level employment, lack of autonomy and time. DiMaggio et al. (2001) also argue that the digital divide "can also apply to extent of use, knowledge of search engines, quality of technical connections and social supports ability to evaluate the quality of information, and diversity of uses" (cited in Simms 2006).

[6] The term black refers to all black ethnic groups living in the United States. I use the terms black and African Americans interchangeably. When referring explicitly to African immigrants, I use the terms neo-Diaspora and African immigrants interchangeably.

[7] To date, no surveys that focus on technology use have disaggregated black ethnic and national groups. The use of ICT by Africans is purely speculative.

Table 1

Share of All U.S. Households and Individuals with Internet and Broadband Access

	September 2001	October 2003	Percent Increase
Share of households with Internet access	50.3% (54.6 million)	54.6% (61.5 million)	12.6%
Share of households with Broadband access	9.1% (9.6 million)	19.9% (21.6 million)	>100%

Despite these barriers, there is reason to believe that an increase in Broadband and Internet access and high-speed Internet and Broadband[8] use are occurring across all racial and ethnic social groups.[9] According to the U.S. Commerce Department's 2004 report, *A Nation Online: Entering the Broadband Age*[10] in October 2003, 58.7% of the U.S. population used the Internet from any location while 54.6% of households had Internet access. The share of households using the Internet in August 2001 rose by 12.6% by October 2003 (see Table 1). Comparing Pew survey and other data sources indicates that there has been an increase in Internet use among white and African Americans; however, the racial disparity still persists (Simms 2006). The use of Broadband technology has expanded rapidly within households from 9.1% in 2001 to 19.9% in 2003 more than doubling. Respectively, 25.7% and 14.2% of whites and blacks live in a Broadband household.

Moreover, the gap between men and women has largely disappeared;[11] however, within the African American community, a gender gap still persists between Black males (50%) and females (67%), while white users are more or less split between men (70%) and women (67%).[12]

The picture of Internet access and use among African immigrants is quite different given their relatively high educational status and income level (Takougang 2003; U.S. Department of Homeland Security 2003;

[8] Refers to digital subscriber lines (DSL), Cable modems, satellite, and fixed wireless Multi-Media Distribution Systems (MMDS).

[9] US Commerce Department's 2004 report, *A Nation Online: Entering the Broadband Age.* Also see Pew Internet American Life Project 2005 Report, *How Women and Men Use the Internet*, http://www.pewinternet.org.

[10] This is the sixth report released by the U.S. Department of Commerce on computers, Internet, and other information technology tools by the American people.

[11] Ibid.

[12] Ibid.

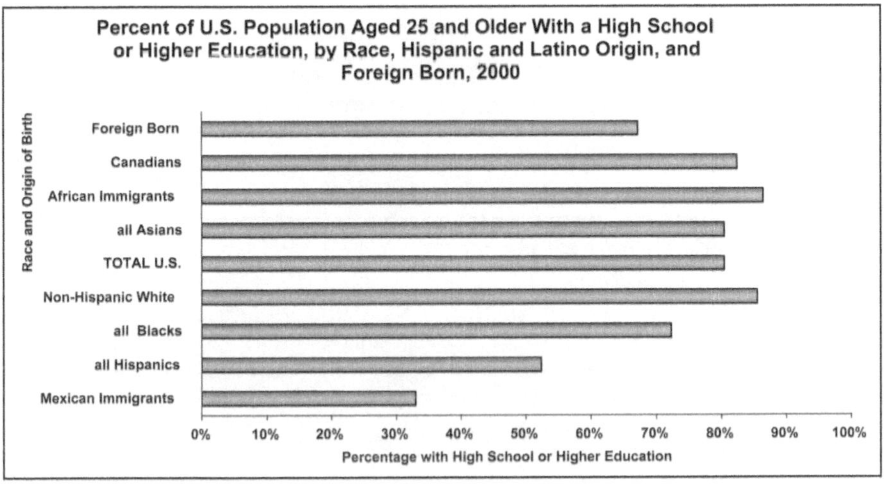

Source: U.S. Census Bureau, Census 2000 Summary File 4 and Special Tabulation (STP-159).

Figure 1. Educational Attainment Between U.S. Native and Foreign Born

U.S. Bureau of Census 2000). The majority of African immigrants who migrate to the United States tend to be "well-schooled urbanites" and from the professional classes (Austin 2006; Read and Emerson 2005; Takougang 2003; Djamba 1999; Speer 1994). Over 85% of African adult immigrants have a high school degree or higher compared to the national average of 80% for native-born Americans (Figure 1).

Africans are also the most educated regional immigrant population.[13] More African immigrants have bachelor's, graduate, and professional degrees than white and black Americans (see Table 2). Therefore, one would expect from the socio-demographic profile of African immigrants that they would tend to behave like their middle-to-upper-class American counterparts and have high Broadband and Internet access and use.

In this paper I attempt to clarify and expound on socioeconomic characteristics of African immigrants, native-born blacks and whites by focusing on five fundamental questions: (1) What barriers to mobilization confronted the participants of the National Summit? (2) How did these barriers affect the participants' ability to carry out organizing activities? (3) What was the character of technology use? (4) To what extent did

[13] Dianne A. Schmidley, U.S. Census Bureau, Current Population Reports, Series P23-206, Profile of the Foreign-Born Population in the United States: 2000 (Washington D.C.: U.S. Government Printing Office, 2001), 37.

Table 2

Socioeconomic Characteristics of African Immigrants, Native-born Blacks, and Whites, 1999/2000

	All African Immigrants	All Blacks	All Whites
% with Bachelor's Degrees or Higher	42.9	14.3	26.1
% Managers or Professionals	40.3	25.2	35.6
Median Household Income (1999)	$41,196	$29,423	$44,687
% in Poverty (1999)	17.3	24.9	9.1

Source: U.S. Census Bureau, Census 2000 Summary File 4 and Special Tabulation (STP-159).

technology support, mobilize action, and make up for lack of resources? (5) What type of communication did delegate's prefer to use based on their race, gender, and citizenship status? Before describing the case study, the following section provides a brief overview of the research methodology used for the study.

METHODOLOGY

This study was conducted over a twenty-four-month period (May 1999-May 2001) in primarily two settings, while I was serving as a California state delegate, Southern California policy and legislative officer, and as a National Summit delegate in Washington, D.C. As legislative officer I was responsible for tracking, compiling, and reporting U.S.-African legislation to the state delegation and attending the National Summit in Washington, D.C. I used a range of data collection techniques, including participant observation, interviewing, archival, and survey data collection. The strength of this design allows for a variety of data collection techniques and sources of evidence to study the same phenomenon (Denzin 1978), and to establish internal validity and consistency of data and interpretation (Cresswell 1998; Spradlely 1980).

Formation of State Delegation and State Leadership Selection Process

The formation of state delegations and selection of state leadership occurred at the six Regional Summits that were held from May 1998 to 1999. The purpose of the regional summits was twofold: first, to convene the states within a particular region to develop a regional policy plan-of-action; and second, to select state leadership to represent the formal state delegations to the National Summit on Africa Washington,

D.C., conference. Interested candidates were free to run for leadership positions, chair and co-chair(s), who were voted on by the wider body.[14]

Procedure and Questionnaire Development

The National Summit on Africa State Chair Survey was developed as a four-page 55-item questionnaire with 14 open-ended questions. I administered the survey in multiple stages: first, I conducted in-person interviews with a convenience sample of state leaders at the National Summit in Washington, D.C.; second, I followed-up with telephone calls and a mailed survey to the remaining state leadership. Questionnaires were mailed in an envelope with a pre-stamped, pre-addressed return envelope. A cover letter was inserted informing participants about the purpose of the study and the protection of their privacy as well as a support letter from Leonard Robinson, Executive Director of the National Summit on Africa. The entire survey process spanned over 10 months (January 2000-October 2000), achieving a 72% (N = 36) response rate.[15]

Overall state characteristics were examined to explore resource ability, mobilization, capacity, and ICT usage. As a participant-observer, I attended weekly organizing meetings in Southern California, regional and National Summit activities in San Francisco, California, and Washington, D.C. Primary observations focused on observing communication patterns and interactions between state leaders and delegates, among the state leadership, and with the National Secretariat. Likewise, interviews were conducted with state chairs and co-chairs to describe and interpret common everyday activities, events, and processes (Fontana 1994). Moreover, I monitored e-mail, on-line conference texts, e-groups, group meeting

[14] Governance structures varied across state delegations, as in the California delegation case the state delegation decided to partition the state along regional lines—Northern, Central and Southern California. The objective was to maximize regional representation, insure inclusiveness and diversity of state delegate perspectives and full participation in the formation of the delegation and policy positions.

[15] The moderate response rate (72%) may have resulted from the politically charged nature of the National Summit and the perception that it might have been portrayed in a negative light. Moreover, an on-line disagreement between Executive Director Leonard Robinson and California State Chair Ramona Tascoe regarding the legitimacy of this project contributed to confusion and mistrust that may have influenced some delegates not to participate in the survey (Delegate interview, 2000). For a more detailed discussion about the politically charged environment with which the Summit occurred please read Humphries' *The Role of Race, Ethnicity, and Nationality in United States-Africa Coalition Building* (2003).

minutes, and correspondence. Archival data from the state delegations and my field notes complemented the state chair survey findings.

Questionnaire Content

The questionnaire assessed a range of socio-demographic information, such as gender, age, citizenship status, race and ethnicity, religion, education, and income level and employment, and occupational status typically linked to the use of high-speed and Internet use (Simms 2006; DiMaggio et al. 2001).[16] State leaders were asked a variety of questions as to whether they were able to mobilize adequate resources both human and financial to fulfill their mandate and participate at the National Summit; in addition, did they request assistance from the National Secretariat and if so, was it adequate enough to fulfill their objectives? Primary sectors from which funds were raised were also identified.

I asked a series of questions on the mode of communication, such as e-mail, e-groups, web-page, and teleconferencing that state leaders employed for planning, information sharing, and alliance-building to communicate with delegates and to interact with the National Secretariat and other state leaders. State leaders also were asked to rate their perceived sense of usefulness of each communication medium. Finally, state leaders were requested to rank order communication mediums—such as, in-person, phone, fax, e-mail, web-page, and e-groups—with the highest level of usage by their state delegation.

Data were analyzed using descriptive statistics, content analysis, and rank order scores for modes of communication used by state delegations. Open-ended survey questions were organized categorically and coded. A list of emerging themes was identified and documented (Creswell 1998; Miles 1984). Non-parametric data such as rank order measures were first transposed into a column of ranks in preparation for analysis with general linear modeling techniques (Marden 1995; Canover 1980). This process entailed transposing cases into a column of variables while the variable or mode of communication becomes the treatment. This procedure was applied first before ranking the data within each subject from lowest to highest value. The Friedman's test was used to analyze least square means among treatments in this case mode of communication to contact policymakers (Canover 1980).

Post hoc tests were not required for this analysis when actual least square means were compared and when the interaction involved a covariate. The Levene's test was applied to check for equality of variance violations (Norusis 2000); and histograms of the groups were examined

[16] U.S. Commerce Department's 2004 report, *A Nation Online: Entering the Broadband Age.*

to ensure that the populations were normal and did not violate the normality assumption (Norusis 2000; Jaccard 1984).

The National Summit in Historical Context

In this section, I provide a brief history of the National Summit on Africa, a presentation of the results from the state leadership survey, and a discussion of implications for future use of advanced communications and political organizing. The history of the National Summit on Africa is a story about negotiating personal relationships along multiple ideological, political, and racial terrains with the intent of building a multiracial U.S.-Africa constituency. The concept of a National Summit on Africa was strongly influenced by the 1994 White House Conference on Africa (Bork Interview 2000). The purpose of the conference was, first to address the declining and changing role of U.S.-Africa relations in foreign policy; second, to broaden the range of actors operating in foreign policy; and third, to reinvigorate an interest in Africa, not only within the government sector, but within U.S. society at large (NSA Staff Member 2000). While the National Summit was originally conceived to be a government-led initiative, it was thought to be too costly and time consuming to be led solely by the government (NSA Staff Member 2000). It was envisioned that the National Summit would become a private sector initiative in order to leverage the necessary resources. According to Walters (2004), this shift in U.S. policy toward Africa signaled a major change "from an emphasis upon public sector-sponsored development assistance to private sector-driven trade and investment."

Timothy Bork, who was a program officer for the African and Middle East Division at the Ford Foundation and who attended the White House Conference on Africa, promoted the idea of the National Summit on Africa (Bork Interview 2000).[17] While Mr. Bork is credited with being the "Father" of the National Summit, its birth is actually attributed to several individuals who were involved in the initial planning process. The initial concept paper, *The African and Middle East Strategy Concept Paper: Improving The United States Policy Environment For Africa's Renewed Development*, was co-authored by Cherrie Waters and Salih Booker, two long-time African activists who envisioned the National Summit "to be a catalytic vehicle to facilitate the process . . . to allow other NGO's, African Americans, and women to voice interest in Africa . . ." (NSA Board Member, 2000).

The Ford Foundation and Carnegie Corporation funded the National Summit initiative for eight million dollars over a three-year period from

[17] Timothy Bork is currently a Resident Associate with the Carnegie Endowment.

1996 through 1999 (Foundation Program Officer Interview 2000).[18] The shape of the National Summit would forever reflect the competing conceptions and interests of the initial players.

The conceptual framework for the National Summit was modeled after the United Nations World Summits. It was envisioned to be a national convening body of U.S. Africa-specific constituencies mandated to develop a comprehensive policy plan-of-action to help guide United States foreign policy toward Africa; to educate the American public about Africa; and to broaden and strengthen the network of Africa's supporters in the United States (Ford Foundation African and Middle East Program Strategy Concept Paper 1996). The creation of this initiative aims to improve the policy environment for Africa by strengthening the key Africa-specific institutions in the U.S., and launching a three-pronged communications effort that would raise Africa's visibility among the U.S. public and policymakers alike.

The Summit was designed to include key stakeholders from various sectors of society, from politicians, representatives from Africa-specific organizations, private businesses, and citizens. Each individual would have an equal opportunity to participate as a state delegate, inform the deliberative process, and shape the national policy plan-of-action.[19] The National Summit was organized geographically along six regions: Southeast, Midwest, Pacific Coast, New England, East Coast, and Mountain West. The regions were composed of fifty states and four U.S. territories. Six regional summits were held over a two-year period whereby state delegates crafted individual regional policy plan-of-actions.[20] The deliberative process was structured such that state delegates participated in five thematic working groups[21] and were tasked with the responsibility of revising and editing the original draft policy plan-of-action. This iterative process occurred throughout the entire National Summit at the local, state, regional, and national levels. The five draft regional policy plan-of-action documents were synthesized into a working draft national policy plan-

[18] See Humphries' *The Role of Race, Ethnicity, and Nationality in United States/Africa Coalition Building* (2003).

[19] The original draft policy plan-of-action was developed by five expert working groups composed of academics, professionals, and other African experts.

[20] The six regional summits spanned from May 1998 to September 1999 culminating with the National Summit in Washington, D.C., February 2000.

[21] To facilitate the deliberative process, the Summit is composed of five thematic working groups that include: 1) Economic Development, Trade and Investment, and Job Creation; 2) Democracy and Human Rights; 3) Sustainable Development, Quality of Life, and the Environment; 4) Peace and Security; and 5) Education and Culture.

of-action document that culminated in the final document, *The National Policy Plan of Action for U.S.-Africa Relations in the 21st Century.*

The elected state leadership was responsible for organizing and mobilizing delegates, redrafting the regional policy plan-of-action, as well as raising money to facilitate delegate participation at the National Summit. Given this ambitious goal, there would appear to be opportunity for advanced communication technology to be instrumental at facilitating state organizing and mobilizing efforts at both the state and regional level.

Results

In this section, I present the results from the state leadership survey to answer the previous questions: What is the relationship between resource mobilization and the potential for advanced communication technology as an enabling agent for political organizing by the National Secretariat and state delegations? The state leadership (composed of chairs and co-chairs) was representative of the various racial/ethnic groups that participated in the Summit process. Forty-three percent of state leadership positions were held by African immigrants, 31% by African Americans, and 23% by white Americans. Men held 67% of the leadership positions, with women holding 33%. Individuals between the ages of 41-60 years of age held 60% of the leadership positions. Eighty-nine percent of the state leadership were U.S. or naturalized citizens while 44% were natives from an African country.[22] The state leadership was extremely well educated, with 46% holding doctorates and 43% with graduate or professional degrees. Thirty-six percent of the leadership made between $50,000-$74,999 dollars per year (see Table 3).

The state leaders and delegates are primarily elites who consequently would be expected to be technology savvy. There is reason to believe that the heavy reliance on digital communication mediums created barriers to participation for some groups. A State Chair suggested that some groups were in fact excluded from participating in the process because they lacked both the technical skills to negotiate a technological environment as well as computer and Internet access (State Chair Interview 2000). State delegations that had individuals from black grassroots and community-based organizations and participants from lower socioeconomic strata were excluded from receiving up-to-date information and participating in on-line deliberative sessions (State Chair Interview 2002). Ultimately, the policy plan-of-action(s) developed by state delegates reflected primarily the interest of a well-educated professional class of individuals.

[22] Some countries represented were Cameroon, Ethiopia, Ghana, Nigeria, Senegal, South Africa, and Uganda.

Table 3

State Chair Leadership Socio-Demographic Characteristics (n = 36)[23]

Race/Ethnic Heritage	
White/Caucasian	22.9% (n = 8)
Black/Afro-American/Caribbean	31.4% (n = 11)
Black/African	42.9% (n = 15)
Other	2.9% (n = 1)
Gender	
Women	33.3% (n = 12)
Men	66.7% (n = 24)
Education	
Some College	2.9% (n = 1)
College Degree	8.6% (n = 3)
Graduate or Professional Degree	42.9% (n = 15)
Ph.D./Ed.D., or terminal Degree	45.7% (n = 16)
Income	
Less than $25,000	6.1% (n = 2)
$25,000 to $49,000	24.2% (n = 8)
$50,000 to $74,999	36.4% (n = 12)
$75,000 to $94,999	12.1% (n = 4)
$95,000+	21.2% (n = 7)
Age	
31–40	22.9% (n = 8)
41–50	31.4% (n = 11)
51–60	34.3% (n = 12)
61–65	2.9% (n = 1)
65+	8.6% (n = 3)

Resources and Barriers to Participation

Resource mobilization. As mentioned earlier, the National Summit received over $8,000,000 over a three-year period (Martin and West 1999). These funds were allocated to administer and manage the day-to-day operations of the Secretariat and to host the six regional summits. Seed money was not initially allocated to state delegations to offset the expenses associated with organizing activities, including public education and outreach activities. The national organization gave $1,000 to state leaders to reimburse them for associated costs with summit activities at the National Summit. State leaders and regional partners questioned the discrepancy between regional summit expenditures that ranged from $500,000 for the Southeast Regional Summit held in Atlanta to approx-

[23] I achieved a 72% response rate for the State Chair Survey.

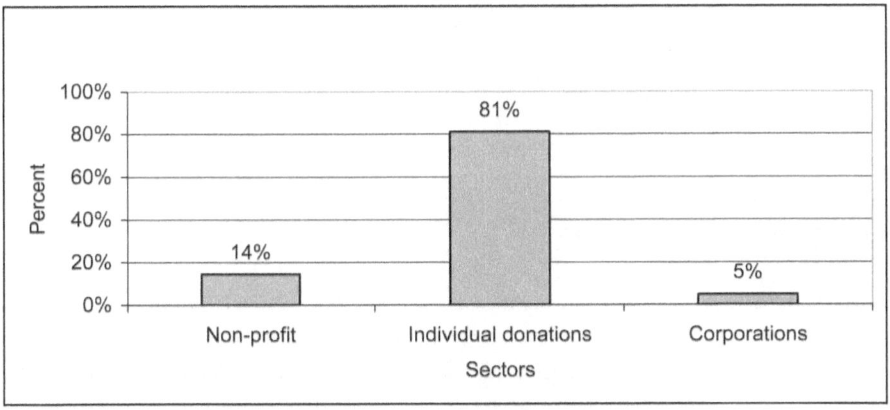

Figure 2. Money Raised by State Delegates by Primary Sector

imately $125,000 for the Pacific Regional Summit in San Francisco and the relative lack of financial assistance for state organizing activities (Regional Partner interview 2000).[24]

The ability of state delegations to accomplish the associated tasks of organizing and mobilizing delegates, communication and outreach, hosting state/regional events and assisting state delegates to the National Summit was contingent upon their ability to raise adequate financial resources or find alternative resources to supplement for the lack of financial capacity. The state leader's inability to raise adequate resources was evident by an overwhelming request (63%) for financial assistance from the Secretariat. When asked if the National Summit provided adequate financial assistance to fulfill its objectives, one chair responded, "it was appropriate for one person, had we been able to fill our delegate slots it would have been woefully short." The survey data reflects that 52% of the state leaders who requested financial assistance felt they received inadequate assistance from the Secretariat to assist them with their organizing and mobilization efforts. As a result, the primary task of fund-raising fell on the shoulders of the delegates who raised 80% of the majority of funds through individual and out-of-pocket donations to attend the National Summit (Fig. 2).

The state leaders overwhelmingly felt that they were unable to raise adequate funds for any of the associated tasks that were necessary to galvanize state delegates. Only 44% of the state leaders were able to

[24] Ten regional summits were initially planned; however, the Secretariat did not have enough money or time for additional summits. Additionally, the Secretariat was under pressure to complete the initiative from their funding agencies.

Table 4

Type of Barriers to Participation

Level	Inadequate finances	Time constraint	Lack information	Feeling frustration	Interpersonal conflict with others	Insufficient time for meetings	Insufficient energy/effort
State	16.3%	26.7%	16.8%	7.9%	5.4%	14.9%	5.4%
Regional	14.9%	26.2%	15.3%	5.9%	2.0%	11.4%	1.0%
National	30.2%	33.7%	11.9%	15.8%	4.5%	17.8%	4.5%

fulfill their number of designated delegate slots to attend the National Summit. According to state leaders, "our inability to fill the allotted number of state delegates to the National Summit was due in part to inadequate publicity at all levels of the groups that are likely to be interested in African issues" (State Leader 2001).

The lack of financial resources also affected the ability of state leaders to plan activities. While 62% of the state leaders felt that they had inadequate financial resources for such activities, 59% felt they had inadequate resources to assist state delegates with transportation and accommodations to the National Summit in Washington, D.C.

Furthermore, some delegates felt a disproportionate burden by participating in the Summit process. As Table 4 shows, participants experienced a range of barriers; the most commonly cited barrier was time constraint, followed by inadequate resources and lack of information. At the national level, inadequate finances and time constraints were cited as problems by a higher percentage of respondents, despite that they had better access to resources. The impact of these barriers, time, information, and finances, was no doubt harder for individuals from lower socioeconomic status, many of whom worked in the non-profit sector.

In sum, the ability of state leaders to mobilize delegates and raise adequate financial resources was constrained by two primary factors, an unrealistic time constraint imposed on the Summit process by the funders, and the lack of financial assistance by the Secretariat to provide "seed money" for state delegation outreach and mobilization efforts. Moreover, the lack of organic link of leaders to the community may have also played a role.[25] This hindered the ability of state leaders to develop and implement effective fund-raising strategies and to engage in outreach and public education activities to attract delegates. Furthermore, the inability of the state delegations to raise adequate funds, coupled

[25] I discuss this issue further in a forthcoming article, entitled "Resisting 'Race': Organizing African Transnational Identities in the United States" or also Humphries *The Role of Race, Ethnicity, and Nationality in United States/African Coalition Building*, 2003.

with the short time horizon, restricted individuals from grassroots, community-based, and non-profit organizations from participating in the Summit process. Individuals from the non-profit sector expressed frustration at the lack of understanding and constraints (time and money) they faced as a result of the lack of discretionary funds to justify activities associated with the Summit (Executive Director, Black Women's Organization 2000). Participants from grassroots and community-based organizations as well as individuals from lower socioeconomic strata experienced more financial barriers that prohibited them from participating in various activities. This, in turn, also affected the composition of the delegation and the content of the national policy plan-of-action.

Additionally, the inability of state leaders to attract delegates also negatively impacted the need for a variety of human resources to carry out necessary tasks such as attending meetings, making phone calls, working on the policy plan-of-action, and demonstrating expert working knowledge of the foreign policymaking institutions (Freeman 1979). Because financial resources were sparse, digital technologies would seem to be the natural means of developing this network.

Use of Technology in National Coordination Efforts by Secretariat

The Secretariat established three communication mechanisms—a web-page, state chair e-group, and teleconferencing—to facilitate communication with state leadership and between state chairs and delegates. For the purposes of this study, I will only focus on the web-page and teleconferencing technologies since I was unable to monitor the state leaders' e-group logs or content of their messages. The primary purpose of the web-page was to disseminate information in an interactive mode to state delegates, while the weekly teleconferences were designed to coordinate Secretariat and state actions, provide up-to-date information and to assist state leaders with any problems associated with Summit activities: "The web-page was extremely useful providing a wide-range of information about the Washington Summit and the build-up to the Summit" (State Chair 2000).

Web-page. The National Summit web-page was designed as a multi-purpose interactive tool to assist state leaders, delegates, and interested individuals with up-to-date news bulletins, national and regional summit policy plan-of-action documents, and links to Africa-specific organizations.[26] Over 69% of the State Leadership felt that the web-page was useful for disseminating information in a timely fashion (Fig. 3). State leaders felt the web-page was useful for a variety of reasons:

[26] See http://www.africasummit.org.

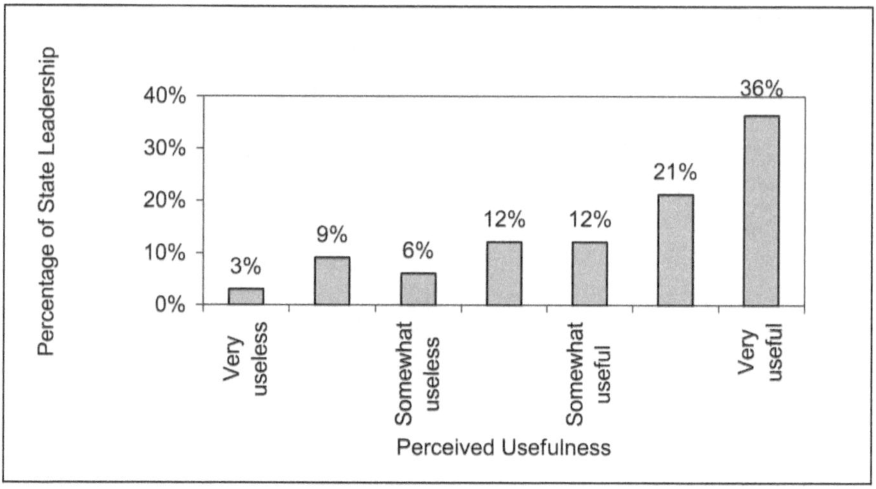

Figure 3. Secretariat Web-Page Usefulness

> "Because we got involved so late, we were able to download all the information, assemble packets, and deliver them before my packet arrived by mail from D.C."
> "All information such as document and housing information was present and convenient."
> "Liked the way they organized the information. Easy to find what one needs and used it to share information."
> "Access could get information easily; self-explanatory, didn't need much computer knowledge."
> "Since we didn't attend the Regional Summits, we relied heavily on information from the National Summit on Africa web-site and write-ups."

Teleconferencing. State leaders felt ambivalent about the usefulness of the weekly teleconferences with the Secretariat. To manage the process, states were divided into two regions: East and West of the Mississippi River. A password was provided to all state leaders who were responsible for dialing the Secretariat at a specific time during the week to participate. The purpose of the teleconferences was to assist with coordinating activities, to share information, and to answer questions and assist state leaders with problem-solving. Twenty-seven percent of the state leaders felt that the weekly teleconferences were very useful for state chair planning efforts, while only 19% reported them to be very useful for sharing information, and 16% stated they were very useful for problem-solving. Overall, the state leaders did not view the use of teleconferencing positively but rather felt it to be too directive in nature and not interactive enough to address their specific concerns and issues (State Chair Interview 2000).

The state chair survey data results support existing studies that the implementation of a user-friendly web-site can assist organizations with

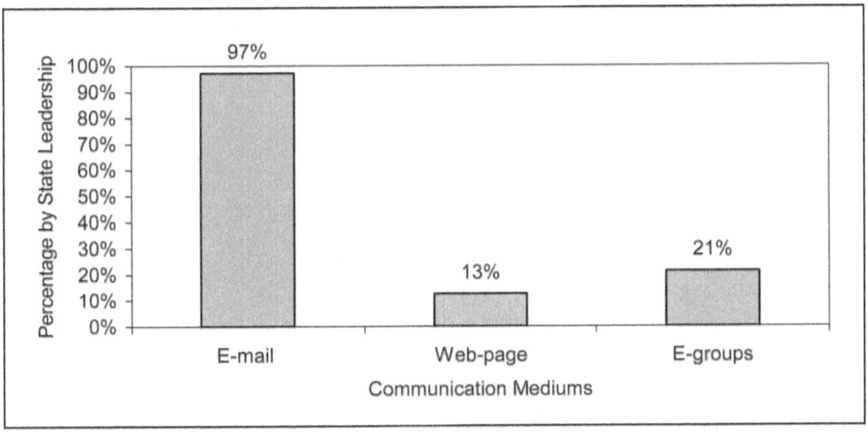

Figure 4. Technology Use by State Leadership

political organizing efforts. A wide array of information can be disseminated in a cost-efficient manner by distributing information across geographical borders and to many individuals simultaneously. In contrast, implementing an effective teleconferencing session requires structuring a relationship that is more interactive in nature. As indicated by the state chair interview data, the state leaders wanted to have more input to shape the structure and content of the teleconference sessions. The one-way interaction and dissemination of information was not adequate enough for state chairs. In order to clarify and supplement the teleconference sessions, many state leaders contacted their regional coordinators for further assistance.[27]

Technology Use by State Leadership

The state leadership employed a variety of communication mediums to accomplish the related tasks associated with preparing for the National Summit. As Figure 4 shows, 97% of the state leadership used e-mail in some capacity, 22% employed e-groups, and only 13% used a web-page.

Intra-state communication use patterns. By far e-mail was used more frequently as a communication tool and for a variety of tasks than e-groups or web-pages. For the purposes of this discussion, I will only focus on e-mail use for planning efforts between state leaders and with state delegates, for the dissemination of information, and for intra-state communication.

[27] The Secretariat staffed two regional coordinators who were responsible for addressing questions from state leaders. State delegations were divided into two regions: East and West of the Mississippi River.

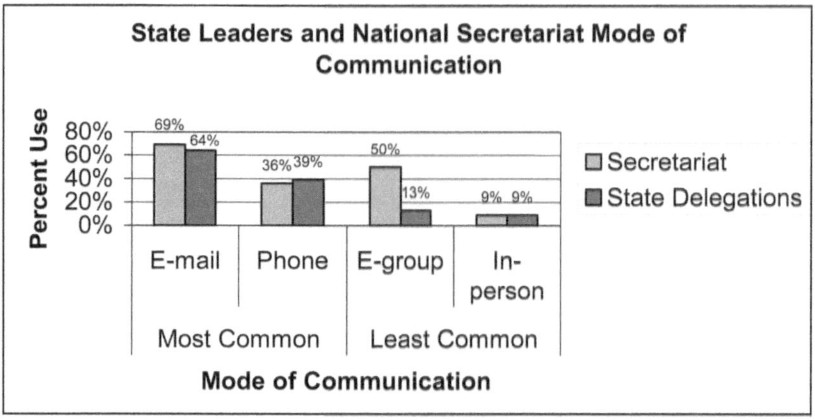

Figure 5. State Leaders and National Secretariat Mode of Communication

Over 50% of state leaders reported using e-mail frequently for planning purposes with each other while close to 30% felt as if they used e-mail infrequently. Interview data with state leaders from smaller states revealed that they preferred face-to-face interaction rather than using electronic forms of communication for planning purposes. Using e-mail to plan with state delegates mirrored a similar pattern, with state leaders reporting 52% frequency.

Sixty-five percent of state leaders reported using e-mail frequently for disseminating information to state delegates. However, when asked how frequently they e-mailed African-specific information to state delegates, only (33%) reported that they did.

Surprisingly, state leaders did not report using e-mail frequently to communicate with other state chairs. Survey and interview data revealed that state chairs were communicating with each other; however, they preferred to use the telephone to speak directly with each other to protect confidentiality and not leave a record of their interaction.

Communicating with the National Secretariat. Figure 5 illustrates the most commonly used modes of communication used in State Leader/Secretariat communication as well as state leader/delegate communication. The use of e-mail (69%, 64%), followed by placing a phone call (36%, 39%), were the most common mode of communication used by state leaders to communicate with the Secretariat and state delegations, respectively. E-groups were not commonly used by leaders to communicate with the Secretariat (50%) or state delegation (13%). Nor was in-person communication commonly used (9%).

In sum, the survey data tend to support the claim that state leaders supplemented a lack of funding resources with a variety of digital technologies to overcome organizing constraints. By far, e-mail was the medium of choice and was used consistently by state delegations for planning, coordinating, and disseminating information. E-groups and web-pages were rarely used by state delegations for such efforts. Only a few states (N = 2) used e-groups for revising the thematic working papers, while three states used web-pages to disseminate information to other state delegations and interested parties. According to the interview data, it appears as if these states were more influential in the agenda-setting process because of their ability to disseminate their policy preferences to other state delegations and build state consensus around specific key policies prior to the National Summit.

Despite the positive indicators that digital technologies do in fact facilitate planning, coordinating, and mobilizing efforts, interviews suggest that respondents from smaller states and states that had individuals who either lacked computer skills or computer and Internet access were unable to leverage digital technologies as easily. Similarly, the use of communication technologies may filter out certain personal, social, and behavioral cues that are necessary to sustain interpersonal relationships and that regulate interaction in face-to-face communication (Sproul and Kessler 1986; Short, Williams, and Christie 1976).

Use of Technology by Delegates: Cyber-Advocacy and the African Constituency

Recent studies primarily focus on how digital technologies are used for political organizing purposes (Elin 2003; Denning 2001; Danitz and Strobel 2001; Castells 1997). Few studies examine how preferences about technology use contribute to our understanding of how technology use can promote organizing. Moreover, differences in preference would raise concerns about how less empowered groups are likely to fare in an increasingly technologically sophisticated political environment. This section examines communication medium use patterns for National Summit participants to contact policymakers.

I first examine how delegates rank order their most favorite mode of communication used to contact policymakers. Second, I compare preferences for the type of communication across different groups, including state leaders/rank and file members, gender, and citizenship status.

Overall delegate preferences. There were statistically significant differences in delegate preferences for the type of communication used to contact policymakers ($p = .0001$). Overall, delegates favored using e-mail and sending a letter to contact policymakers rather than placing a phone call, speaking in-person, or faxing policymakers (see Table 5).

Table 5

Rank Means for All Delegates

Type of Communication	All delegates (n = 157; p = .0001)
E-mail	2.19
Fax	3.30
In-person	3.28
Letter	2.42
Phone	2.44

Table 6

Rank Means by Race

Type of Communication	White (n = 63, p = .0001)	Afro-American/ Caribbean (n = 66, p = .0001)	Black/African (n = 56, p = .0001)	Other (n = 8, p = 0.49)
E-mail	1.84	2.51	2.15	2.25
Fax	3.49	3.13	3.37	3.25
In-person	3.35	3.43	2.95	3.29
Letter	2.34	2.03	3.01	2.57
Phone	2.41	2.56	2.18	3.25

Preferences by race. As shown in Table 6, there were statistically significant differences for the type of communication used to contact policymakers (p = .0001) for all racial categories except for "other" (p = 0.49). E-mail was the preferred mode of communication for all racial groups except for Afro-American/Caribbeans, who preferred to send a letter to contact a policymaker. Sending a letter and placing a phone call were the second preferred modes of communication to contact policymakers. The interaction effect between mode of communication and race is significant (p = 0.0038) indicating that the race of a person does have an effect on which mode of communication that person prefers.

Elite preferences. There were also statistically significant differences in the preferences of state leaders versus rank-and-file members' preferences for type of communication to contact policymakers (p = 0.0379). When preferences across state leaders and rank-and-file members are compared, using e-mail, sending a letter, and placing a phone call were ranked as more favorable than sending a fax or speaking in-person to contact a policymaker (see Table 7).

Table 7

Rank Means for State Leaders and Rank and File Members

Type of Communication	State Leaders (n = 9; p = .04)	Rank and File Members (n = 193; p = .0001)
E-mail	2.00	2.20
Fax	3.38	3.30
In-person	4.00	3.25
Letter	2.25	2.43
Phone	2.57	2.43

Table 8

Rank Means for Women and Men

Type of Communication	Women (n = 86; p = .0001)	Men (n = 111; p = .0001)
E-mail	2.25	2.17
Fax	3.29	3.33
In-person	3.40	3.19
Letter	2.23	2.60
Phone	2.49	2.34

Gender preferences. Men and women showed statistically significant differences in their choice of communication medium (p = .0001). As indicated in Table 8, women were more likely to send a letter or to use e-mail to contact a policymaker, while men clearly preferred to use e-mail and to make a phone call rather than any other form of communication to contact policy-makers. These results to some extent support existing studies that the gender-gap between men and women is closing. Regardless of socioeconomic status women are now more likely to use advanced communication technology for a variety of purposes (see http://www.pewinternet.org/PPF/r/171/report_display.asp.).

American citizenship. There were also significant differences in communication preferences between delegates with American citizenship and non-citizens (p = .0001). Both citizens and non-citizens ranked e-mail as their preferred mode of communication to contact policymakers (see Table 9). However, non-citizens were more likely to place a phone call rather than send a letter to contact a policymaker when compared to American citizens. These results tend to support my earlier proposition that African immigrants who occupy the same socioeconomic status as

Table 9

Rank Means for Citizens and Non-citizens

Type of Communication	Citizens (n = 163; p = .0001)	Non-citizens (n = 31; p = .01)
E-mail	2.21	1.80
Fax	3.32	3.12
In-person	3.45	2.62
Letter	2.32	2.68
Phone	2.46	2.43

their American counterparts are just as likely to be technology savvy when contacting policymakers. Further, analysis revealed that an interaction effect between citizenship status and mode of communication was slightly significant (p = 0.08). This leads me to believe that there is some indication that the variable "delegate citizenship status" does help explain some of the differences in preferences that exist between citizens and non-citizens and their choice of communication medium to contact policymakers.

In summary, e-mail is clearly the preferred communication medium for all participants except for African Americans/Caribbeans who preferred to send a letter to contact their policymakers. Further research is needed in order to determine why African Americans/Caribbeans prefer to send a letter to contact their policymakers. This study, however, suggests that e-mail is transforming the character of political communication. Differences between secondary preferences varied between sending a letter and placing a phone call. The only variation was that non-citizens preferred to speak in-person to contact a policymaker.

DISCUSSION

Political Organizing and Resource Mobilization Capacity

The National Summit on Africa provides us with another example for examining political organizing and the benefits and constraints of shifting from more traditional forms of organizing tools, such as phone-banking, fax blasts, and public forums, towards digital technologies. In summary, I have argued that state delegations suffered from a lack of financial resources and less so from a lack of delegates. The decision by the Secretariat not to provide seed money to state delegations hindered their ability to adequately engage in outreach activities and, as such, selected for a more "elite" group of participants (Kleidman 1993). Although the

Secretariat provided technical assistance to state leaders, it was often too late to galvanize potential volunteers. While all participants experienced a wide range of barriers (e.g., time constraints, lack of information and finances) participants experienced these constraints differently, given their occupational and class status. For example, individuals who worked in higher education and/or the business community had more flex time and access to a wider range of personal and institutional resources, thus facilitating their ability to participate in summit activities. In contrast, less affluent participants and those who worked in the non-profit sector had less control over how they spent their time had to justify their participation in summit activities, and were affected more negatively by a range of barriers.

How did these various constraints and barriers affect the summit process? And more specifically, how did these barriers affect the representation of participants, impact the character and nature of the deliberative process and eventual policy position document? The socio-demographic profile of the participants reflected a change from grassroots, student-led initiatives and an absence of Pan-African and Black Nationalist groups to a more professional group of participants. The Black Left boycotted the event since they did not see the National Summit as being legitimate, given its ideological, formalization, national level affiliation and top-down approach to organizing. This shift to a more affluent group of participants may potentially have led to more moderate positions being reflected in the final regional and national policy documents.

Given the lack of adequate financial resources, state delegations were hindered in their ability to engage in traditional outreach activities such as mailings, phone-banks, and public education forums and travel-related expenses to attract volunteers. As such, state delegations relied more heavily on digital technologies for political organizing activities. Given that some delegates did not have computer or Internet access, coupled with the lack of computer skills, created barriers for them to participate in organizing, planning, and deliberative activities.

Digital technologies are changing the character and nature of political organizing. As observed in the case of the National Summit, the National Secretariat used a range of technologies for planning and coordinating efforts with state delegations across the United States. Using a web-site and teleconferencing as organizing tools, the Secretariat disseminated information in a timely and cost-efficient manner, and created a network of individuals and organizations engaged in African initiatives. Although the weekly teleconference sessions provided a vehicle for statewide problem-solving, particular attention is required to ensure interactivity between national and local organizations.

The Use of Digital Technologies in Statewide Organizing Efforts

As observed, state leaders used a variety of communication mediums to accomplish the associated tasks of organizing, mobilizing, and public outreach. While e-mail was clearly the most used digital technology, to some extent the use of various technologies was task-specific. For example, e-groups were more likely to be used for revising the thematic working papers in contrast to e-mail that was used for four out of five activities, for example, planning state/regional events; information dissemination; state leadership communication; and sharing Africa-specific information. In contrast, web-sites were used primarily to disseminate information and to share Africa-specific information. State leaders used more traditional communication mediums (e.g., in-person, phone, fax, and surface mail) for planning purposes, revising thematic working papers, and disseminating information.

Although a range of technologies were used for organizing purposes, it appears that state leaders preferred to speak in-person or use the telephone when communicating with other state leaders. This leads us to believe that privacy and confidentiality are valued over convenience. Likewise, not all state delegations preferred to use digital technologies; rather, smaller state delegations preferred to meet in person to organize and to work on the thematic working papers. State leaders articulated that the deliberative process required face-to-face interaction and dialogue in order to work through and thrash out difficult points. In-person contact also facilitated relationship-building between state delegates who perceived the use of technology to be too impersonal (Sproul and Kessler 1986; Short, Williams, and Christie 1976). Furthermore, State Leader/Secretariat and State Leader/Delegate communication-use patterns confirm existing use of e-mail and phone calls as the preferred modes of communication (see Fig. 5).

With a shift away from more traditional forms of communication mediums used as organizing tools (such as phone-banking, fax blasts, surface mail, and in-person contact) towards more intensive digital technologies, political organizers need to pay more attention to potential barriers created by the use of information and communication technologies. Likewise, particular care should be given to the types of technologies preferred by Summit participants to contact policymakers. Overall, it appears that delegates favored using e-mail to contact policymakers, thus supporting existing evidence that specific technologies are changing political communication between citizens and their representatives. While there was slight preference variation between categories (race, elite, gender, and citizenship status), e-mail still remained as the favorite mode of communication except for African American/Caribbeans, who preferred to send a letter to contact their policymakers.

Perhaps, African Americans/Caribbean's preference to send a letter is reflective of the digital divide that still exists between white Americans and racial minorities (Simms 2006; DiMaggio et al. 2001; U.S. Census Current Population Reports 2003). Coupled with poor computer and Internet access as well as low computer skills, trust and privacy issues may help explain why some participants still prefer to use traditional communication mediums to contact their policymakers. Strikingly, African immigrants also ranked the use of e-mail as their preferred medium to contact policymakers, thus supporting the previous proposition that African immigrants with professional backgrounds would also rely on technology like their U.S. counterparts. This case study, therefore, has attempted to illustrate the increasing importance of digital technology use by African advocacy organizations in their organizing efforts and the need for special emphasis on both the benefits and constraints of technology use.

REFERENCES

Adler, E.S., Gent, C.E., & Overmeyer, C.B. 1997. "The Home-style Homepage: Legislator Use of the World Wide Web for Constituency Service." American Political Science Association. Washington, DC. August.

Austin, A. 2006. "Are Africans in America African American?" *Black Directions* 2:1-7.

Bennet, L. 2004. "Communicating Global Activism: Strengths and Vulnerabilities of Networked Politics." Pp. 1-26 in *Cyberprotest New Media, Citizens, and Social Movements*, edited by Wim Van de Donk, Brian D. Loader, Paul G. Nixon, Dieter Rucht. New York: Routledge.

Booker, S. 1993. *A Review of Public Education and Constituency Building Programs for Africa.* New York: Ford Foundation.

——. 1996. "Thinking Regionally Priorities for U.S. Policy Toward Africa. Background paper." Washington, D.C.: African Policy Information Center.

——. 1999. "Thinking Regionally: A Framework for U.S. Policy Toward Africa." Unpublished Manuscript.

Brainard, L., & Siplon, P. 2002. "Cyberspace Challenges to Mainstream Non-profit Health Organizations" *Administration and Society* 34:141-175.

Brown, W. 1991. *Manhood and Politics.* Lanham, MD: Rowman and Littlefield.

Canover, W.J. 1980. *Practical Nonparametric Statistics.* New York: John Wiley & Sons.

Castells, M. 1997. *The Rise of The Networks Society: The Power of Identity, Vol. 2.* Oxford: Blackwell Publishers Inc.

Clough, M. 1992. *Free at Last: U.S. Policy Toward Africa and the End of the Cold War.* Washington, D.C.: Council on Foreign Relations Press.

Coombs, K. 1999. "Online Voter Mobilization: The Gilmore Model. Grassroots Lobbying and The Internet Explosion: New Opportunities For Issue Campaigning." *Campaigns and Elections* 20:3.

Creswell, J.W. 1998. *Qualitative Inquiry and Research Design Choosing Among Five raditions.* Thousand Oaks: Sage Publications.

Culan, M.J., & Markus, M.L. eds. 1987. *Information Technologies.* Newbury Park: Sage Publications, Ltd.

Danitz, T., & Strobel, W.P. 2001. "Networking Dissent: Cyber Activists Use the Internet to Promote Democracy in Burma." Pp. In *Networks, and Netwars: The Future of Terror, Crime, and Militancy*, edited by J. Arquilla &. D. Ronfeldt. Santa Monica: RAND Corporation.

Denning, D.E. 2001. "Activism, Hactivism, and Cyberterrorism: The Internet as a Tool for Influencing Foreign Policy." Pp. 239-288 in *Networks and Netwars: The Future of Terror, Crime, and Militancy*, edited by J. Arquilla &. D. Ronfeldt. Santa Monica: RAND Corporation.

Denzin, N.K. 1978. "The Logic of Naturalistic Inquiry." *In Sociological Methods: A Sourcebook*, edited by N.K. Denzin. New York: McGraw-Hill.
Diamond, L.J. and Plattner, M.F. 1999. *Democratization in Africa.* Baltimore, Md: Johns Hopkins University Press.
Di Maggio, P., Hargittai, E., Neuman, W.R., and Robinson, J.P. 2001. "Social Implications of the Internet." *Annual Review of Sociology* 27:307-336.
Djamba, Y.K. 1999. "African Immigrants in The United States: A Socio-demographic Profile In Comparison to Native Blacks." *Journal of Asian and African Studies* 34:210-216.
Dumbrell, J. 1997. *The Making of U.S. Foreign Policy.* Oxford Road: Manchester University Press.
Elin, L. 2003. "The Radicalization of Zeke Spier: How the Internet Contributes to Civic Engagement and New Forms of Social Capital." Pp. 97-116 in *Cyberactivism Online Activism in Theory and Practice.* New York: Routledge.
Faigley, L. 1992. *Fragments of Rationality: Postmodernity and The Subject of Composition.* Pittsburgh: University of Pittsburgh Press.
Fontana, A. and Frey, J. 1994. "Interviewing The Art of Science." Pp. 361-376 in *Handbook of Qualitative Research*, edited by and Yvonna Lincoln Norman Denzin. Newbury Park: Sage Publications.
Freeman, J. 1979. "Resource Mobilization and Strategy." Pp. 167-189 in *Dynamics of Social Movements*, edited by M.N. Zald & J.M. McCarthy. Cambridge: Winthrop.
Gordon, D.F., D.C. Miller, and H. Wolpe. 1998. *The United States and Africa A Post-cold War Perspective.* New York: W.W. and Norton Company.
Grossman, L.K. 1995. *The Electronic Republic: Reshaping Democracy In The Information Age.* Harlow: Viking Publishers.
Gurak, L. 1997. *Persuasion and Privacy In Cyberspace.* Chelsea: Book Crafters, Inc.
Hochschild, A. 1999. *King Leopold's Ghost: A Story of Greed, Terror and Heroism In Colonial Africa.* New York: Houghton Mifflin Co.
Hoffman, D., and Novak, T. 1998. "Bridging the Digital Divide: The Impact of Race on Computer Access and Internet Use." Unpublished Working Paper.
Horne, G. 1999. "Race for Power: U.S. Foreign Power and The General Crisis of "White Supremacy." *Diplomatic History* 23:437-461.
Humphries, J. 2003. *The Role of Race, Ethnicity, and Nationality in United States—Africa Coalition Building.* Ann Arbor: ProQuest UMI Dissertation Services.
Huyer, S. 1997. *Supporting Women's Use of Information Technologies for Sustainable Development.* Retrieved July 14, 2006 (http://www.wigsat.org/it/womenicts.html).
Jaccard, J., Becker, M. & Wood, G. 1984. "Pairwise Multiple Comparison Procedures: A Review." *Psychological Bulletin.* 96:589-596.
Jeffreys-Jones, R. 1995. *Changing Differences: Women and The Shaping of American Foreign Policy, 1917-1994.* New Jersey: Rutgers University Press.
Jenkins, J. 1983. "Resource Mobilization Theory And The Study Of Social Movements." *Annual Review of Sociology* 9:527-553.
Kang, J. 2000. "Cyber-Race." *Harvard Law Review* 113:1130-1208.
Kilson, M. 1992. "African Americans and Africa a Critical Nexus." *Dissent*, 39:361-369.
Kleidman, R. 1993. *Organizing for Peace: Neutrality, the Test Ban, and the Freeze.* Syracuse: Syracuse University Press.
Krenn, M. ed. 1999. *The Impact of Race on U.S. Foreign Policy: A Reader.* New York: Garland Publishing, Inc.
Marden, J.I. 1995. *Analyzing and Modeling Rank Data.* Oxfordshire: Chapman and Hall.
Martin, W.G. and West, M.O. 1999. *Out of One, Many Africas Reconstructing The Study and eaning of Africa.* Chicago: University of Illinois Press.
McAdam, D.J., McCarthy, J.D., & Zald, M.N. ed. 1988. *Social Movements.* Beverly Hills: Sage.
McCarthy, J.D., & Wolfson, M. 1996. "Resource Mobilization by Local Social Movement Organizations: Agency, Strategy, and Organization. In The Movement Against Drinking and Driving." Pp. *American Sociological Review* 61:1070-1088.
McCaughey M. and Ayers M.D. eds. 2003. *Cyberactivism Online Activism in Theory and Practice.* New York: Routledge.

Negroponte, N. 1998. "The Third Shall Be First: The Net Leverages Latecomers in the Developing World." *Wired*. Retrieved on July 14, 2006 (http://www.wired.com/wired/archive/6.01/negroponte.html).

Norusis, M.J. 2000. *SPSS 10.0 Guide to Data Analysis*. Upper Saddle River: Prentice Hall.

Oliver, P., & Furman, M. 1989. Contradictions Between National and Local Organizational Strength: The Case of the John Birch Society. *International Social Movement Research* 2:155-177.

Pew Internet & American Life Project. 2006. *How Women and Men Use the Internet*. Retrieved July 14, 2006 (http://www.pewinternet.org/PPF/r/171/report_display.asp. Washington, D.C.: Pew Institute).

Piven, F., & Cloward, R. 1979. *Poor People's Movements*. New York: Vintage.

Read, J.G., and Emerson, M.O. 2005. "Racial Context, Black Immigration and U.S. Black/White Health Disparity." *Social Forces* 84:181-199.

Seifert, J.W. and Petersen, R.E. 2002. The Promise of All Things E? Expectations and Challenges of Emergent Electronic Government. *Perspectives on Global Development and Technology* 1:193-212.

Schraeder, P.J. 1991. "Speaking With Many Voices: Continuity and Change in U.S. Africa Policies." *The Journal of Modern African Studies* 29:373-412.

——. 1994. *United States Foreign Policy Toward Africa, Incrementalism, Crisis and Changes*. Berkeley: University Press.

——. 1996. "Removing the Shackles? U.S. Foreign Policy Toward Africa After The End of The Cold War." Pp. 187-205 in AFRICA In *The New International Order*, edited by Edmond J. Keller and Donald Rothchild. Boulder: Lynne Rienner Publishers.

Schwartz, E. 1998. An Internet Resource for Neighborhoods. Pp. 110-124 in *Cyberdemocracy: Technology, Cities and Civic Networks*. edited by R. Tsagaroursianou, D. Tambini, and C. Bryan, London & New York: Routledge.

Short, J., Williams, E., and Christie, B. 1976. *The Social Psychology of Telecommunications*. Indianapolis: Wiley and Sons Publishing.

Siegel, J., Dubrovsky, V., Kiesler, S., & McGuire, T.W. 1986. "Group Processes in Computer-Mediated Communication." *Organizational Behaviour and Human Decision* 37:157-187.

Simms, M.C. 2006. *Measuring the Divide: African Americans' Access to the Online Universe*. Washington, D.C.: Joint Center For Political And Economic Studies.

Speer, T. 1994. "The Newest African Americans Aren't Black." *American Demographics* 16:1-3.

Spooner T., and Rainie, L. 2000. African-Americans and The Internet. Pew Internet & American Life Project. Retrieved July 14, 2006 (http://www.pewinternet.org).

Spradley, J.P. 1980. *Participant Observation*. Chicago: Holt, Rinehart and Winston, Inc.

Sproul, L & Kessler, S. 1986. "Reducing Social Context Cues: Electronic Mail in Organizational Communication." *Management Science* 32:1492-1512.

Staggenborg, S. 1991. *The Pro-Choice Movement: Organization and Activism In The Abortion Conflict*. New York: Oxford University Press.

Stoecker, R. 2004. "Cyberspace vs. Face-to-Face: Community Organizing in the New Millennium." *Perspectives on Global Development and Technology* 1:143-164.

Takougang, J. 2003. "Contemporary African Immigrants to The United States." Ìrìnkèrindò: A Journal of African Migration, Retrieved July 14, 2006 (http://www.africamigration.com/).

Tsagarousianou, R., Tambini, D., and Bryan C. ed. 1998. *Cyberdemocracy: Technology, Cities and Civic Networks*. New York: Routledge.

U.S. Census Bureau. 2000. *Current Population Reports, Series: Profile of the Foreign-Born Population in the United States*. Washington, D.C.: Government Printing Office.

——. 2003. "Computer and Internet Use in the United States." Retrieved July 14, 2006 (http://www.census.gov/prod/2005pubs/p23-208.pdf).

U.S. Department of Commerce. 2004. "A Nation Online: Entering the Broadband Age." ashington, D.C.: Government Printing Office.

U.S. Department of Homeland Security. 2003. *Yearbook of Immigration Statistics*. Washington, D.C.: Government Printing Office.

Van Aelst, P. and Walgrave, S. 2004. "New Media, New Movements? The Role of the Internet in Shaping the 'Anti-Globalization' Movement." Pp. 97-122 in *Cyberprotest New Media, Citizens, and Social Movements.* edited by Wim V.D., Loader B.D. Nixon P.G., and Rucht D. New York: Routledge.
Van de Donk, Wim, Brian D. Loader, Paul G. Nixon, and Dieter Rucht, eds. 2004. *Cyberprotest New Media, Citizens, and Social Movements.* New York: Routledge.
Walters, R. 2004. "The African Growth and Opportunity Act Changing Foreign Policy Priorities Toward Africa in a Conservative Political Culture." Pp. 288-306 in *Diversity and U.S. Foreign Policy: A Reader*, edited by Ernest J. Wilson III. New York: Routledge.
Williams, L. 1997. *Making Connections for Africa Report from a Constituency Builder's Dialogue.* Retrieved July 14, 2006 (http://www.africaaction.org/bp/cbd.htm).
Wittig, M.A., and Schmitz, J. 1996. "Electronic Grassroots Organizing." *Journal of Social Issues*, 52:53-69.
Young, D.R. 1989. "Local Autonomy in a Franchise Age: Structural Change in National Voluntary Associations." *Nonprofit and Voluntary Sector Quarterly*, 18:101-117.
Zald, M.N. 1970. *Organizational Change.* Chicago: University of Chicago Press.

6. Biodiversity Management: A Current Trace of the African Diaspora

*Paula Moreno-Zapata**

Abstract

This study investigates an aspect of the African Diaspora that, to date, has received scant attention. Environmental affairs of African Colombians have been woefully understudied and largely undocumented in major international scholarship. This is surprising since Colombia has the second largest African-descendant population in Latin America, and the African-Colombian territory in the Pacific coast is one of the most biologically diverse regions on the entire planet. The potential economic advantages of this could be enormous for African Colombians and has affected their models of development. However, African Colombians are like other African Diasporas—they are presently disproportionately poor, uneducated, and powerless in their respective societies. A principal objective of this study is to discuss the political-economic and environmental aspects inherent to high biodiversity presence in the African Colombians' territories, identifying the advantages and obstacles standing in the way of realizing the real dimension of these natural endowments.

INTRODUCTION

The African Diaspora remains integrally connected to the natural resources of the settlements, where African-descendants were mostly forced to migrate. In the last decades, some of these settlements (e.g. tropical forests), have reached a significant global level of discussion due to the growing environmental concern about the loss of biodiversity and its impact on human survival. This concern has also revealed the crucial

* Cambridge University, Centre of Latin American Studies, Cambridge, England. E-mail: pmm39@cam.ac.uk, p.moreno.03@cantab.net.

role that ethnic communities have played in conservation and sustainable use of these unique natural resources. In particular, ethnic communities have constructed their lives and cultures in direct connection with nature. African-descendants, as one of the largest ethnic communities in high biodiversity areas, have been forced to recognize and reinforce their African roots in order to establish their own role and perspective in this environmental global concern. In Colombia, this perspective has been based on the institutional strengthening of the grassroots organizations and the recognition of an ethno-development approach that is based on their identity.

Globalization, as a process of high and accelerated interconnectedness of different areas of contemporary life, has integrated diverse actors and common causes, while at the same time influencing historical processes in different corners of the world. The interrelationship between global issues, such as ethnicity, gender, development, and environmental concerns has accelerated the emergence of a growing network of interest and solidarity groups.

The African Diaspora movement is one such interest group. It represents a contemporary recognition of forced migration from Africa, particularly for the purpose of enslavement, throughout the world. In this regard, historical background is the point of reference relating to the challenges faced by the global African Diaspora community to actively participate in the process of globalization. This community is directly affected by major global issues such as poverty and environmental depletion. In particular, the social crisis has been the main concern of most African-descendants, regardless of their location. Hence, the African Diaspora impels the global solidarity of people who share not only the same skin color (to some degree), but who also have a connection to the environment, in a manner reflective of the African continuum.

Nature has been an important actor and witness of this Diaspora; it has embodied the set of material and immaterial components, which has allowed the permanence and transmission of the African roots. The biological diversity of genes, species and ecosystems was also influenced by the new migrants to the tropical areas.

Biodiversity, a rather new term, raised awareness on the key role of ethnic local communities within the global environmental system of governance. The Convention on Biological Diversity emphasizes in its preamble, and in Article 8 addressing the *In situ* conservation, the role of indigenous and *local communities* in biodiversity conservation. African-descendant communities are included under the term *local communities*, from which indigenous groups are differentiated. Such rhetoric, grouping the African-descendants in the *local communities*' category, while the indigenous remain autonomous, neglects the contribution that African-descendants have made to biodiversity. The invisibility of the African-descendant in the environmental arena is evidenced in this omission in one of the most important multilateral environmental agreements.

The case of Colombia is particularly interesting because it holds the second largest African-descendant population in Latin America with approximately 11,745,403 African Colombians, which represents 26% of the total Colombian population. Moreover, it is considered the second most megadiverse country in the world[1] with the Pacific coast classified as a biodiversity hotspot (Mitterneier 1999).[2] In the Pacific coast region, African Colombian communities account for 90% of its total population, with collective land rights in 5,000,000 of the 10,000,000 hectares of its total extension (Escobar 2004). In fact, the Pacific coast represents the region with the highest levels of poverty, lowest coverage of public services, and lowest economic growth in the country. The wealth of natural resources and the harsh social reality faced by most African Colombians have generated the armed conflict sharpened in regions like the Pacific coast (Restrepo 2004).[3]

This paper studies the relationship between biodiversity and the African Diaspora in light of the process of globalization and attempts to answer the following questions: What does biodiversity mean for African-descendants? How do the ethnic and environmental concerns determine the process of social advancement of African-descendants, in light of the Colombian case? To what extent could the megadiversity conditions potentially make in the African Colombian development? For the most part, these questions can be answered through a discussion of global trends and the relationships between development, environment, and the African Diaspora. From this overview, the study of the African Colombian organizational structure for managing biodiversity will also provide key elements for understanding the African Diaspora in the biodiversity network.

[1] The group of megadiverse countries, which comprehends 17 countries: Brazil, China, Australia, Madagascar, USA, Papua N. Guinea, D.R. of Congo, Colombia, Ecuador, India, Indonesia, Malaysia, Mexico, Peru, Philippines, South Africa and Venezuela.

[2] The Colombian Pacific coast makes part of the group of biodiversity hotspots, 14 places in the world where more than 70% of the world's biodiversity is concentrated. The Pacific coast's profile is available online (http://www.biodiversityhotspots.org).

[3] According to CODHES, African Colombians account for almost 40% of the main victims of displacement in the country.

GLOBALIZATION, ETHNICITY, AND THE ENVIRONMENT: FINDING SIMILARITIES, BUILDING GLOBAL COMMUNITIES

In a recent analysis about the reality of several municipalities within major African Colombian populations located in the Pacific coast region of Colombia, some of the participants suggested that the reality of these municipalities and their problems were similar to the situation of several African countries or Caribbean islands. The similarities not only stemmed from the ethnic component but also from the problems of underdevelopment. For instance, the main explanation for the African Colombian social crisis given by most of the government authorities in Colombia is a similar explanation for this crisis in Africa. The two main explanations are the widespread phenomena of corruption and laziness of the population and its leaders,[4] which correspond to an ancient African stigma. Jeffrey Sachs (2005) argues that corruption and laziness offer a too simplistic explanation for the complex situation and reality of the African crisis, which also applies for the major problems of African-descendant population in Colombia.

Another example of this existing social connection between Africans and African-descendants can be exemplified by the comparable situations of African Americans before their achievements in reducing discrimination in the United States, vis-à-vis the reality of African Colombians. This solidarity reflects the lack of representation in the decision-making positions in the main national institutions, the low access to basic services, limited opportunities and high rates of poverty. Despite the different historical processes and settings, these communities find similarities in their goals and fights. From different national and international perspectives, the African Diaspora shares not only an ancient movement and transmission of several components (e.g., culture, plants) but also the main social, economic, and political challenges faced by its populations.

Several authors have mentioned ethnicity as a cornerstone in the growing global civil society, which is one of the outstanding phenomena in the globalization process (Kamal 2004; Wade 1996). This ethnic role enters into the so-called "globalization of resistance" and "integration of the global democracy" (Oslesden 2004; Esteva and Suri 2004). This social side of globalization stems from the response of groups that feel marginalized from the global scenario. These marginalized groups have

[4] See the Colombian Vice-president speech for the opening event of the Third Conference on the African Colombian Institutional Strengthening held in Cali from 4th to 6th August 2005.

become a socially synergic force that puts pressure on the public and private sector, advocating a defense for their own diverse perspectives and resisting the homogenized models of the so-called "global village."

One specific action undertaken by ethnic communities in order to raise awareness of their difference has been the active participation in the global system of governance composed of a set of international conventions. Some of these conventions exclusively address the global ethnical discussion (e.g., Durban), and others, the contribution of ethnic communities for major global concerns (e.g., Convention on Biological Diversity and the Convention to Combat Desertification). As another action, the international cooperation and the influence of Diaspora interest groups in developed countries have been important in consolidating the goals and projects of the African-descendant communities, especially in developing countries.[5] Finally, academia and its process of reflecting on Diaspora realities constitute a main force of memory and influence as a reminder of the social connections between the national and international African-descendant communities.

The ethnic component is a crosscutting issue that is also influencing other dimensions of globalization. For example, the political role of religious groups has been decisive in the formation and consolidation of the ethnic grassroots movements and the enforcement of the global civil society. The economic dimension relates to some issues (e.g. traditional knowledge, property rights, workforce or corporate image) to which ethnic groups could contribute and build an advantage in the market place. Ethnicity becomes a key aspect that has built historical models and determined the different sides of contemporary life.

Ethnicity and the environment have had a close connection. African-descendants and indigenous communities have created their life models with an ancestral relationship with nature. Life models are constructed around the dependency on natural resources in order to survive physically (e.g., food, medicine, housing) and spiritually (e.g., spiritual beliefs, music). This relationship has provided an invaluable knowledge about the various existing species. Ethnic communities have also provided an invaluable knowledge about the different species, and through their traditional knowledge they became the main inventory of biological wealth and its different uses. Furthermore, these communities have conserved the environment without intensive use of the resources. Enslaved Africans were forced to

---

[5] For instance, the influence of African-American congressional members' emphasis on the African Colombian community in USAID programes for Colombia (2006-2008). See the report of the Department of State, Foreign Operations and related programs appropriation bills 2006, page 64, Calendar 150, Report 109-96.

become the workforce of extractivist activities by the colonialist power. Therefore, slavery not only took away their freedom and dignity, but also the ancient tradition of respect and conservation of the environment.

In the global agenda, the environment, has been one of the foremost concerns under a phenomenon called "ecological or environmental globalization" (Rodriguez 2005; Agarwal 2001). From the ethnic perspective, the environmental side of globalization contradicts itself. On one hand, it declares the importance and contribution of local groups to the conservation of the global environment, particularly regarding biodiversity protection and its sustainable use. On the other hand, it is also creating what Vandana Shiva calls "globalization as environmental apartheid," in which some of the local groups participate in the global environmental system of governance without being considered in final decisions.

In this regard, some environmental experts have affirmed that African-descendant communities have not had environmentally friendly attitudes, mainly connected to their participation in extractive activities with industries like mining and timber. However, they do not consider that the colonialist power imposed this extractive approach on African-descendants. These experts have not analyzed the ancient and traditional use of the natural resources by African communities before they were forced to respond to the economic interests of the colonialists. In the Colombian case, an alarming fact shows how this colonialist approach continues to be the attitude of some mining, African palm, and timber industries, and is now the interest of the drug trafficking businesses. The so-called non-environmentally friendly attitude of African-descendants corresponds to a historical pattern of economic globalizing forces, which by means of slavery imposed accelerated extractivist regimes.

Globalization reinforces the transnational nature of the African Diaspora based on the re-creation of a global ethnic identity. This identity is closely related to the environment, which allowed the Diaspora to recreate its ancestral roots. The environment becomes a key element in the process of social advancement of African-descendants, in particular in megadiverse countries where there is a worldwide interest in sustainable use and conservation. The conservation of the environment should be accompanied and developed in a close consultation with the local ethnic communities.

ETHNO-DEVELOPMENT AND TERRITORY

Some authors mention that *development* has been one of the inventions by which the powerful forces have imposed their economic and social models on most populations in the world (Shiva 2005; Escobar 1995). This initial Western-oriented model of development has surprisingly engendered reflection and actions that arise from groups that want to posit "difference" as a key factor in global trends. As a result, *development* has become a more plural concept transformed by different groups.

Sachs (1996) posits a broader definition: "Development is much more than just a socio-economic endeavour; it is a perception which models reality, a myth which comforts societies and a fantasy which unleashes passions." Charlton (2005) defines development as "the human capacity to influence and control the natural and social environment." These definitions reveal the level of subjectivity and particular interpretation of the *development* discourse. However, the latter definition is remarkably important for African-descendants in major biodiverse areas, because development for them depends on their capacity to influence and control their natural and social environment.

The ethnic Diaspora encounters have proposed their own conception, entitled ethno-development. The concept of ethno-development brings together the preservation of cultural identity, the institutional strengthening, and the creation of business opportunities in line with the traditional practices and the conservation and sustainable use of the natural resources (Moreno 2005). The World Bank defines ethno-development as "an autonomous process representing a community's vision of its history, its values, and its future goals as it seeks for a better quality of life" (Partridge, Urquillas and Johns 1996). The ethno-developmental approach emerges in response to the traditional model of development, which suggests a singular route to development.

Megadiverse countries have a direct correlation to ethno-development and biodiversity. The high level of endemism in Colombia, Ecuador, Brazil, among other countries has been related to the migratory phenomenon in the fifteenth century. Some of the diverse species found in high biodiversity areas in the Americas are native to Africa (Carney and Acevedo 2003). African slaves brought their traditional knowledge and practices. For this reason, African-descendants are regarded as "guardians of biodiversity," because even under the forced migratory phenomenon they remained intimately related to the environment (Wade 1999).

The aforementioned correlation also corresponds to the biological and cultural components of the meaning of biodiversity. As Zweilfel (1997) pointed out, "*the diversity in nature corresponds to, and results from, a diversity of culture.*" African-descendants print their essence in the way they establish their settlements and transform the ecosystems. For instance, African Colombians are water-oriented and are mainly located next to the river; thus, the river became a major source of inspiration for survival for the African slaves. Apart from that, the traditional practices determined the way to use or not to use the land and the different natural species.

Biodiversity management has substantially determined the process of ethno-development. To some extent, the economic interest that focused on the high biodiverse regions has demanded different levels of organization from the ethnic grassroots communities. Some of these communities have possession of collective property rights to territory. Historically, the lack of determination and organizational structure allowed different economic forces to take advantage of the ancient natural resources preserved by local communities, who, coincidentally, received little or no benefit from the powers that be.

The management approach depends on the development agenda of the different stakeholders of biodiversity. Ethnic communities have determined that their development perspective is rooted in their identity and differs from the capitalist approach to exploit the natural resources. An illustrative example is the ethnic communities' concept of territory, which differs from the traditional concept of land. Territory entails a Diaspora foundation, in which communities have their cultural milestone and define their life projects (PCN 2005). It also implies a historical process in which the Diaspora demands from the State recognition and support for their initiatives and acceptance of their identity based on a sense of ownership.

In light of the Colombian case, African Colombians are called on to be social and environmental authorities under the ethno-development approach. Property rights in these biodiverse areas constitute a strength that is widely unrealized. The environmental advantage should be used as an instrument of social advancement and a means to political and economic empowerment, based on the African-descendant contribution to the knowledge, conservation, and ancestral sustainable use of the environment.

BIODIVERSITY: THE CASE OF AFRICAN COLOMBIANS IN THE PACIFIC COAST

In the earliest publication where the term "biodiversity" was first mentioned, Choco, one of the regions of the Colombian Pacific coast, was alluded to as a place with major biodiversity (Wilson 1986). Later on, international environmental NGOs and agencies established that this region possesses "the greatest plant biodiversity in the planet" (GEF 1999). Over 9000 vascular plants species have been classified and biologists declare that most of the species are still unknown (Mittermeier et al. 1997).[6]

[6] Another biologist was Alwyn Gentry who wrote, among others, an article titled "*We Know More About the Moon than About Choco,*" in which he discussed the national ignorance about this invaluable hotspot (Gentry 1993:56).

At present, the area is the country's main producer of platinum and the second highest domestic producer of gold. The region accounts for approximately 60 per cent of Colombia's wood and paper pulp production. The Colombian Pacific coast is made up of 10 million hectares of tropical forests, from which 5 million have been given as territorial rights to African Colombians communities (Restrepo 2004).

The African Colombian population has traditionally settled on the coasts of the Pacific Ocean and the Caribbean Sea, but not always by choice. In the middle of the twentieth century, this population started moving to major urban centers, located in the central regions of the country, mainly in search of job opportunities and a better quality of life. On the Pacific coast, the African-descendant tradition remained and the race mixture was minimal compared to the Caribbean Sea coast (Wade 1997). This accounts for one of the reasons why the African-descendant political movement has been more dynamic in the Pacific region.

Historically, the major presence of the African-descendant population on the Pacific coast—largely undesirable by colonialists—may be explained by the colonialist's lack of knowledge and adaptability to the tropical forests. This is depicted by Warwick, "historically in the colonial tropics, virgin forests were perceived as a challenge for Western colonialists to domesticate and civilize, not only actions but also their inhabitants' minds" (cited in Greenough and Lowenhaupt 2003). The colonialists also perceived the similarity of this region to some African countries, which facilitated the exploitation of the natural resources, using the traditional knowledge and practices of the African slaves. Apart from this mainly economic exploitation, some enslaved Africans escaped from Spanish oppression by fleeing into the heart of the forest.

African Colombians are not fully accepted as a community with an important contribution to Colombian development. However, they have not only enriched and preserved natural resources, but also constituted a fundamental and skilled workforce. Their contribution to biodiversity incorporates the presence of some African native species, landscape transformation, traditional knowledge, cultural practices, ecosystem management, and the consolidation of an organizational structure to develop, protect and defend their territory and its inhabitants.

Unfortunately, the lack of recognition of the African-descendants' historical connection to the environment to some other crucial areas of the contemporary life is exacerbated by the high level of vulnerability of these communities. African Colombians are one of the most vulnerable groups in Colombia. The vulnerability integrates a series of factors, such as violence, displacement, natural disasters, unemployment, and low access to education, healthcare, job opportunities, and housing. The African Colombian population has, in all basic indicators, a lower level of existence compared to the rest of the population (CONPES 2004).

The Pacific coast exemplifies a development paradox. One of the richest areas, in terms of natural resources, is Colombia's poorest and most underdeveloped region where 80 percent of the population live in extreme poverty with a high level of malnutrition. One hundred and twenty-five children out of every 1000 die before reaching their first birthday; the illiteracy rate is three times the national average; two out of a hundred African Colombians have access to higher education. Most of the population have no access to electricity and potable water. The infrastructure is deficient; the means of transportation are precarious, and in most municipalities mainly fluvial. As one leader of an African Colombian social movement declared, "Biodiversity becomes nothing more than some resources which enable a population living in misery to barely survive."

The environment and development have a close relationship, which in the Colombian case is also exacerbated by the violence and armed conflict. The armed conflict threatens and generates a new internal African Colombian Diaspora marked by displacement and nurtured by drug trafficking. These latter phenomena imply not only the loss of the territory, culture, and values but also the increase of poverty and vulnerability.

A main concern for African Colombians is how the ethno-development approach, intimately related to the environment, becomes a cornerstone for improving the life conditions and vulnerability of most African Colombians. Megadiversity is a comparative advantage, which has become a competitive advantage in several countries by means of economically sustainable activities and research. This competitive advantage has had an impact on development by assuring the equal benefit of the local communities, mainly by the determination of these communities to be actors and not spectators of the decision-making process on biodiversity.

THE AFRICAN COLOMBIAN INSTITUTIONAL STRENGTHENING AND THE BIODIVERSITY NETWORK

In order to face the complexity of their situation, some African Colombians in the 1970s started political and civil society organizations in an effort to represent their position. They became interlocutors with the different power brokers (e.g., the government and businesses) and responded to the need to defend African Colombian rights and gain major control of the environment and social life.

These organizations could be classified into three main categories: social movements, ethno-territorial entities, and interest groups. One category represents the social movements (e.g., Movimiento Cimarron, Proceso de Comunidades Negras), which the main feature was the advocacy of nature in a call for autonomy, territorial and political rights, cultural legacy, and the defense of life. This latter aspect has been crucial, given the sharpening of the armed conflict and the continuous attack on the ethnic communities (Wade 1995).

Another category is represented by the communitarian councils, which arose from a response to Law 70 based on the necessity of organizational performance and synergy to defend and validate collective land titles management. Communitarian councils are ethno-territorial entities with autonomy over the collective titles of African Colombians. Currently, there are 160 communitarian councils, which defend the African Colombian rights from the State, economic forces, and even the illegal networks such as guerrilla and paramilitary groups. As the leader of one communitarian council in Tumaco mentioned "we are the State in regions where there is no State, we gather together to defend our lives, and we have achieved consideration as a community from the armed groups, the economic groups and the State."[7]

African Colombian communitarian councils, recognizing their different perspectives towards development and the environment, have established their life projects, which can be said to have the same relevance as the official municipalities' development projects. Likewise, for biodiversity management, they have established their plans for Integral Environmental Management (Planes de Manejo Ambiental Integral (PMAI)), in which these communities establish their land rights, principles for protection of the environment, and the improvement of the agricultural traditional practices (Gallo 2004; ACIA 2002; PCN 2003, 1999).

Among the African Colombian organizations, which have been formed more recently, interest groups may be considered as the third category. Some of the main interest groups are the politically-oriented associations. Of these groups is the Colombian Association of African-descendant Mayors (AMUNAFRICAN), an Association of mostly African-descendant municipalities in different parts of the Pacific coast, such as AMUNORCA and FEDEMPACIFICO. These associations strengthen and enhance the political participation of African Colombian leaders in order to include the ethnic perspectives in the major decision-making instances of the country, the region, and the municipality.

Other interest groups are the African Colombian network of women and the Young African Colombian network. In particular, the gender

[7] Translation made by the author, from an interview made with the leaders of the Communitarian councils in Tumaco (RECOMPAS) on 15th May 2005.

perspective of the African Colombian institutional framework has gained importance and there exists more than 200 female groups on the Pacific coast, which gathered more than 10,000 African Colombian women. The harsh reality of women's issues on the Pacific coast is demonstrated by the high percentage of female-headed households, for example, on the Pacific coast where over 40% of women with children are single mothers (Grumer 2003). This situation is partially attributed to violence; the male-heads of the family are members of illegal groups, or were killed or forced to leave due to the lack of job opportunities. In most municipalities of the Pacific coast, women are responsible for the economic maintenance of the households and directly responsible for biodiversity management.

In the consolidation of the African Colombian organizations, part of an important global African Diasporan and civil society force, international cooperation has played a crucial role in providing resources for their development. Many of these organizations have utilized international aid in the creation and formalization of Communitarian councils[8] and social movements.[9] The African Colombian Institutional Network (ACIN), which is comprised of unions and other civil society organizations with international outreach and aspirations, is a key player in advancing solidarity in the ethnic community. ACIN works within a strategic framework to prevent history form repeating itself, that is, division among Colombians leading to more vulnerability. This framework needs to devise different economic, political, environmental, and social scenarios with attendant programmatic steps that lead to success.

CONCLUSIONS

The African Diaspora is not only a dynamic concept with historical and multidimensional connotations, it is also a framework that enables its global community to define and examine issues that are crucial for advancement in the global political economy. In particular, biodiversity, a growing global environmental concern, is emerging as a potential source of economic development for African Colombians. For centuries, Africans initially were forced to live on the coastal areas, which were considered the least desireable areas by colonialists. Now, with the potential boon

[8] According to ACIA, the main comunitarian council of Choco, the process of conformation and consolidation of their organization was mainly due to the support of Dutch aid through the DIAR project.

[9] The PCN (Black Communities Process) acknowledge the support of Danish aid for their organizational strengthening.

that could conceivably come from a myriad of new products resulting from the biological diversity concentrated in this area—half of which African Colombians have land rights to—the centuries-long oppressed African Diasporans in Colombia stand to benefit economically from a region once regarded as undesirable. To turn this potential into a reality, African Colombians need to continue with their political and civil society organizing as pressures from major domestic and international interests will have designs on the unique environmentally-based products from the region. African Colombians are also in need of additional education in environmental sciences, business management, and public policy in order for their community to maximize economic benefits for themselves.

Through the continuous process of understanding biodiversity, not only does one come to appreciate the wealth of biological resources, but also its inherent connection with the ancient communities. Therefore, the diversity in nature also corresponds to a cultural wealth constructed by the different roles and perspectives of African-descendants. Throughout their presence in Colombia, the environment has been closely related to the process of empowerment of the African-descendant communities. Through the environment, many important issues emerge, such as land rights and institutional strengthening, which require a holistic approach.

Reflecting on global prospects, the future of African Colombians and most African-descendants in the Diaspora, not only in the developing world, but also in the developed world, turns in part on the fulcrum of their global connections. These connections should embrace a sense of unity without trying to impose singular models, but instead increasing the global support for advancement pursued in various ways to different regions throughout the world. In general, there is considerable need for more serious research on the extent to which African-descendants can benefit from biodiversity.

ACKNOWLEDGEMENT

I truly thank the Inter-American Foundation for its support in the process of preparing this paper.

REFERENCES

ACIA. 2002. *La defensa del territorio: una historia de vida—Comunidades negras del Medio Atrato–. Bogotá: Red de Solidaridad Social.*

Agarwal, A., Narain, S., Sharma, A. and Imchen A. 2001. *Poles Apart. Global Environmental Negotiations.* Centre for Science and Environment. New Delhi: Thomson Press.

Brannstrom, C. 2004. *Territories, Commodities and Knowledges: Latin American Environmental Histories in the Nineteeenth and Twentieh Centuries.* Institute for the Study of the Americas.

Boli, J. and Lechner, F. 2004. *The Globalization Reader.* New York: Blackwell Publishing.

Escobar, A. 1998. Whose Knowledge, Whose Nature? Biodiversity Conservation and Social Movements' Political Ecology. *Journal of Political Ecology* 5.

——. 1997. *Biodiversidad, Naturaleza y cultura: localidad y globalidad en las estrategias de conservación*. First edition. Mexico city: Universidad Nacional Autonoma de Mexico. Centro de Investigaciones Interdisciplinarias en Ciencias y Humanidades.
——. 1995. *Encountering Development: The Making and the Unmaking of the Third World.* Princeton: Princeton University Press.
Gallo, V. 2003. Una propuesta de etnodesarrollo sostenible. *El Molino No 15. Retrieved July 16, 2006* (*http.//www.paisrural.org/El Molino.*)
Gardner, J. and Mitchell, P. 2003. *Integrating Biodiversity into Environmental Management Systems and Community Development Programmes.* Geneva: IUCN.
Grueso, L. 2003. *Territorios de vida, alegría y libertad.* Documento del comité ambiental del PCN.
Held, D., McGrew A., Goldblatt D. and Perraton J. 1999. *Global Transformations. Politics, Economics and Culture.* Oxford: Polity Press.
Hofstede, G. 1991. *Cultures and organisations: Software of the Mind.* London: McGraw Hill.
Igliori, D, Goeschl, T. 2003. *Property Rights for Conservation and Development: An Analysis of Extractive Reserves in the Brazilian Amazon.* Unpublished manuscript.
Lessen, R. 1998. *Management Development Through Cultural Diversity.* London: Routledge.
Moreno, P. 2005. *An Organizational Approach to the Biodiversity Management by Local Communities in Developing Countries.* Paper presented at the Critical Management Studies conference, Cambridge, U.K.
——. 2004. *What Does Biodiversity Mean for a Country like Colombia?* Unpublished manuscript. *To What Extent Can Local Communities Benefit from Biodiversity? Management Studies.* M. Phil Dissertation. Judge Business School. Department of Management Studies University of Cambridge.
O'Riordan, T. and Stooll-Kleemann. 2002. *Biodiversity, Sustainability and Human Communities: Protecting Beyond the Protected.* Cambridge: Cambridge University Press.
Parker, M. 2000. *Organisational Culture and Identity.* London: Sage publications.
Patridge, W., Uquillas, J. and Johns K. 1996. *Including the Excluded: Ethno-development in Latin America.* Working paper 27202. Washington, D.C. The World Bank.
PCN. 1999. *Proceso de Comunidades Negras: Territorio región del Pacífico Colombiano.* Documento interno PCN.
——. 2003. *Proceso de Comunidades Negras. Participación.* Documento interno: PCN.
Ramakrishnan, P. 1998. Ecology, Economics and Ethics. Some Key Issues Relevant to Natural Resource Management in Developing Countries. *International Journal of Social Economics.* 25: 207-225.
Restrepo, E. & Rojas A. 2004. *Conflicto e invisibilidad: Retos en los estudios de la gente negra en Colombia.* Editorial Universidad del Cauca. Colección Políticas de Alteridad.
Sachs, J. 2005. The End of Poverty. *Time.* March 14, 2005. Pp. 42-49.
Sachs, W. 1996. *The Development Dictionary: A Guide to Knowledge as Power.* London: Zed Books.
Sen, A. 1999. *Development as Freedom.* New York: Knopf.
Shiva, V. 2000. Ecological Balance in an Era of Globalization. In Paul Wapner and Lester Edwin, *Principled World Politics: The Challenge of Normative International Relations.* London: Rowman & Littlefield Publishing group.
Sponsel, L. 1993. "The Potential Contribution of Buddhism in Developing an Environmental Ethic for the Conservation of Biodiversity." pp. 75-97, Ch. 4 in *Ethics, Religion, and Biodiversity: Relations Between Conservation and Cultural Values*, edited by Lawrence S. Hamlton. Cambridge, U.K.: White Horse Press.
Thompson, P. & McHugh, D. 2002. *Work Organisations.* 3rd Ed. New York: Palgrave.
Vallejo, A. 2000. *Modernising Nature: Sustainable Development, Biodiversity Conservation and Indigenous Peoples: The Case of the Yasuni National Park.* Environment and Development M. Phil Dissertation Department of Geography. University of Cambridge.
Vira, B. 2003. *Stakeholder Interaction and Collaborative Forest Management; Theory and Analysis of the Indian Experience.* PhD thesis of the Department of Geography. University of Cambridge.
Visvanathan, N., Duggan, L., Nisonoff L. and Wiegersma, N. 2005. *Women, Gender & Development Reader.* London: Zed Brooks.

UNDP. 2003. *Local Business for Global Biodiversity Conservation: Small Business Development Strategies In Biodiversity Projects*. Retrieved November 5, 2003 (http://www.undp.org/gef/undp-gef_publications).

——. 1999. *Human Development Report 1999: Globalization with a Human Face*. Retrieved October 25, 2003 (http://hdr.undp.org/reports/global/1999).

Vermeulen, S. 2004. Biodiversity Planning: Why and How Should Local Opinions Matter? *Gatekeeper series* No. 115, IIED.

Wade, P. 1999. *The Guardians of Biodiversity. The Antropology of Power: Empowerment and Disempowerment in Changing Structures*. London Routledge) pp. 73-87.

——. 1997. *Race and Ethnicity in Latin America*. London: Pluto Press.

——. 1993. *Blackness and Race Mixture: the Dynamics of Racial Identity in Colombia*. Baltimore: John Hopkins University Press.

Wilson, E. 1986. *Biodiversity*. National Forum on Biodiversity. Washington D.C.: National Academy of Sciences.

Zweifel, H. 1997. The Gendered Nature of Biodiversity Conservation. *Nwsa Journal* Vol. 9, Issue 3. Bloomington pp. 107-123.

7. Building the New African Eco-Industrial Economy: Circulating Brains and Recycling Materials

*Rubin Patterson**

Abstract

This paper develops an original proposition for debate in the fields of African studies, transnationalism, environmental studies, and technology studies. Essentially, the paper posits that, for a few key reasons, Sub-Saharan Africa will not likely have an opportunity to experience industrialization with the reigning "destructo-industrial" technologies pioneered by Europeans and Americans. An industrial experience appears achievable for Sub-Saharan Africans only in the context of a new ecological economy. Not only are there no unassailable national frontrunners in this future area, but Sub-Saharan Africans have a credible opportunity of being among the leaders in the future. The process would commence with "brain circulation," the movement of Africans into rich, technologically advanced countries to have their human, economic, and social capital enhanced, some of which to be reinvested in their respective homelands, particularly in ecological industrial areas.

INTRODUCTION

Students of Africa's development may have noticed that the once gushing flow of publications regarding industrialization strategies for the continent has diminished to barely a trickle. One explanation for this decline, a conclusion likely but quietly held by many analysts, is that African nations are simply too far behind in this post-industrial age to undergo

* University of Toledo, Department of Sociology & Anthropology, Toledo, Ohio. Email: rpatter@utnet.utoledo.edu.

industrialization. Skipping landline telephony and leapfrogging right into cellular telephony are part of the overall migration of economic focus from "atoms to bits." I posit that there are two principal reasons to account for why many analysts and powerbrokers alike are, in a sense, "writing off" Africa's industrial future—one of these two reasons is the focus of this paper.

Extraordinarily high global industrial productivity may potentially account for why development strategists do not see industrialization in Africa's future. Consider that a single company in Taiwan with 5,000 employees produces over 40% of all the world's notebook computers, and Taiwanese companies collectively produce 75% of the world's notebook computers (Amsden and Chu 2003). As for all of information and communications technologies (ICT), OECD nations plus China, Malaysia, Singapore, Taiwan, Thailand, the Philippines, and India produced 95% of the entire world's ICT output (Patterson 2005). And the superfluity of Sub-Saharan Africa to global production is not limited to high technology. Mainland China produces 70% of the world's toys; 60% of its bicycles; 50% of its shoes and microwave ovens; 33% of its air conditioners, television sets, and luggage; 25% of its washing machines; and 20% of its refrigerators (Shenkar 2005). Hence, these trends suggest that there is no reason for Africa to participate in industrial production.

The other reason why Africa may remain non-industrialized, if the big powers have their way, is due to environmental destruction. The industrialized world has been accelerating towards depletion of minerals and damaging the environment over the past century, but now with massive and momentous China and India's rapid development, there is a growing concern about the sustainability of our tenuous planet. The soot, toxic chemicals and climate-altering gases spewed into the atmosphere, as required for China and India to approach the West industrially, is environmentally troubling to say the least. As Bradsher and Barboz (2006) have noted, "The increase in global-warming gases from China's coal use [alone] will probably exceed that for all industrialized countries combined over the next 25 years, surpassing by five times the reduction in such emissions that the Kyoto Protocol seeks" (p. A1). China opens a new coal-fired power plant somewhere in the country every week to ten days, each one generating enough power to serve all the households in Dallas and San Diego (Bradsher and Barboza). Given these environmental challenges that emerging powers are presenting for established powers, why would either be interested in additional planetary stress by acquiescing to the industrialization of the world's least industrialized populated continent, and politically among the least powerful at this juncture? My argument here is not a simple reprise of the 1972 Club of

Rome clarion call about Limits to Growth.[1] Critics have unfortunately derided the Club's model as unduly pessimistic. Instead, this paper is about much more than the acknowledged biophysical limits that are being overshot with the destructo-industrial approach to economic growth. Thus, I focus here optimistically yet realistically on how growth can continue with an eco-industrial approach.

This paper rests on the assumption that established and emerging powers have a stake in Africa never experiencing industrialization. Whatever industrialization the continent experiences will likely come despite that opposition. From that assumption, the paper attempts to advance the discussion by asserting and developing a proposition for a "non-environmentally-threatening" form of industrialization for Africa. The timing may be fortuitous since there is a creeping consciousness settling in the minds and attitudes of Western corporate and venture capitalists that the "new new" economy is likely to be more of an ecological economy. The "old new" economy was the Internet-platformed production and globalization. Production that uses less material and less energy, that is less toxic and less greenhouse gas-inducing, and that is recyclable, is likely to attract more global investment and be more attractive to global consumers. In the world today, there are no unassailable frontrunners in ecological industrial production and economy. The gap between African nations today and those nations that are presently in the lead in ecological production is far smaller than the gap between African nations and leading nations in areas of physical industrial and digital knowledge sectors of the economy, which means Africans can make more gains in a growth area that has just begun. And considering that African nations may have a comparative advantage because of their ecological endowments, plus with ecological production being the wave of the future, preparing for an ecological economy today seems both prudent and potentially lucrative. If African nations were to start moving now decisively and systematically, they may accrue more benefits as a result of being among the pioneers and early adopters of a global ecological economy.

Africans can no more commence to help pioneer an ecological economy today without first studying and working in Western universities, research institutes, and corporations than Asians could help pioneer an

[1] Three of the four chief architects of the Club of Rome's paradigm (Meadows, Randers, and Meadows (2004)) illustrate in their 30-year update just how correct their original claims were. They made no attempt to predict the future, only to shine a light on various possible scenarios given trends toward overshooting the world's carrying capacity.

information economy three decades ago without first studying and working in such Western institutions. Similar to the way Asian recent graduates of baccalaureate programs in engineering and the physical sciences entered graduate programs in such fields in large numbers throughout the 1970s and '80s, African governments can encourage and facilitate graduates of engineering and life science undergraduate programs at home to seek graduate education in those fields in the United States and other Western countries throughout the next decade to be in position to help pioneer and early adopt the ecological economy possibly just over the horizon.[2] If Africans were to do this strategically and successfully, they would be establishing systematic brain circulation similar to what some Asian transnational groups have done around the digital knowledge economy.

I should hasten to add that I am not suggesting that the mere absorption and co-production of new technical knowledge are sufficient for economic growth in one's homeland. For one thing, before Asians began streaming into America's graduate programs, they had already established economic bases of growth. Additional studies are needed to tease out the more subtle mechanisms operating between the economic bases of growth, technical educational attainment, and catalysts for "take off" in developing nations. I focus here on technical educational attainment via brain circulation since it is an often overlooked component of transformative development in Southern societies.

A NEW PRODUCTION GENUS: FROM DESTRUCTO-INDUSTRIAL TO ECO-INDUSTRIAL

State-of-the-art industrial technologies and production are so wasteful, toxic, and resource-depleting until we may as well refer to the hitherto

[2] This by no means suggests that Westerners are inherently smarter, of course; rather it is only consistent with how knowledge has grown and diffused throughout the world for centuries. Notes Jared Diamond (1999: 255), "When a widely useful invention does crop up in one society, it then tends to spread in either of two ways. One way is that other societies see or learn of the invention, are receptive to it, and adopt it. The second is that societies lacking the invention find themselves at a disadvantage vis-à-vis inventing society, and they become overwhelmed and replaced if the disadvantage is sufficiently great." There is no denying that the United States is, on the whole, the world's frontier R&D center, just as other nations have been in the past. But neither the United States nor any other nation has even established an R&D paradigm of an ecological economy, so as Africans study and work in core institutions, they won't be mere receptacles of such new knowledge; instead, they will be among the inventing peers. Again, this is replicating the Asian experience in Silicon Valley in the information economy.

industrialization as the "Destructo-industrial" Age, which could not be more different from its likely successor, the "Eco-industrial Age." Destructo-industrial technologies are those technologies that focus on enhancing labor productivity with little if any regard for consequential harm to environmental sources and sinks. Conversely, eco-industrial technologies are those that focus on enhancing natural resource productivity by increasing performance and recycling with continuously less material usage. Moreover, destructo-industrial technologies cannot be sustained environmentally even for the mere 15% of the world's population who currently "benefit" from them. In fact, less than 1% of the North American materials flow remains useful in a product only a few months after purchase (Hawken, Lovins, and Lovins 1999). Approximately 80% of ore mass is unwanted impurities that are discarded (Das 2005). The impure ores and the surrounding earth as well as organic and inorganic byproducts are dumped back onto or into the earth or released into the atmosphere, which, due to the way materials were previously processed, some toxic materials leach into water tables and the soil or are inhaled, whereupon such agents enter into the food chain and are ultimately consumed and breathed by humans. And, of course, extracting billions of tons of raw earth every year requires enormous amounts of energy that is generated largely by greenhouse gas-producing fossil fuels. The metals, nonmetallic minerals, and agricultural topsoil that took billions of years to form could, at the present rate, be exhausted in many geographical locations during this century. All of this destruction is just to provide a high standard of living and comfortable existence for 15% of the world's population (i.e., 975 million out of 6.5 billion).

The Chinese and Indian masses—in particular—and others are fast and resolutely arriving to experience similar lifestyles, largely via the same wasteful, toxic, and resource-depleting technologies. The industrial approach pioneered by Europeans a couple of centuries ago and ratcheted up throughout the twentieth century to enhance labor productivity is no longer sustainable for the current 975 million principal beneficiaries, let alone the more than 2.4 billion Chinese and Indians, and billions more of others who dream of such a materialistic, consumer-oriented quality of life. The 15% that presently benefits from state-of-the-art industrial technologies purchase three-quarters of the world's 60 million automobiles produced annually (*The Economist* 2004). But today China, already the world's second largest car market, experienced a 54% growth in the first quarter of 2006 over the same period the previous year. If the present growth rate continues, China will have 130 million cars on the road in 2020, a fourfold increase over the 2006 level (Fairclough and Oster 2006).

Under these constraining environmental conditions, and having missed out on much of the industrial revolution, while still struggling to rock into forward motion with the digital revolution, the question becomes: What can Sub-Saharan Africans possibly do to improve their socioeconomic circumstances in an era of intense global competition? China and India, both very far behind the West, are moving ahead swiftly and confidently while Sub-Saharan Africans continue to struggle with their footing: to wit, extreme poverty (i.e., subsisting on less than $1/day) was cut between 1980 and 2001 from two-thirds to 17% in China while in India the rate fell from half to 35% (Starke 2006). Meanwhile, Sub-Saharan Africa went in the wrong direction: the share of their population living in extreme poverty increased from 41% to 46%. Intense global competition is one challenge, but insufficient resources, toxic byproducts, and immense waste of resources prevent Sub-Saharan Africa from *ever* developing socio-economically with current state-of-the-art destructo-industrial technologies. In order for the rest of the world to live on a socioeconomic scale as Americans or Canadians (but fortunately many do not aspire to do so), "two additional earths" comprised with today's resources and sinks would be needed. The 1.3 billion Chinese are in a strong position to compete for declining shares of natural resources to improve their living conditions—at least for the next few decades until "depletion-approach" begins to act as dirt thrown into the gears of the global economy. The opposite is the case for the 775 million Sub-Saharan Africans who are among the least able to compete for today's insufficient natural resources, despite, ironically, their disproportionately lucrative endowment of natural resources. Competition for those resources will only become substantially more intense during depletion-approach. So the situation is doubly dire for Sub-Saharan Africans. On the one hand, they cannot consume the limited materials and requisite technology to meet today's industrial development needs, and on the other hand, those very resources threaten their long-term existence (and that of the rest of the world for that matter).

In 2005, China alone consumed 25% of the world's crude steel, 33% of the rice, nearly 40% of the cotton, and nearly 50% of the cement (Starke 2006). Oil consumption doubled in China in a ten-year period, catapulting the nation into the second position behind the United States. If China continues growing at this pace, in 25 years it will be consuming 99 million barrels of oil per day. This is more than what the entire world currently uses, some 87 million barrels a day (Brown 2006). Considering that, as experts contend, the world has probably already drilled and burned into the world's oil deposits at such a rapid pace until we have likely reached the peak of oil production or have reached peak capacity. And the pace at which the remainder is being exhausted (e.g., India doubled its oil consumption in twelve years), oil and the entire global industrial edifice pioneered by the West are not accommodating for future Sub-Saharan African development.

The global economy is outgrowing the earth's capacity to support it (Meadows, Randers, and Meadows 2004), and billions of the world's citizens, particularly Sub-Saharan Africans, are not benefiting from the overshooting of the planet's capacity to generate natural resource sustenance as well as absorb industrial pollution. Ecologists contend that the world is in an overshoot-and-collapse mode of existence. Scientists such as Jared Diamond (2005) illustrate how many earlier societies have overshot their natural environment's capacity to meet the demands of inhabitants, and, over time, those societies inevitably collapsed. In some cases, sedentary populations grew, which caused them to destroy the forest for fuel wood and extend crop production areas, which helped increase the population, requiring still more crops and depleting more of the forest, further eroding the soil, and finally sealing the harsh fate of the population. When those societies trekked along such ill-fated production paths, they overshot-and-collapsed largely in isolation. But in today's integrated global economy, the overshooting-and-collapsing may be global in scope (Brown 2006). For this reason, it is in the interest of all nations to work within the global system to build eco-technologies and a strong international regime to enforce rigorous standards for sustainability.

The inevitability of life beyond fossil fuels is due to exhaustion primarily, but also due to environmental destruction. In order to improve the quality of life for the 5.6 billion left behind and all of the 6.5 billion today and the billions to come in the future, a gigantic paradigmatic shift in economic production is mandatory. Since there are no unassailable frontrunners of an ecological economy today, some Sub-Saharan Africans can become such a frontrunner about as much as any other nation.

PIONEERING AN ECOLOGICAL ECONOMY

Today's environmentally-destructive global economy has been shaped by politicoeconomic forces rather than by the principles of ecology. In other words, we should say that the economy has been shaped by politicoeconomic forces and not by mere market forces since the mobilization of states has always been crucial in shaping markets. Perverse tax reductions and subsidies to aid companies degrade the environment as a byproduct were politically influenced, not generated by mere market forces. In the larger scheme of things, it is rarely a matter of markets simply being an aggregation of specific products and preferences. Sub-Saharan Africans do not have the political and economic muscle to elbow their way presently to more of a declining share of the requisite resources for industrial development. Stronger nations of the South with relatively elevated positions within the global economy are able to temporarily extract wealth that in previous centuries and even earlier decades would have gone almost exclusively to Western powers. China is investing heavily all across Africa to feed its voracious appetite for energy and industry-related minerals, such as copper and platinum. China is canvassing the continent to buy as much industrial mineral resources as possible. As a result, China-Africa trade jumped fourfold between 2000 and 2005: from $10.6 billion to $40 billion. This helped to nearly double Africa's growth rate, increasing from 3% to 5.8% (Timberg 2006).

If this were the end of the story, we would have yet another reason to wallow in "Afropessimism." The thinking would be that since Sub-Saharan Africans are too poor and too weak with respect to political influence, science and technology knowledge, and skills possession to restructure their economies in a manner to have a higher value-added role in the global economy, then consequently they are destined to become progressively poorer in both absolute terms and in relation to wealthier nations.

At present, there are no detailed mental models, let alone actual precedence, for transforming an economy configured by the principles of capitalist politicoeconomic forces into an economy congruent with the principles of ecology. Sub-Saharan Africans have less to lose and possibly the most to gain from devising intellectual frameworks, mental models, rigorous research, and policy formulation to construct a new, twenty-first century eco-industrial economy. The wealthy nations with their reputed industrial prowess, and the rising wealthy nations with their celebrated S&T knowledge possession are largely hampered from pioneering a new eco-industrial economy due primarily to existing perverse tax and subsidy schemes,[3] political patronage, existing upward social mobility, and "a bird in the hand . . ." mentality that discourage states from taking the initiative to steering their respective economies to longer term security against overshoot-and-collapse.

[3] Some rich nations are pursuing alternative energy sources for Kyoto compliance among other reasons, particularly economic. Western Europeans because of environmental politics and Japan because of necessity resulting from a dearth of natural resources are more attentive to a future of alternatives than Americans. That said, no country is well on its way toward heretically transforming its economy ecologically by a measure according to what is possible: Factor 10. Factor 10 involves eliminating 90% of the materials and energy for a similar level in quality of life.

Sub-Saharan Africans can begin right away at understanding how to pioneer economies that mimic nature. Pioneering industrial biomimicry involves promoting the synergy between industrial ecology, ecological and environmental engineering, business and management, and public policy. Industrial ecology represents an effort to ecologize industry as opposed to industrializing ecology. After all, it is industry that is derived from the ecology rather than industry as the force of sustenance for the ecology. Industrial ecology is thought of as the science of sustainability. In other words, to the extent that one is serious about sustainable industrial production and large-scale agriculture, industrial ecology provides the scientific wherewithal for these two to occur whereas they have been in conflict since the industrial revolution. Ecological engineering represents an emerging branch of engineering that organically links, on the one hand, traditional environmental fields such as ecology, agro-ecology and restoration ecology with, on the other hand, traditional branches of engineering such as electrical, mechanical, civil, and materials. The unique skills possessed by ecological engineers enable them to engage in special kinds of design and environmentally-friendly production and environmental repair. With respect to design and production, ecological engineers, when teaming up with other engineers (e.g., electrical, environmental, chemical, mechanical, civil, and product) design products and processes that move toward zero emissions, biodegradable, and low energy consumption. Ecological engineers work collaboratively to design the products—and the production processes for generating them (e.g., food, houses, pharmaceuticals, transportation, clothing, and mobile phones, among countless other products)—in a manner that is consistent with nature's methods of efficiently consuming energy and materials before generating waste that serves as sustenance for additional useful products. As ecological engineers mimic nature, they lay the groundwork of a circulating economy free of waste. Many refer to this as the "cradle-to-cradle" model of production as opposed to what the world has largely experienced to date under destructo-industrialization, namely, "cradle-to-grave" model of production.

The final two disciplinary components for making an ecological economy, namely, business and management plus public policy, need no explanation except to discuss the role they may play in the ecological economy. Ecological engineering, as a nascent branch of engineering, is like other engineering branches that can serve any type of economy, from capitalist to socialist and the infinite nuanced varieties in between. As market economics effectively predominate in nearly all countries today, practitioners of the field ply their trade by working with business managers, economists, investors, and marketers to efficiently produce useful and desired products by employing biomimicry methods.

Ecological engineers hardly exist in rich countries, let alone in Sub-Saharan Africa. Among other things, public policy has to be formulated and implemented in order for ecological engineers and industrial ecologists to be generated in sufficient numbers in the future. Once such a vision takes root, something not easily achieved, since such a vision requires a long-term commitment that does not have a lot of immediate benefits, the requisite educational infrastructure has to be designed and funded. The entire educational infrastructure would have to be strengthened to start teaching with hands-on practice-orientation involving ecological restoration, ethnobotony, pollution, earth science, recycling, renewable energy, ecology, and environmental citizenship (Lynch and Hutchinson 1992).

In addition to the traditional fields of study, students would have to enroll at the graduate level, such as ecology, biology, materials science; chemical, electrical and mechanical engineering; and they would also study emerging related fields, namely, industrial ecology and ecological engineering.[4] The two fields have new professional societies: International Society for Industrial Ecology (formed in 2001), American Ecological Engineering Society (also formed in 2001), and International Ecological Engineering Society (formed in 1993). Industrial Ecology strives to make industrial production emulate the energy efficiencies and material recycling of natural ecosystems. To make this work practically in an economy, students would have to know how to establish eco-industrial parks, "which are industrial parks that facilitate material by-product exchange, recycling, cogeneration of energy from waste, and preservation of natural habitat, represent the physical space that emulates the energy flow and material cycles of an ecosystem" (Tilley 2003:15). As for ecological engineering, it "combines the disciplines of ecology and engineering in order to solve environmental problems" (Kangas 2004). Moreover, notes Kangas, "Ecological engineers design, build, and operate new ecosystems for human purposes" (p. 13).

Ecological economies subscribe to the biologically mimicked industrial ecology model, which means that only salable and useful goods are manufactured without waste. Hence, whatever materials are superfluous to the manufactured goods produced within a facility serve as feedstocks to other products. An economy without waste is an economy without pollution, since pollution is the release of waste into the environment. Ecological economy professionals refer to production processes without waste as zero discharge or zero emissions. The concept of zero emissions

[4] For an introductory discussion of industrial ecology and ecological engineering, see Tilley (2003).

is modeled on W. Edwards Deming's "zero defects" and Toyota Taiichi Ohno's "zero (or just it time) inventory." The Japanese cases serve to underscore the importance of moving decisively to a new revolutionary production paradigm to challenge established powers successfully.

Internet visionaries such as Bill Gates (Microsoft), Steve Case (AOL TimeWarner original broker), and John Doerr (among the earliest significant investors in Google and Amazon.com) see eco-technologies, as the next great leverage, as disruptive, consequential, universally impacting, and as profitable—certainly for early investors—as the Internet (Shin 2006). These technologists and venture capitalists see eco-technologies as being on the verge of not only going mainstream, but acquiring an appealing cachet. With the right public policy mix and broad execution, it is possible for Sub-Saharan African nations to be among the pioneers and early beneficiaries.

Examples abound of venture capitalists and corporations investing in eco-technologies. However, no nation has a comprehensive strategy to build an eco-economy (Brown 2001). Pioneers and early adopters of comprehensive green-friendly materials and processes stand to benefit as much as if not more than pioneers and early adopters of new information and communications technologies (ICT) in the 1980s. Sub-Saharan Africans largely came around to adopting ICT grudgingly at the end of the 1990s. The slow adoption came despite the tremendous efforts of national technology and business leaders, United Nations Economic Commission for Africa, United Nations Development Program, International Telecommunication Union, and many technology- and policy-oriented friends of Africa. In addition to being preoccupied with a host of other crises with which to deal, government officials were first concerned about loss of public revenues as a result of losing its telecom monopoly, and second they were concerned about losing control of its information flow monopoly in the country. Advisors were able to eventually break through on the first area of resistance by patiently demonstrating how governments stood to have even greater public revenue streams as a result of opening up the network to competition and investment throughout the economy (Hafkin 2002; James 1999; Mansell and Wehn 1998). New FDI and technology transfers occurred, which served as a stimulus to more economic activity, and expanded public coffers. As for the second issue, Sub-Saharan African governments continue to harbor concerns about losing monopoly control of information flow in the country. This, of course, is not unlike the case of China today, which appreciates the enormous economic benefits of ICT, though remains vehement about keeping in place what has been dubbed the "Great FireWall" in China, which strives to keep out "seditious" information flow.

Though the idea of helping Sub-Saharan African leaders to move forward in ICT was challenging, at least there were established intellectual frameworks, models, and empirical data about the processes and benefits of adopting competitive ICT strategies. Like the eco-industrial revolution, the digital revolution before it is one that all nations will certainly undergo, making it only a question of whether one will be a leader or a follower. Accrued ICT gains were measurable for Sub-Saharan Africans, but those gains were smaller than for those who pioneered ICT and for those who adopted the technologies earlier. Now, with the eco-industrial technologies, again, because there are no unassailable frontrunners, Africans have an opportunity to be pioneers and even be early adopters, which would likely culminate into substantially larger benefits than pioneers and early adopters received with respect to ICT.

BRAIN CIRCULATION: DIGITAL ASIA AND ECO-INDUSTRIAL AFRICA

Though Westerners were the original pioneers of new ICT, Asians have emerged over the past twenty-five years or so as subsequent ICT trailblazers in design, application, and new product development. Arguably, one of the greatest explanations of this positioning came as a result of Asians immigrating to the United States in very large numbers since the mid-1960s. Many of the students and working professionals were in engineering and physical science fields. Because ICT-related works were among the hottest technologies being developed at the time, thereby attracting more venture and other development capital, and since there was a gargantuan shortage of Americans with the requisite human capital to engage in that area of work, Asian immigrants found themselves helping to pioneer new ICT when those technologies were in their infancy. Now, a generation later, ICT constitutes a two trillion dollar plus global industry and Asians have been in a position to help reinvest some of their human and economic capital in ICT fields in their respective ancestral homelands.

In other words, brain circulation around ICT has worked well for some Asian transnational communities, particularly Chinese, Taiwanese, Koreans, and Indians. It is simultaneously possible for brain circulation around the recycling of environmental and engineered materials to work well in the future for African transnational communities. In the 1970s, these Asian nations did not have the requisite rigorous graduate programs at their respective national universities in applied mathematics, physics, chemistry, electrical engineering, and materials science, let alone the industrial enterprises where the cutting-edge R&D could occur. Asian students principally did not just come to the United States on student visas, get their technical education and degrees, and then immediately returned home. Instead, upon graduating, they mostly went to work for S&T-oriented businesses and other institutions, thereby further enhancing their technical and managerial human capital, business networks (i.e., social capital), and economic capital. Some of this capital was reinvested into their ancestral homeland.

Similar to the way Asian diasporans in the United States utilized brain circulation to benefit from helping to pioneer and early adopt the new revolutionary technology platform of ICT, Sub-Saharan Africans can possibly utilize brain circulation today to benefit from helping to pioneer and early adopt the new revolutionary technology platform of eco-industrialization. Since Sub-Saharan Africans do not have educational facilities that offer students the requisite rigorous graduate programs in biomimicry, industrial ecology, ethnobotany, environmental engineering, mechanical engineering, genetic engineering, biology, and materials science, they can utilize brain circulation to help pioneer a new global industry.

In preparation for graduate and professional work and ultimately employment in these fields to occur among Africans in rich economies, Sub-Saharan Africans must have access to primary, secondary, and baccalaureate curriculums that emphasize practice-orientation, teamwork, holistic and analytic problem solving, and context-specific solution implementation. Universities with some leading graduate programs in these fields include Ohio State, Stanford, University of Michigan, Johns Hopkins, UC Berkeley, University of Texas, University of Maryland (both College Park and Baltimore County), University of Washington, and Oregon State. Of course, there are many other graduate programs across the United States that could serve as great training grounds in emerging eco-industrial fields for students from Sub-Saharan Africa.

At this juncture, African governments by and large think in terms of preventing the emigration of raw human capital (i.e., students) and refined human capital (i.e., working professionals) to rich societies. If those governments were to facilitate such emigration, while simultaneously following up in helping to establish an atmosphere that welcomes and supports their subsequent investment of some portion of their enhanced human, economic, and social capital in a society of transparent governance, those African economies may grow stronger in areas of commerce and civil society (Patterson 2006).

As those Sub-Saharan African nationals and coethnics ascend in corporations, gain the intellectual wherewithal to develop original marketable products, meet immediate needs, earn very high salaries and stock options, and enter into lucrative business networks (i.e., become notable players in their industrial fields), governments, universities, civil society and business groups who support such diasporans abroad have a greater chance of emigrants investing some of their capital back home. Perhaps the eco-industrialist will lecture at a university for a term, or conduct an R&D workshop, or advise a start-up company, or advise the government about creating the enabling conditions and specific subsidies to start a new eco-industrial sector, or they may even invest their own economic capital to found some new company in such a sector, or some may even want to repatriate.

Sub-Saharan Africans concentrating their brain circulation in the ecological economy areas are likely to bear more fruit for three reasons. First, pursuing this tactical approach improves the prospect of the creation of a critical mass of talent and S&T-focused capital to have a measurable economic impact as opposed to being spread too thin. Second, eco-industrial technologies will reign supreme in the future due to today's unsustainable depletion of natural resources and pollution-generating, wasteful twentieth-century industrial technologies. Third, as stated earlier, no nation even has a comprehensive, transformative national plan of action in the area of ecological economy, let alone a cornered market. Sub-Saharan Africans are noncompetitive in nearly every aspect of today's major markets. However, gearing up for and competing successfully in such markets, given the experiences of established players, would be far more challenging than gearing up to help pioneer a new market by utilizing a tried and tested strategy.

Sub-Saharan Africans are so far behind and their number of immigrants into the United States is so small in comparison to the number of Asians since the mid-1960s, that the former group should think of their US-based diasporans as beyond those who have emigrated from their given homeland, say, from Nigeria, or Ghana, or Kenya. Very few Africans, relatively speaking, immigrate to the United States. For instance, Africans constituted only 1.8%, 2.4%, and 3.9% of all US immigrants in the 1970s, 1980s, and 1990s. Over the 10-year period between 1993 and 2002, the top five Asian source countries (Philippines, PRC, India, Vietnam, and Korea) sent 1,933,079 immigrants, whereas the top five African senders (Nigeria, Ethiopia, Egypt, Ghana, and South Africa) sent 236,085 immigrants, only 12% as many over the same period.[5] Because

[5] It is recognized that over 40% of immigrants from Africa are not "black Africans." Those from places like South Africa are primarily white and those from places like Tanzania are primarily Indians. Nevertheless, irrespective of their racial-ethnic makeup and identity, the model is still applicable to the extent they are interested in "doing well and doing good" by investing some of their human economic capital back home.

of these current trends in US immigration, and the fact that the overwhelming majority of the African diaspora in the United States is comprised of those descendants from Africans enslaved in this country, the share of new immigrants to the total US-based African diaspora, only about 8%, will remain very small in comparison to the Asian counterpart, of whom as many as 60% or more are foreign born.

Since most Asian Americans were born in their ancestral homeland and likely retain kith and kin relations in specific hamlets and cities in those homelands, they are more likely to want to help out "home" and to have a better angle on how to succeed in a specific business there. In recent decades, forward looking, savvy governments have been courting their diasporans to remit to kith and kin, and to invest some to their human and economic capital more broadly into money-making and employment-creating ventures in their homeland as a way of doing well and doing good. The point is that the number of immigrants from a given African country is likely to be so tiny—perhaps with the Nigerian exception—until a critical mass would not likely be established. For this reason, it is useful for African Americans, those descendants from enslaved Africans in the United States and who have never lived in Africa, nor have any of their known relatives lived there, to be a part of the transnational African development agenda to do well and do good as well. Bridging the gap between this group of descendants and the recent voluntary immigrants from Africa is admittedly a difficult proposition. Dialogue, understanding, and coordination between leaders from both these sections of the US-based African diaspora on the one hand, and dialogue, understanding, and coordination among the government, the business community, and civil society groups in Africa on the other represent early requisite steps. The African Union and NEPAD are moving in this direction.

The long-term paradigmatic economic shift from destructo-industrial to eco-industrial is to begin by getting a critical mass of intellectuals and professionals ready to carry out the work. Each Sub-Saharan African nation would identify youths who demonstrate scientific, imaginative, and entrepreneurial talent for preparatory work and careers in an ecological industrial economy. Scores of students could be prepared at national undergraduate universities for graduate training in the United States and in other technologically advanced economies that offer graduate and professional degrees in a host of related fields such as those cited earlier in this paper.

For two principal reasons, regional nations within Sub-Saharan Africa could collaborate in this eco-industrial transformative enterprise. First, the idea of educating young citizens in these technical fields, knowing full well that many if not the majority will be encouraged—even by the government as an investment in the nation's future—to leave the country upon graduation for advanced education and employment is a costly undertaking. And helping them gain student visas as well as helping to defray the cost for graduate education in these fields in the United States is also demanding, even when they receive graduate education assistantships to cover tuition and provide a stipend to cover living expenses. Second, since regional nations within Africa, particularly those contiguous, share a common ecological system, which means that they have similar comparative advantages and disadvantages, they could collaborate to avoid blindspots and costly duplication. Such neighbors are in position to share both costs and benefits. For example, the Upper Guinea Forest zone, a biologically diverse hotspot, straddles Sierra Leon, Liberia, Cote d'Ivorie, and Ghana. Since the costs of educating tomorrow's ecological scientists, engineers, business managers, and public policy practitioners can be prohibitive for each country whereas as they all stand to gain economically from the common ecosystem, they can specialize in particular and complementary areas. A given country may specialize in a given area of the sciences, another in a particular field of engineering.

If the twentieth century was a century of building national economies, the twenty-first century is a century of transnational economics. TNCs have stretched across the globe with FDI, subcontract manufacturing, licensing design, and distribution in their economic interests. Since thousands of corporations can straddle the planet, entering deals in their best interest, it is reasonable to think that neighboring African nations could forge transnational economic projects around their common ecological and economic system.

BUILDING AN ECOLOGICAL ECONOMY: THE POTENTIAL CASE OF LIBERIA

Because Liberia is just getting underway with a legitimately elected government and a peaceful atmosphere is holding, after twenty-five years of wanton destruction and civil war, the Liberian government understandably will focus on rapid impact programs, not long-term heretical economics. Nevertheless, this does not have to be at the expense of long-term pioneering of an eco-industrial economy.

There are over 40,000 Liberians living in the United States. Using tactics of Indian, Mexican, and other governments as guides for consideration, the Liberian government or, for example, a quasi-government entity in Monrovia, could work principally with several offices in US cities such as in Washington, DC and Atlanta where a significant percentage of Liberian professionals live. In addition to encouraging the organizations to provide fellowship, they would also help connect with other Liberian Americans scattered around the United States. These clearinghouse organizations could incubate ideas about what they would like to see their ancestral homeland become and massage the ideas into a few common themes that would subsequently affect Monrovia's policy agenda. As the federal government, the business community, and civil society groups learn what is needed before human and economic capital-rich Liberian Americans begin investing in the country, subsequent adjustments made could result in increased investment flows.

Initiating investment ties in a variety of economic areas would be the founding of an important tradition for African transnational societies. Over time, as those Liberian students complete their graduate programs and acquire professional status in fields such as materials science, agriscience, biotech, environmental and chemical engineering, biological and pharmaceutical industries, relationships between Liberian and diasporan institutions would mature. Some recent graduates would likely want to return to Liberia right away, but most others, as history has documented, would want to remain in the United States for varying lengths of time as they work not only to increase their net worth and enrich their business networks, but also to avoid the day-to-day difficulties of low-level development back home. Myriad ways exist for those Liberian and Liberian diasporan graduates from US universities to contribute to development in the homeland. Singaporeans, Taiwanese, Koreans and other groups that have benefited handsomely from such brain circulation did not just leave questions of emigration and investment back home and possibly even repatriation up to chance. The state, with the assistance of the commercial class and intellectual elites helped with coordinating human and economic capital contributions to the homeland. On an ongoing basis each of these states hosted gatherings in places such as Silicon Valley as well as back home. The idea was to keep the scientists, engineers, entrepreneurs, investors, policy experts, and professors in the broad transnational community talking to their counterparts and related professionals.

With regard to agriculture in Liberia today, immediate issues for resolution involve unemployment, deforestation, malnourishment, and near absence of medicine. Liberia can be a case in study to illustrate these problems that are replicated in different ways and to different degrees throughout the region. Unemployment in Liberia is estimated at 80%, with 85% of the population living on less than $1 per day and 52% eking out an existence on less than $0.50 per day (UNEP 2004). Under these severe conditions, the government is not likely to prioritize an eco-industrial economy. It is only when there is a framework for addressing these immediate, pressing needs within the context of pioneering twenty-first century eco-economic practices that Liberians will see it as potentially prudent to walk simultaneously on both legs—short-term actions to meet pressing needs and long-term actions to transform the economy consistent with ecological principles.

Between 1990 and 2000, forest cover in Liberia was reduced from 38.1% to 31.3%. Up to 99% of the population depends on charcoal and fuel wood to satisfy basic cooking and heating needs (UNEP). As we know from Haiti and other cases, first populations clear the forest for energy and agricultural production, then the soil erodes, and then the population is threatened. Restoration activities can be a means of attending to both unemployment and environmental issues such as deforestation. With the assistance of the donor community, Liberians can be employed as tree planters to restore not only the forest but also other areas of the environment that were particularly heavily damaged since the 1980 Doe coup.

Engaging primarily in extractive economic activities today while the world is characterized by a global knowledge economy is not a prescription for economic success. Again, the real challenge is to address the short-term difficulties of unemployment and illiteracy while simultaneously preparing society for an economic revolution over the long term. Nationwide illiteracy is estimated at 63%. Now that a democratically-elected president is in power and peace has taken hold, children, many of whom having been enlisted as soldiers in the war, are now returning to the classroom. As they get their primary and secondary education, their curriculum can emphasize many aspects of environmentalism, herbal medicine, and other ecological principles, not to mention hands-on crop and mineral development. Conceptual and analytical principles can be linked with practice. For instance, according to a 2003 FAO report, with less than 10% of the nation's 4.6 million hectares of arable land cultivated, a part of the curriculum might involve hands-on practice as a follow-up to and reinforcement of principles learned in the classroom.

Over 40% of the Upper Guinea Forrest, one of the world's richest areas of biodiversity, is located within Liberia. Botanical knowledge of Liberia is probably poorer than for any other country where the Upper Guinean ecosystem is located (UNEP). A comprehensive development strategy that provides for environmental education, protection, and restoration can help reduce illiteracy, unemployment, and a degraded environment simultaneously.

Upon graduation, assistance can be provided for many of the Liberian students to receive graduate assistantships at American and other Western research universities in ecological industry-related fields of study. At the same time, in light of the new US government's expressed interests in "helping Liberia's Johnson-Sirleaf government succeed," something yet to be demonstrated substantively, it may be possible to successfully lobby to have H-1B-type visas set aside for Liberians in ecological industrial economy areas of work. H-1B visas are technical visas awarded to talented foreigners who have private sector sponsorship in technical fields where, at least theoretically, Americans exist in short supply. By special arrangement, 6,800 such visas are set-aside for Chileans and Singaporians (U.S. Citizenship and Immigration Services 2006). The H-1B1 visa program is earmarked exclusively for Chileans and Singaporians with at least a baccalaureate degree that relates directly to technical employment. If the program could be expanded to include Liberians and other Sub-Saharan Africans, when they graduate they would be in position to compete for sponsorship from the private sector to work in ecological industry-related employment fields. The H-1B1 visa program did not just come about serendipitously. Instead, such programs occur out of lobbying by transnational societies (out of concern for coethnics and the homeland) and transnational corporations (out of concern for higher earnings and market share). Liberian Americans and African Americans, descendants and others, could engage in such lobbying, as well as attempt to enlist TNCs to help mobilize for student and employment visas.

To better appreciate the importance of political mobilization to do well and do good for oneself and one's transnational community, one might look at Indians in the United States. Consider a case of Indians seeking green cards. There are about two million Indians living in the United States, many having entered the country on student and H-1B visas. Thousands who are seeking green card status but are unsatisfied with the long delay have taken to lobbying action. In just a few months, thousands of Indians organized into a new group known as Immigrant Voices, and were on their way to reaching an achievable target of $200,000, principally to hire a top-drawer K Street Washington lobbying firm to help expedite their being granted citizenship (Kalita 2006) so that they could continue their human and economic capital enhancement and brain circulation. Indians are by far the largest recipients of H-1B visas, with lobbying occurring within the United States and in India to increase their numbers as H-1Bs. Opportunities are likely to exist for Liberians and other Sub-Saharan Africans if focused political action could be brought to bear on the issue.

Liberians who enter into graduate study and employment in ecological industry-related fields after earning baccalaureate degrees would have the opportunity to help start the pioneering work of circulating natural materials in a manner to restructure the economy around eco-industrialization. Biofuels are one form of sustainable production. Brazil has helped pioneer this area with the successful growth of sugarcane as a feedstock to ethanol. In 2006, Brazil declared itself energy independent as a result of ethanol accounting for over 20% of its transport fuel market. Massive sugarcane growth for such feedstock only requires a lot of arable land, plenty of rainfall, and low-cost labor. Liberia has all three. Ramping up sugarcane—which is already a major crop in Liberia—growth is a way to soak up unemployment, reduce the energy crunch, and lessen environmental degradation. Running automobiles on carbohydrates instead of fossil fuels, though significantly less stressful on the environment than fossil fuels, the former causes some problems too. Among the problems is the extensive use of agrichemicals of herbicides and pesticides as well as the related pollution runoff and damage to the soil. But having Liberians receiving advanced rigorous university study and private-sector employment can help tackle these and other problems. Increasing yields are a means of mitigating the damage. Between 1975 and 2005, Brazil's gallons of per hector (GPH) jumped from 520 to 1,360. Biotech is another path to mitigating environmental damage. Brazilian scientists and engineers decoded the DNA of sugarcane, which helped them produce more drought and pest resistance. As a result, less herbicides and pesticides are required (Luhnow and Samor 2006).

Just as recycling organic materials can be done to help meet today's needs and reposition society to an elevated position in the world's economy, recycling inorganic materials, particularly metals can do much of the same. New, engineered materials such as superalloys, high-performance polymers, polymer matrix composites, electronic materials, photonic materials, shape-memory alloys, and nanoparticles, among others, are the materials technologies that are going forward[6] (Geiser 2001). Producing these materials technologies is challenging enough, but doing so while emphasizing detoxification and dematerialization is likely to be the touchstone of twenty-first century eco-industrial pioneers. Methods of extracting the ore and removing impurities are frequently highly toxic. Such methods are not exhaustive and can be replaced by other methods, some of which are yet to be devised, that obviate the generation of toxicity. Another aspect of zero emissions is dematerialization, which involves the production of materials and end-use consumables with declining quantities of materials. All products would embody less material and

[6] Also see the works of Prof. Soboyejo, director of US/Africa Materials Institute and a director at the Princeton Institute of Science and Technology of Materials.

weight while embodying more intelligence, which would yield greater performance per quantity of material. Rather than embedding the product with the extra materials to handle different situations and objectives, the smarter product will be intelligent enough to provide the performance as required for different situations.

CONCLUSION

As this article makes clear, Sub-Saharan Africans can walk on both short-term and long-term legs towards an eco-industrial transformation, thereby meeting immediate pressing needs while elevating the economies within the overall global economy. The opportunities associated with an eco-industrial transformation for Sub-Saharan Africa appear both propitious and challenging. This moment is propitious because the world appears on the cusp of demanding and receiving products through processes that are significantly less environmentally destructive and even environmentally enhancing. At present, no nation has mastered this. No nation, not even the "environmentally advanced" nations such as Sweden and Denmark, is beyond only a few percentage points in terms of environmental efficiency. Internet visionaries and technology's original intellectual and financial backers have begun investing heavily in eco-industrial technologies. They see the eco-economy as being as disruptive and lucrative as the digital economy they helped to found.

The future eco-economy will represent a significant production paradigm shift by its focus on resource productivity instead of labor productivity, which has been the focus of the destructo-industrial economy. Sub-Saharan Africa can make a concerted effort to help pioneer this new eco-industrial economy. The gap between Sub-Saharan Africa and the established and emerging economic powers is significantly lower with regards to eco-industry than to the physical and digital industries.

Building an eco-industrial economy in Sub-Saharan Africa will be challenging since it would have to be done without any historical precedent. It would also be difficult since the region lacks the intellectual R&D capital in the requisite life and material sciences and engineering, as well as the requisite economic capital. This is where brain circulation enters the picture. Sub-Saharan Africans, upon completing their undergraduate training in related fields, can compete and lobby to earn more graduate assistantships in eco-industrial graduate programs around the United States and other rich nations with such programs. If Sub-Saharan Africans were to become eco-industrial pioneers, they would have new markets just as Brazil finds itself today with being a celebrated pioneer of biofuels. To help them meet their Kyoto targets, Japan and Sweden are purchasing sugarcane-based ethanol from Brazil. And Southern S&T

superpowers, India and China, are sending numerous technologists to help those countries undergo similar transformations. Going all out green can turn out to be a rousing success for Sub-Saharan Africans at this critical juncture in history.

As we say in technology studies, we project probabilities, forecast possibilities, and predict the unknown. Projections deal with the shortest timeframe, forecasts with intermediate timeframes, and predictions with long-range issues over the horizon. This paper, rather than simply trying to predict future technological development as the be-it-all and end-all, starts with what is realistically possible as suggested by short-term projected trend lines. Thus, we project a continuation of what we see among venture capitalists and technology revolutionaries who are investing economic and intellectual capital into eco-industrial technologies. We can forecast continued recognition by leaders and regular citizens that the peak-oil phenomenon is here, and that the so-called BRIC (i.e., Brazil, Russia, India, and China) national economic juggernauts have stepped up to demand, not only their share but, like the Western powers, more than their share of the world's natural resources. This development leaves less for the West and degrades the environment more for all. Results can only be the acceptance of lower standards of living in the West or a new way of meeting expectations with alternative technologies. Finally, we can predict, based on these projected and forecasted trends that a new eco-industrial economy represents the next substantial tectonic shift in human production history. With early efforts and the right policy mix and political will, Sub-Saharan Africans have a credible chance at being among the leaders in this newly emerging production paradigm. It is obviously unknown whether they will succeed in such an endeavor. All that is predicted is that such an opportunity is likely to emerge.

ACKNOWLEDGMENT

The principal proposition of this study would not have been formulated without several months of extensive and intensive debates with Professor Cynthia Hewitt of Morehouse College in Atlanta, Georgia, which occurred during my visiting fellowship there in 2005-06.

REFERENCES

Bapat, Jyotsna. 2005. *Development Projects and Critical Theory of Environment.* Thousand Oaks, CA: Sage.

Bradsher, Keith, and David Barboza. 2006. "Pollution from Chinese Coal Casts a Global Shadow." *New York Times.* June 11, p. A1.

Brown, Lester R. 2001. *Eco-Economy: Building an Economy for the Earth.* New York: W.W. Norton & Co.

——. 2006. *Plan B 2.0: Rescuing a Planet Under Stress and a Civilization in Trouble.* New York: W.W. Norton & Co.
Das, Tapas, ed. 2005. *Toward Zero Discharge: Innovative Methodology and Technologies for Process Pollution Prevention.* Hoboken, NJ: Wiley Interscience.
Diamond, Jared. 2005. *Collapse: How Societies Choose to Fail or Succeed.* New York: Viking.
1998. *Guns, Germs, and Steel: A Short History of Everybody for the Last 13,000 Years.* London: Vintage.
Economist, The. 2004. "Perpetual Motion." Retrieved June 28, 2006 (http://www.economist.com/surveys/showsurvey.cfm?issue=20040904.)
Fairclough, Gordon, and Shai Oster. 2006. "As China's Auto Market Booms, Leaders Clash Over Heavy Toll." *Wall Street Journal.* June 13, p. A1.
Geiser, Ken. 2001. *Materials Matter: Toward a Sustainable Materials Policy.* Cambridge, MA: MIT Press.
Hafkin, Nancy. 2002. "The African Information Society Initiative: A Five-Year Assessment." *Perspectives on Global Development and Technology.* 1:101-142.
Hawken, Paul, Amory Lovins, and L. Hunter Lovins. 1999. *Natural Capitalism: Creating The Next Industrial Revolution.* New York, NY: Little, Brown and Company.
James, Jeffrey. 1999. *Globalization, Information Technology and Development.* New York: St. Martin's Press.
Jeong, Ho-fion. 2006. *Globalization and the Physical Environment.* Philadelphia: Chelsea House.
Luhnow, David and Geraldo Samor. 2006. "As Brazil Fills Up on Ethanol, It Weans Off Energy Imports." *Wall Street Journal.* January 16, p. A1.
Lynch, Daniel R. and Charles E. Hutchinson. 1992. "Environmental Education." *Proceedings of the National Academy of Sciences.* 89:864-67.
Kalita, S. Mitra. 2006. "Skilled Immigrants Turn to K Street." *Washington Post.* April 26, p. D1.
Kangas, Patrick. 2004. *Ecological Engineering: Principles and Practice.* Boca Raton, FL: Lewis Publishers.
Mansell, Robin and Uta When. 1998. *Knowledge Societies: Information Technology For Sustainable Development.* New York: Oxford University Press.
Meadows, Donella, Jorgen Randers, and Dennis Meadows. 2004. *Limits to Growth: The 30-Year Update.* White River Junction, VT: Chelsea Green Publishing Company.
Mitsch, William. 2004. *Ecological Engineering and Ecosystem Restoration.* Hoboken, NJ: John Wiley & Sons.
Patterson, Rubin. 2005. "Global Trade and Technology Regimes: The South's Asymmetrical Struggle." *Perspectives on Global Development and Technology.* 4.3-4:379-396.
——. 2006. "US Diasporas and Their Contributions to Homeland Development in the Global South: A Study of Transnationalism." *Social Forces* 86:1891-1908.
Olson, Robert and David Rejeski, eds. 2005. *Environmentalism & the Technologies of Tomorrow.* Washington, DC: Island Press.
Roodman, David. 1998. *The Natural Wealth of Nations: Harnessing the Market for the Environment.* New York: W.W. Norton & Co.
Shin, Annys. 2006. "Internet Visionaries Betting on Green Technology Boom." *Washington Post.* April 18, p. D1. Retrieved May 24, 2006 (http://www.washingtonpost.com/wp-dyn/content/article/2006/04/17/AR2006041701563_pf.html)
Tilley, David. 2003. "Industrial Ecology and Ecological Engineering: Opportunities for Symbiosis." *Journal of Industrial Ecology.* 7:13-32.
U.S. Citizenship and Immigration Services. 2006. *Current Cap Count for Non-Immigrant Worker Visas for Fiscal Year 2007.* Washington, DC: U.S.C.IS. Retrieved July 15, 2006 (http://www.uscis.gov/graphics/services/tempbenefits/cap.htm).

8. Brain Drain and Its Impact on Ethiopia's Higher Learning Institutions: Medical Establishments and the Military Academies Between 1970s and 2000

*Solomon A. Getahun**

Abstract

Africa is beset with problems that range from natural calamities to civil wars and epidemics such as HIV-AIDS. Ironically, countries like Ethiopia, which badly need trained manpower, continued to lose highly skilled professionals, both military and civilian, to Western Europe and the United States. Ethiopia, for instance, loses more than a third of all its students who were sent for further education to Europe and the U.S. This is in addition to those who leave the country for various reasons but refuse to return home and those educated Ethiopians who became refugees in African countries. One of the consequences of the outflow of highly educated Ethiopians is that today there are more Ethiopian professionals, including MDs, working in the U.S. than in Ethiopia. However, not all Ethiopian professionals are successful in practicing their profession. Among these professionals, highly trained military officers constituted the largest group. They end up being taxi drivers and security guards; they represent the worst case of brain drain—brain hemorrhage. My paper will examine the causes and processes of migration of highly educated Ethiopians to the U.S. and its impact on higher education, both military and civilian, and health institutions in Ethiopia—a country with the least developed higher education establishments, even by African standards, and one of the worst HIV-AIDS affected areas in the world.

* Central Michigan University, History, Mt. Pleasant, MI 48859. Email: getah1sa@cmich.edu.

INTRODUCTION

Africa in general and Ethiopia in particular have been noted for political tremor, drought, and famine for the past three decades. The scenario in Ethiopia seems to be even worse. The country's population of 72 million, which is the second largest in sub-Saharan Africa, has a per capita income of $110.00, one-fourth the average for the continent. Its education sector, at all levels, indicates the lowest participation rates in the world, and even in Africa: 30 percent at primary, 13 percent at secondary, and less than 1 percent at the tertiary levels (World Bank 2001). The country's health sector (all the country's medical colleges are attached to hospitals), too, is in no better condition. Health expenditure between 1990 and 1995 was 1.7 percent of the GDP. In the same period, population per physician ratio was 35,051, while population per hospital bed was 4,141. Life expectancy at birth is 49 years. The country has been identified as one of the highest HIV-AIDS affected parts of the world. According to a report during the latter part of the 20th century, there were 9.3 HIV positive individuals per 100 adults (World Bank 1998).

In spite of this bleak reality, Ethiopia has been providing the Western World and parts of Africa with highly educated professionals. How did this happen? This paper examines the causes and processes of migration of highly educated Ethiopians to the Western World, mainly to the U.S., and its impact on Ethiopia's institutions of higher education. It also assesses the possibility of "brain gain" from the Ethiopian immigrant community in the U.S.

CONTEXT OF MIGRATION: THE DEVELOPMENT OF HIGHER EDUCATION IN ETHIOPIA

Apart from its traditional educational establishment, which was primarily based on the teachings of the Ethiopian Orthodox Church, Ethiopia did not have a Western modeled institution of higher learning until the 1960s. Nevertheless, it does not mean that the country has never had a Western trained and educated professional until that time. Since the mid-19th century, Ethiopian emperors had been trying to introduce Western education into the country. The purpose, however, was very limited. For example, while Emperor Tewodros II (r. 1855-1868) wanted to educate Ethiopians so that the latter could build weapons for him, Menelik II (r. 1889-1916) and his immediate successors sought Western educated Ethiopians to serve as interpreters in the royal court. Emperor Haile Sillassie I (r. 1930-1974), on his part, needed Western educated Ethiopians to fill his "modern" bureaucracy, which was also partly intended to neutralize the nobility. Therefore, it was Haile Sillassie's drive to modernize the bureaucracy that really necessitated the introduction of "modern" higher education in Ethiopia and the training of Ethiopians abroad.

Although initially Ethiopians were sent to the various parts of the world such as Europe, the Middle East, and the U.S., the latter began to take the lion's share in the post-1945 period. This focus on the U.S. seems due to the following reasons. Ethiopia had never been colonized and thus, like most African countries, could not send its students to former colonial powers for further education. Though Italy had occupied Ethiopia between 1936 and 1941, its positive impact on education was almost none.[1] Even if this had not been the case, Italy was too weak of a colonial power, compared to others, to sustain its former colonial bond with Ethiopia. Hence, Ethiopia could not benefit from relations with the "mother country." Second, the absence of such a colonial past seemed to have created a favorable circumstance for the U.S. Unlike in other parts of the world where the U.S. has to do much maneuvering to supplant the former imperial powers, it was relatively easier for America to lay its foundations in Ethiopia. Third, the decision of the Ethiopian government to use English as a medium of instruction, as opposed to the earlier practice that employed French and other languages, further paved the way for the development of Anglo-oriented education in Ethiopia. Finally, the emergence of the U.S. as one of the "Big Powers" in the post-1945 period and yet with no colonial legacy (at least in Africa) or interest in Africa seemed to have attracted Ethiopians, especially Haile Sillassie, toward the U.S. for virtually everything. Consequently, the training of Ethiopians in America that commenced with two medical students in the 1920s surpassed the thousand mark by early 1970s, which made Ethiopia the third African country (next to Nigeria and Egypt) with the largest number of students in the U.S. By 1973, Nigeria had 4,092; Egypt, 1,148; and Ethiopia, 1,046 students in the U.S. (Institute of International Education 1973).

[1] Italy's impact on "modern" education in Ethiopia is rather negative: After the assassination attempt on General Graziani in February 1937, the Italian government hunted down all Western educated Ethiopians throughout the country and killed them. In addition, it had also tried to decimate the highly educated Orthodox clergy by ransacking their abode, such as the Dabra Libanos Monastery. The Italian Black Shirts and their collaborators killed more than 1000 learned men from that monastery alone. For the Italian massacre of Ethiopian intellectuals of the early twentieth century, see John Markakis (1974), *Ethiopia: Anatomy and a Traditional Polity*, Oxford: Clarendon Press, p. 146; Bahru Zewde (2002), *Pioneers of Change in Ethiopia: The Reformist Intellectuals of the Early Twentieth Century*, Athens: Ohio University Press, pp. 204, 210–211.

The U.S. involvement in education in Ethiopia was not limited to the civilian sector. Prior to the 1974 Ethiopian Revolution, America provided almost all weapons as well as education and communication equipment to the Ethiopian Armed Forces. Between 1953 and 1968, over 2,500 Ethiopians had been given military training in the U.S. Between 1946 and 1972, U.S. military aid amounted to over $180 million—an assistance that made Ethiopia the largest recipient of U.S. military aid—which was 60 per cent of the total U.S. military aid for sub-Saharan Africa (Markakis 1974; Marcus 1983).[2] A further testimony to Ethiopia's military dependence on the U.S. and the latter's deeper involvement in Ethiopia was the Qagnaw Station, an American Military base in Ethiopia, which, by the 1970s, had over 3,000 U.S. military personnel and their dependents. In addition to this, the U.S sent an American unit, Military Assistance Advisory Group (MAAG) to Ethiopia to train a 40,000 strong Ethiopian army. MAAG remained active in Ethiopia until the 1974 Revolution.

Therefore, the presence of Ethiopians in America was related to the evolution of America as a world power since 1945 and to the Cold War politics since then. As Ruben G. Rumbaut (1996: 24) noted "migration to the United States . . . may be seen as the complex and deeply ironic social consequences of the expansion of the nation to its post-World War II position of global hegemony. *As the United States has become more deeply involved in the world, the world has become more deeply involved in America* [emphasis added]—Indeed, in diverse ways, it has come to America."

CONTEXT OF MIGRATION: POLITICAL REPRESSION

Until the 1974 Revolution and subsequent developments such as the "Red Terror," almost no Ethiopian wanted to reside in the U.S. It is said that between 1945 and the early 1970s only four Ethiopians who were educated in the U.S. had chosen not to return to Ethiopia (Personal communication). It was also noted that some Ethiopian students did not even wait for their diplomas as they were in such a rush to depart from the U.S. The diplomas were mailed to them in Ethiopia. Although the bureaucracy that was the main employer of educated Ethiopians was becoming saturated by the early 1970s, jobs were waiting for them. By

[2] For a detailed account of U.S. military assistance such as type of weapons and manpower training, see Department of Defense Security Assistance Agency: Military Assistance and Foreign Military Sales, May 1973; Foreign Military Assistance Facts, November 1975; December 1976; December 1977; and December 1978.

then, the private sector also had begun employing some of them. The society, too, treasured and even revered these educated Ethiopians.

Here, one has to also note that it is not poverty, population pressure, drought, and famine that trigger migration as classical migration theorists have indicated. Ethiopia was poor even prior to the Revolution. What is more, as migration studies inform us, the first to migrate are usually the affluent class but not the famished and the poor (Castles and Miller, 1993). Accordingly, by the time of the Revolution, the 5,000 or so Ethiopians who were residing in the U.S. were businessmen, tourists, diplomats, students, and others of comparable backgrounds. Such individuals, however, failed to return home because of the political upheaval and uncertainty in Ethiopia. The bloodshed that commenced with the massacre of 63 former government officials was soon followed by so-called "red" and "white" terrors, which were conducted on the streets of Addis Ababa and other provincial towns by both the military junta and its supporters, such as the All Ethiopian People Socialist Movement (AEPSM) and the political oppositions that were spearheaded by the Ethiopian Peoples Revolutionary Party (EPRP). These "red" and "white" terrors that claimed the lives of thousands of political activists and innocent bystanders (Kiflu 1998; Halliday & Molyneux 1981)[3]—a significant number of whom were highly educated Ethiopians—also drove the multitudes out of Ethiopia, to the neighboring countries.

Meanwhile, changes in U.S. immigration policy, which now included provisions for refugee resettlement, further attracted Ethiopians to the U.S. Hence, by 1990 the number of Ethiopians residing in the U.S. grew to more than 33,000. Of these, some 28,000 were political refugees whom the U.S. Refugee Resettlement Bureau brought into the U.S. from refugee campuses in the Horn of Africa, mainly from Sudan (U.S. Census 1990).[4] These were primarily victims of the "Red" and "White" terrors, and in the global scheme of politics, the U.S. regarded them as people who "voted on their feet" against communism. The refugees ranged from

[3] For detailed information on prison condition, torture and the killings in Ethiopia, see Amnesty International (1978), *Human Rights Violation in Ethiopia*, London November, AI Index: AFR 25/10/78 pp. 14–17.

[4] See also Report to the Congress: FY 1996 Refugee Resettlement Program, U.S. Department of Health and Human Services, Administration for Children and Families Office of Refugee Resettlement; Refugee Admission Proposal: Hearing Before the Committee on the Judiciary House of Representatives, Ninety-seventh Congress, 1st Session, September 29, 1981. For the relatively recent number of refugees in Sub-Saharan Africa and other parts of the world, see Jonathan Baker (1995), *Studies On Emergencies and Disaster Relief, Report No. 2, Refugee and Labor Movements in Sub-Saharan Africa*, Nordiska Afrikainstitute. According to his work, Sudan is the main center for Ethiopian refugees in Africa, p. 10.

the politically conscious yet illiterate peasants to high school students and university professors.

By the 1990s, the number of Ethiopian refugees admitted into the U.S. continually declined from more than 3,000 in the 1980s to less than two hundred in the mid-1990s. This was so not because there was no political repression in Ethiopia and thus there were no Ethiopian refugees found in the neighboring countries, but because the new government in Ethiopia, unlike the former military regime that ruled Ethiopia between 1974 and 1991, was "friendly" to the U.S. Besides, the Cold War was over. Otherwise, Ethiopia still produced refugees, though their numbers were relatively fewer compared to the number of refugees during the *Derg* regime (another name for the military junta). While the number of Ethiopian refugees admitted into the U.S. declined steadily in the 1990s compared to the 1980s, the number of Ethiopian political asylum seekers in the U.S. has continued to grow—from 348 in 1993 to 1,092 in 1999 (Immigration and Naturalization Services 1999).[5] Worth noting is the correlation between the decline of Ethiopian refugee admittance into the U.S. and the increase in the number of Ethiopian asylum seekers in the U.S. Ethiopians who realized that their chances of being admitted into the U.S. as refugees was slim decided to go directly to the U.S. under various guises (as visitors, businessmen/women, diplomats, short-term trainees, athletes, etc.) and refused to return home rather than become a refugee in one of the neighboring African countries and wait for a response from the U.S. refugee admittance program in Africa. Also, worthy of note is that most of these asylum seekers were among the highly educated and affluent Ethiopians.

As time went on, however, the nature and pattern of migration to the U.S. seemed to shift. It appeared to become more network driven. The shift was further strengthened due to America's immigration policy that gave priority to family reunion. In addition, the Diversity Visa (DV) Lottery, which the U.S. introduced in the 1990s, opened additional venues for Ethiopians to immigrate to the U.S. The DV, despite being a lottery, is selective. Applicants must at least have completed high school. The DV winners also must have a sponsor. It is apparent that the flight of the affluent and educated Ethiopians continued on a much larger scale. This did not include Ethiopians who were sent to the U.S. for education and other reasons but declined to return. A closer scrutiny of one of America's institutions of higher learning, the graduate program

[5] In the same period, 1993 to 1999, the INS data indicated that Ethiopia was the 3rd largest refugee-sending country to the U.S. next to Somalia and Sudan.

in history at Michigan State University (MSU), further reveals the continued flight of educated Ethiopians and the severity of the problem. Since the 1980s, the history department had given fellowships, scholarships and assistantships to eleven Ethiopians. Of these, six had already earned Ph.D. degrees. Nevertheless, except for one, none of them returned to Ethiopia. From among the remaining Ethiopian graduate students, almost all of them have opted to stay in the U.S. Nearly all of them have Green Cards, or are in the process of getting one. Even without it, there is a likelihood of obtaining a working permit in the U.S. Moreover, of the three or more Ethiopians who earned a doctorate in agricultural economics at MSU, only one returned to Ethiopia. Furthermore, the university has six or so Ethiopian/Ethiopian-American professors, with doctorate degrees, teaching and researching in the fields of geography, engineering, biology, biochemistry, agriculture, and other fields. This figure does not include the present-day Eritreans who, however, came to the U.S. as Ethiopians and now work in the university in various departments.

ANOTHER "PUSH" FACTOR: LACK OF INFRASTRUCTURAL DEVELOPMENT AND ABSENCE OF GOVERNMENT INCENTIVE FOR THE EDUCATED

Despite the change of government in Ethiopia in 1991, the absence of a significant improvement in the country's educational establishment remained another source of frustration for Ethiopian educators and medical professionals. Almost all of the country's universities and colleges were built fifty or so years ago where the number of university students throughout the country was barely a thousand. Today, these same institutions are expected to handle 60,000 students in the regular, evening, and summer programs. Yet, according to the Ministry of Education, which oversees Ethiopia's institutions of higher learning, the annual placement of new students in these institutions is an average of 11,000, while around 30,000 students are eligible for placement in these higher education institutions (Genet 2000). Currently, Addis Ababa University alone, with 688 full-time teaching staff members, is handling more than 20,000 students (*Addis Tribune* 2002). Though new private and government-owned colleges and universities were opened in Ethiopia since the mid-1990s, mismatch between the number of students qualified to enter higher learning institutions and the availability of space has continued to this day (Walta Information Center 2005). Even if space is available, there is a lack of qualified university teachers. To mitigate the situation, the Ethiopian Peoples Democratic Front (EPRDF) regime in Addis Ababa has begun bringing in Indian, Nigerian, and Chinese expatriates—the latter barely speaks English.[6]

Most of the books in the Addis Ababa University Kennedy Library, which is also the only library worthy of its name in the country, are old. Most of its "latest" collections of books are from the 1980s and back. It is also said that due to inadequate funds, the Library had even discontinued subscribing to some of the journals. The production of texts for higher learning institutions within the country, which could have solved some of the problem, is almost unknown. The saddest part, however, is that some of the rare collections of books, including senior essays, are often stolen from the library. Mutilating books is also common. Therefore, the lack of adequate infrastructure and qualified instructors, the scarcity of materials and at times the absence of the latest journals, books and texts in Ethiopia's institutions of higher learning further elucidate the sorry state of higher education in Ethiopia and its disheartening effect on the academic staff (Freemantle 2006).[7]

The state of the country's health establishments (all medical colleges are attached to hospitals) is no different from the rest. According to WHO's analysis, a country that spends less than $60 per person on healthcare annually could not claim to have an effective health system. Yet, the same report also indicated that 42 countries spend less than that. Of these, at the bottom were Afghanistan, at $2 a person, and Ethiopia, at $4 (Bowman 2000). So great were the financial constraints, major health institutions like Gondar Medical College were compelled to reuse disposable latex gloves after disinfecting them. Because of the scarcity and at times unavailability of resources, including the most essential ones such as water and electricity, very few people are interested in working in that college which is located in a city where more

[6] Between September 2002 and July 2003, I was in Ethiopia and had the opportunity to meet some of the Chinese instructors in Addis Ababa. They teach in the newly opened technical colleges. During my conversation, I asked the Chinese how and when he learned English. He replied that he had an English immersion for three to six months before his departure from China. He also said that he would continue the English language training in the summer. I met him while he was on his way to China for the summer break.

[7] Charitable contributions by research institutions like the London-based Royal Society of Chemistry that opened its archives for free online access by African universities and the continued digitization of books and academic journals by Google and online service providers can help solve some of the predicaments related to books and journals. Yet, this too requires African institutions of higher learning to overcome the "digital divide." The continent overall trudges far behind in the use of Internet Technology (IT).

than 200,000 people reside (Tobia 2000).[8] The college has only one gynecologist; and, according to WHO, the maternal mortality rate in Ethiopia is higher than in most Sub-Saharan African countries. The main causes of maternal deaths in Ethiopia are also related to emergency obstetric care and complications associated with unsafe abortion. Induced abortion is prevalent and commonly performed by unqualified persons (World Health Organization 2001).

Low pay is another reason for the exodus of educated Ethiopians. For instance, an MD is paid less than $200 per month, while a university instructor with an MA makes even less. Had medical professionals and university professors been allowed to run their own private practice on their free time, low pay might not be an issue. However, because of an ill-advised government policy that inhibits medical professionals and university professors from establishing their own clinics, many MDs and university instructors are forced to leave their post, or they prefer to leave their country (Reporter 2000).

The consequence is devastating. Despite the productions of more than 400 MDs annually since the 1980s from the three medical schools in Ethiopia (Black Lion, Gondar Medical College, and Jimma Health Sciences Institute) and from abroad (Gondar College of Medical Sciences 2001), today the total number of medical doctors in the country is less than 3,000 for a population of more than 70 million (The World Bank 1998). Thus, it is apparent that more than 50 percent of all medical doctors who were trained both in Ethiopia and abroad have left the country for the Western World, mainly the U.S., and southern Africa (*Reporter* 2000; BBC 2001; Samson 2001). So great is the number of Ethiopian medical personnel in some of the U.S. hospitals, the doctors are said to do their rounds in Amharic, the working language of Ethiopia (Personal communication).

An important note also is that the development of faster means of communication such as the Internet had made contact between Ethiopian MDs in the U.S. and in Ethiopia easier. As a result, Ethiopian medical professionals at home and abroad were able to exchange information on living and working conditions, discuss differences between Ethiopia and the U.S. and ultimately the means of getting out of Ethiopia. This development, together with America's insatiable need for medical professionals and highly qualified immigrants and the existence of an already established

[8] A video-supported report concerning the Gondar Medical College at the International Conference of Development Issues in Ethiopia at Kalamazoo, Michigan, in August 2001, further revealed the despicable condition that the Medical College is in.

Ethiopian immigrant network in America, further accelerated the flight of Ethiopians to the U.S.

The migration of educated Ethiopians and highly skilled professionals is neither limited to the civilian sector nor confined to the Western World. Members of the Ethiopian Armed Forces—especially graduates of the Harar Military Academy, an elite military establishment, whose Ethiopian instructors were drawn from very well-known military academies such as Sandurst (England) and St. Cyr in France (Markakis 1974; Bahru 2002)—are found scattered around the world, primarily in the U.S. (Etop 2003). Because their number in the U.S. is so large, they have their own association and even a website. Currently, the Harar Military Academy, which also trained officers for many of the newly independent African countries in the 1960s and 70s, does not exist. Yet, the irony is that Ethiopia today employs foreign nationals to train its troops.

The Ethiopian Air Force Academy—one of the oldest in Africa and which had officers and flight instructors who were trained in countries like Israel, the U.S. and U.S.S.R. and which produced some the finest pilots and flight engineers in Africa—is another higher learning institute that is losing its skilled professionals. Its problem, like the civilian institutions, began with the 1974 revolution. The *Derg*, which espoused Marxist-Leninist principles and which sided with eastern block countries, viewed many of the Western trained air force officers and instructors as puppets of imperialism. Those who survived the periodic purges and killings left their country for the Western World, mainly the U.S. When the current regime came to power in 1991, it accused the air force of genocide, dismantled the academy, and disbanded the military. Some members of the air force managed to escape with their MIG fighter jets and helicopter gunships to neighboring countries before the EPRDF's capture of Addis Ababa. Some managed to come to the U.S. As in the army, today the Ethiopian air force not only employs flight instructors but also is alleged to have used mercenaries to fly some of its planes.

Educated Ethiopians are found in various parts of Africa as well as abroad. While the major concentration of Ethiopians is in South Africa, former Addis Ababa University professors and instructors dominate some departments in the universities of Botswana (*Reporter* 2000).[9] A number of these professors were victims of purges of the EPRDF government.

[9] The number of Ethiopians residing in South Africa is estimated at 3,000. These Ethiopians left their country after paying $1,500 for middlemen who could take them to South Africa with the hope of going abroad from there. The fee for getting legal documents and visas to the U.S. is around $2,500.

In West Africa, too, in addition to Ethiopian civilian professionals, members of highly trained Ethiopian military personnel are found working in various capacities. One BBC (2001) report has it that among the mercenary (South African, Ukrainian, and French) pilots and helicopter gunship maintenance crew in the civil wars in Sierra Leon, Liberia, and Guinea were also Ethiopian military engineers and aircraft mechanics. They were members of the Ethiopian Air Force. They left their country in 1991 for fear of persecution by the new regime, EPRDF.

In the same vain, Ethiopian Air Force pilots and instructors are found working in eastern Africa. Trained by Americans, Israelis, and Russians, these individuals were highly trained professionals who provided a mark of distinction to the Ethiopian Air Force. The latest report concerning the Ethiopian Air Force is not encouraging, either. Very recently, it had lost fifteen of its best pilots and engineers, some of whom with the rank of colonel; most of them have left for the U.S., while some found their way to England. Also in 2005, Ethiopian Air Force pilots who were sent to the Ukraine and Israel for further training sought asylum, protesting against the June massacre of civilian protesters in Addis Ababa (*Addis Tribune* 2005).

The fact that Ethiopian professionals, civilian as well as military, are found employed in parts of Africa, contrary to the commonly held belief that Africans migrate to the Western World only denotes a radical shift in the migratory pattern of African professionals and appears to imply the following. It indicates the despicable situation that forced these highly educated Ethiopians out of their country, and compelled them to seek employment even in Africa, a continent that does not have a good reputation, rather than to leave for the Western World. On the other hand, however, it might also herald a new era. Parts of Africa had developed to the degree of enticing fellow educated Africans to live and work there rather than leave the continent. Partly, the demise of apartheid in South Africa could also be considered as a plausible factor for such development in southern Africa. It could also be the result of the contradictory nature of "globalization." The Western World that advocated the integration of world economies also tightly closed its doors against immigrants.

Some Ethiopians, who were willing to live and work in their country even for low pay, were discouraged because of the lack of either academic freedom or incentive. While higher education institutions are expected to be seedbeds of new ideas, centers of innovation, and birthplaces of responsible citizens, teachers, managers, scientists and leaders, the current government in Ethiopia seemed to think otherwise. According to the *Chronicle of Higher Education* (2001), the country's current leaders "have developed the same fear of intellectuals" that the previous regime had.

As a result, Ethiopia's institutions of higher learning do not have autonomy. Their presidents and administrators are handpicked party affiliates who "are either despots who run these institutions . . . as their own fiefdoms or are 'invalids' who are helpless in the execution of the tasks entrusted to them. . . . Despots . . . together with their loyalists, are turning these institutions into structures that are rigid and unresponsive to the problems and concerns of its staff. These people see the ordinary staff as something disposable; it is only them [sic] who are indispensable" (Tesfa 2000).

Therefore, any opinion from the academics that criticized the government's education policy, ethnocentric principles, and anti-democratic practices was repeatedly met with stringent action. The government expelled forty-two professors and lecturers in 1993 while it closed the university indefinitely in 2001 and 2004. Hence, Addis Ababa University, which was one of the best institutions of higher learning in East Africa, "now, after years of ethnic and political conflict, it is one of the most poverty stricken" and understaffed institutions. Of the 850 academic staff, 70 percent do not have graduate-level training (*Chronicle* 2001). Gondar College of Medical Sciences is 40 percent understaffed. In the past three years alone, the College has lost 25 specialists in the various fields of medicine (Tobia 2000; Walta Information Center 2000).

Meanwhile, the number of highly educated Ethiopians in the U.S. is increasing. A colleague, who is collecting data on Ethiopian medical professionals in the U.S., informed me that he had been able to tally 1,200 MDs in the U.S. Findings from the U.S. Census further underlined his claim. According to the 1990 U.S. Census, there were 33,868 Ethiopians in the U.S. Of these, 29.5 percent have bachelor's degrees and above, while 11.8 percent have graduate degrees or higher. The U.S. national average for immigrant/refugees population is 20.3 percent and 7.8 percent, respectively, which therefore placed Ethiopians among one of the highly educated immigrant groups in America (U.S. Census 1990).

THE POSSIBILITY OF BRAIN GAIN

In the age of globalization physical and psychological distance is becoming less significant because of the availability of faster and easier modes of communications. In addition, the end of the Cold War and related developments increasingly questioned the legitimacy of the nation-state, boundary, and the meaning of citizenship (Nieguth 1999). Thus, today it is not uncommon to see people living and working in two or more worlds, at times simultaneously. What is more, unlike earlier times, citizenship has ceased to mean, as it once did, loyalty and allegiance to a country.

Rather, it is used to facilitate travel (Sassen 1998; Foner, Rumbaut, and Gold 2000). As the result of such developments, it is hoped that the Third World, which suffered most due to "brain drain," might benefit from "brain circulation," as one of the *New York Times* columnist indicated (Dugger 2000; Barber 2000). Today, we have ample evidence that "brain gain" or "brain circulation" is a reality. A good instance is India, which lost some 25,000 of its top scientists to the U.S. since the 1960s. But, now, some of its citizens are returning home. They are establishing some of the best technical institutes in the world in India. Those who are not returning are supplementing the intellectual "remittance" with a substantial financial support.

Though not comparable to Indians in America, Ethiopians, too, are trying to help their home institutions. For instance, an Ethiopian, who was one of the victims of the September eleven tragedy, had been collecting second-hand kidney dialysis machines to send to Addis Ababa University Medical Faculty. By the time of his death, he had already gathered five of these machines. His American colleagues are now continuing to pursue his initiative. They, in addition to gathering dialysis machines, have embarked on fundraising to cover the cost of transportation. They have already raised $30,000. Meanwhile, some pharmaceutical companies have pledged to ship the equipment to Ethiopia free of charge (Carter 2002; Addis Zaman 2002). Currently, the machines have arrived in Addis Ababa, waiting for decisions by the university officials on how to move forward.

Individual initiatives among Ethiopians in America also include spending their sabbaticals in Ethiopia. Those who have done so have indicated that every time they go to their homeland during their sabbatical leave, they take computers, books, journals, and other equipment and materials and leave these items for the department or college in which they once worked. They are also urging their fellow countrymen to do the same.

The greatest contributions of the Ethiopian Diaspora to Ethiopia's higher education institutions, however, seem to come from Ethiopian professional associations in North America. One of such organizations is the Ethiopian American Foundation (EAF), which was established in 1994. The primary objective of this group is to help higher education in Ethiopia. Accordingly, since 1999, in addition to sending books and journals to the higher learning institutions in Ethiopia, the EAF also has granted fellowships worth $2,100 to six Ethiopians (three graduate students and three faculty members) every year since 1999. While each faculty member receives $500, students get $200. The money is disbursed based upon the merits of the research proposal that the candidates submit. The fellowship is not available to Ethiopians in the U.S. EAF has also organized seminars and conferences that focused on issues of education and development in Ethiopia (Personal communication, 2003).

Another Pan-Ethiopian organization, which is helping Ethiopia's higher learning institutions, especially medical colleges, is the Association for Higher Education and Development (AHEAD). It was established in Ottawa, Canada, in 1999. The objectives of the organization are

> to contribute towards development efforts in Ethiopia by mobilizing, coordinating and channeling the necessary resources and relevant expertise to Ethiopian higher academic institutions . . . to assist in the capacity building of the Addis Ababa University by responding to academic, infrastructure and resource needs . . . to mobilize Ethiopians in the Diaspora and facilitate their contributions to and role in development undertakings in higher academic institutions in Ethiopia . . . to facilitate partnership between Ethiopian academic institutions and governmental, non-governmental and international organizations (AHEAD).[10]

In accordance with its principles, AHEAD provided financial support for eighteen undergraduate medical students from the three medical colleges in the country: Addis Ababa University, Gondar School of Medicine, and Jimma Institute of Health Sciences (now Jimma University). Each student receives 30 Birr ($5.56 Canadian) per month for three years. Ethiopia provides free university education, including food and boarding. Currently, AHEAD is also engaged in establishing a resource center in Jimma, which is expected to open soon. The purpose of the center is to supplement the small public library in Jimma and thus cater to a larger community of university students and also to the public. The project is a joint venture between AHEAD, which contributed 12,000 Birr ($1.00 = 8.58 Birr), and the Canadian Embassy in Ethiopia, which donated 150,000 Birr, to finance the project. In addition, AHEAD also embarked on a project to collect and send medical books to the aforementioned institutions in Ethiopia. So far, it had sent hundreds of invaluable medical books, journals, and equipment such as stethoscopes to Addis Ababa University.

Ethiopian North American Health Professional Association (ENAHPA), as its name might imply, is an association of Ethiopian medical professionals residing in America. The organization was founded in 1999 in Detroit, Michigan. Its establishment is a clear indication of the presence of a growing number of Ethiopian medical professionals in America: physicians, dentists, nurses, pharmacists, and healthcare workers. Its mission "is to attend to the specific healthcare needs of women and children; assist in the delivery of medical and surgical services to adults; assist in promoting

[10] See the organization's web page: http://www.aheadonline.org/index.html.

preventive health and provide educational materials and medical supplies to healthcare facilities; transfer skills and state-of-the-art technologies to healthcare professionals in practice and in training in Ethiopia" (ENAHPA).[11] In accordance with its objective, members of the organization provided free training to Ethiopian medical professionals, especially cardiologists, in Ethiopia. A group of cardiologists, led by a known heart specialist, Dr. Ingeda Assafw, has begun providing open-heart surgery in Ethiopia for free. The free medical service is given to Ethiopian heart patents who have no means of getting such service in the country. ENAHPA is also planning to establish a cardiac hospital in Ethiopia. The ENAHPA also collects the latest books and journals from American institutions and philanthropic organizations and individuals and donates them to the various medical institutions in Ethiopia.

Gondar Mutual Association of America is another Ethiopian Diaspora organization that is engaged in helping Ethiopia. Currently, it is busy fund raising to build a well-equipped 400-bed referral hospital in Gondar. At its completion, the hospital is expected to cost the Association some 30 million birr. The association also helps poor students, both high school and university students, who cannot support themselves though they are academically successful. Each student receives 100 birr per month until he/she completes his/her education (Gondar Mutual Association).[12]

CONCLUSION

The Ethiopian government's response to "brain drain" seems mixed. It still considers coercion as a means to alleviate the flight of Ethiopian intellectuals. While requiring university instructors and others who leave for further education to sign an obligation to work for 12 or 15 years (those going for the Ph.D.) or pay compensation of 140,000 Birror more (Tesfa 2000), it is also devising a means to retain and attract academic staff. It proposed an incentive package that includes housing allowance, medicare, staff and family insurance, pensions, schools for children, and other benefits. However, the planned package has not yet been implemented (Walta Information Center 2000).

While considering incentive packages for university instructors and medical professionals, it might also be beneficiary to include such variables as distance from the capital and the availability of adequate infrastructure in a given locality. A teacher or a medical doctor, for example, who is assigned to a remote part of the country should be given more

[11] See their website at http://www.enahpa.org/about/mission.

[12] Information obtained from the Gondar branch of the Association.

incentives than the person who is assigned work in the capital. This, in addition to encouraging employees to work in distant places, might also reduce, to some degree, the risk of intellectual flight.

Recently, the government had also granted "dual" citizenship to all Ethiopians who become foreign citizens. In addition to the various benefits, these Ethiopians are allowed to come and go as they please, which seems partly intended to entice Ethiopians from the Diaspora to offer their knowledge, skills, and other assets as investments in their country.

The country's education and health budget has also exhibited a marked increase. For instance, the country's health budget is growing by 33 percent compared to the budget in the 1980s (*Reporter* 2000). Besides, hospitals, health centers and other health-related facilities are being constructed throughout the country. New universities were also established while the old ones were being rehabilitated and upgraded. Private investors were encouraged to participate in the realm of higher education. Some investors had already opened universities, colleges and nurse-training centers. So far, the Ministry of Education had accredited twenty privately run universities and colleges. Hence, there is a marked increase in the country's higher education institutions: a decade ago, Ethiopia had only sixteen (16) colleges and universities. However, by 2003, the number of institutions of higher learning in the country has grown to one hundred twenty (120). This, in turn, has dramatically increased the country's capacity to admit freshman university students by more than threefold. In the 1990s, the country's universities and colleges could enroll barely ten thousand (10,000) freshman students annually. But, by 2003, according to the Minister of Education, this figure had grown to more than 33,000 (Ethiopian Radio 2003).

Nevertheless, more is still desired in this regard. The number of students completing high school is more than a quarter of a million annually. Besides, most of these universities and colleges, especially privately owned ones, are concentrated, for various reasons, in the capital, Addis Ababa. Though one of the reasons is the lack of an adequate student population that warrants the opening of a college in the provincial capitals, the other is the investment policy of the various Kilils (ethnically based administrative units), which prefer the investment of their co-ethnics rather than "outsiders."

In spite of all these positive developments in the areas of higher education in Ethiopia, according to a relatively recent study of the International Organization for Migration (IOM), one-third of Ethiopians who were sent abroad for further education do not return to their country (Damtew 2000). Thus, the country, which is the poorest on earth, has remained a supplier of trained manpower to the Western World. Another IOM report also revealed that Ethiopian professionals—unlike successful professionals among other African immigrants—have continued to resist attempts to entice them to return home (*Chronicle* 2001). This fact indicates that the government in Ethiopia needs to do more while the Ethiopians in the Diaspora, on their part, might consider lowering their expectations of their home country.

REFERENCES

Addis Tribune. 2002. "AAU Expands Graduate, Continuing and Distance Education Programs . . . Students to Resume Classes." *Addis Tribune*. Retrieved March 29, 2002 (http://www.addistribune.com/Archives/2002/03/29-03-02).

——. 2005. "Ethiopian Pilots: Goodbye to Belarus." *Addis Tribune*. August 5. Retrieved August 29, 2006 (http://www.addistribune.com/Archives/2005/08/05-08-05/Ethiopian%20Pilots.htm).

Addis Zaman. [Ethiopian daily Amharic News paper], *Maskaram* 11, 1995 E.C. September 18, 2002.

Amnesty International. 1978. *Human Rights Violation in Ethiopia*. London November 1978, AI Index: AFR 25/10/78, pp. 14-17.

Bahru Zewde. 2002. *Pioneers of Change In Ethiopia: The Reformist Intellectuals of the Early Twentieth Century*. Athens: Ohio University Press.

Baker, Jonathan. 1995. *Studies On Emergencies and Disaster Relief, Report No. 2, Refugee and Labor Movements in Sub-Saharan Africa*. Nordiska Afrikainstitute.

Barber, Ben. 2000. "Indian-Americans Use Cash to Aid 'Motherland.'" *The Washington Times*. February 25.

Bowman, Lee. 2000. "U.S. Ranks Only 37 for Health System Efficiency in World." *The San Diego Union Tribune*. June 21, Wednesday, p. A-1.

BBC World Service. 2001. "Mercenaries' in West Africa's War: Mark Doyle Investigates the Role Played by Foreign Helicopter Pilots in West Africa's Three-way Border War Involving Guinea, Sierra Leone and Liberia." *BBC World Service*. Wednesday, 28 February, 2001 at 16:31 GMT.

BBC Online. 2001. "Brain Drain Costs Africa Billions." Retrieved October 17, 2001. (http://news.bbc.co.uk/hi/english/world/africa/newsid_1605000/1605242.stm).

Carter, Ryan. 2002. "Still Fulfilling a Doctor's Dream: Colleagues Working to Deliver Dialysis Machines to Man's Native Land after His Death in September 11 Attacks." *Burbank*. Retrieved March 16, 2002 (http://wwwlatimes.com/tcn/burbank/).

Castles, Stephen and Mark J. Miller. 1993. *The Age of Migration: International Population Movements in the Modern World*. II Ed. New York: The Guilford Press.

Damtew Teferra. 2000. "Revisiting the Doctrine of Human Capital Mobility in the Information Age." Regional Conference on Brain Drain and Capacity Building in Africa. February 22-24, Addis Ababa, Ethiopia.

Dugger, Celia W. 2000. "Web Moguls' Return Passage to India." *The New York Times*. February 29, *Ethiopian Radio News*. Tuesday March 25, 2003 @ 1:30 pm local time.

ETOP. 2003. "Air Force Pilot Asked Asylum in London: The Number of Ethiopian Air Force Pilots and Engineers who Fled their Country has Reached Fifteen (15)." *Etop* (an Amharic newspaper) *Magabit* 3, 1995 E.C. [March 12, 2003]. Vol. 9, No. 386.

Foner, Nancy, Ruben G. Rumbaut and Steven J. Gold, ed. 2000. *Immigration Research for a New Century: Multidisciplinary Perspectives*. New York: Russell Sage Foundation.

Freemantle, Michel. 2006. "Archives for Africa: Royal Society of Chemistry Offers Free Online Access to its Scientific Journal Archive." *Chemical & Engineering News*, Volume 84, Number 20, May 15, 2006, pp. 44-45.

Gebre-Igziabiher Elyas. 1994. *Prowess, Piety and Politics: the Chronicle of Abeto Iyasu and Empress Zewditu of Ethiopia (1909-1930)*. Edited and translated by Reidulf K. Molvaer. Koln: Rudiger Koppe Verlag.

Gondar College of Medical Sciences. 2001. *47th Anniversary Information Bulletin*. Gondar: Gondar Printing Press.

Halliday, Fred and Maxine Molyneux. 1981. *The Ethiopian Revolution*. London: NLB.

Institute of International Education. 1973. *Open Doors, 1973*. New York: Institute of International Education.

Kiflu Taddesse. 1998. *The Generation, Part II. Ethiopia: Transformation and Conflict*. Lanham: University Press of America.

Kigotho, Wachira. 2001. "Academics in Ethiopia are Again Under Siege." *The Chronicles of Higher Education*. May 18, 2001, pp. A49-50.

Marcus, Harold G. 1983. *Ethiopia, Great Britain, and the United States, 1941-1974: the Politics of Empire*. Berkeley: University of California Press.

Markakis, John. 1974. *Ethiopia: Anatomy and a Traditional Polity*. Oxford: Clarendon Press.

Nieguth, Tim. 1999. "Beyond Dichotomy: Concepts of the Nation and the Distribution of Membership." *Nations and Nationalism*. Vol. 5, No. 2, April 1999, p. 154.

Reporter. 2000a. "Ethiopian Physicians are Leaving the Country." *Reporter*. Vol. 5, No. 51, No. 259, Retrieved August 21, 2000 (http://www.ethiopianreporter.com/ Archive/ amh_main_259.htm).

——. 2000b. "Badabub Afriqa Yetyopiyawuyan Motina Siqay Eyabrakata Naw." [In South Africa, the Suffering and Death of Ethiopians is Getting Worse]. *Reporter*. Maskram 8, 1993 E.C. September 16, 2000.

Rumbaut, Ruben G. 1996. "Origins and Destinies: Immigration, Race, and Ethnicity in Contemporary America." In Silvia Pedraza and Ruben G. Rumbaut, Ed., *Origins and Destinies: Immigration, Race, and Ethnicity in America*. Belmont: Wadsworth.

Samson Mulugeta, Africa Correspondent. 2001. "Help Wanted: Professionals, Brain Drain Strains Africa." *Newsday*. July 19, 2001. (http://www.newsday.com/pages/fcs.html)

Sassen, Saskia. 1998. *Globalization and its Discontents*. New York: The New Press.

TOBIA. July 29, 2000 (an Amharic Newspaper)

Tesfa H. 2000. "Ongoing Discourse about Higher Education in Ethiopia: The Ministry of Education Needs to Revisit Itself." *Addis Tribune*. Retrieved October 6, 2000 (http:// www.addistribune.com/Archives/2000/10/06-10-00/Ongo.Htm)

U.S. Department of Justice: Immigration and Naturalization Services. 1999. *Statistical Year Book of the Immigration and Naturalization Services Refugees, Asylees Fiscal Year 1999* (Internet release) (http://www.ins.gov/graphics/aboutins/statistics/99YrbkREF/RA99.pdf).

U.S. Department of Commerce Economics and Statistics Administration Bureau of the Census. 1990. *1990 Census Population: Ancestry of the Population of the United States*. Washington, DC: Bureau of the Census

Walta Information Center. 2000. "Education Minister Genet Zawde on Ethiopian Education." *Walta Information Center*. Retrieved December 29, 2000 (http://www.waltainfo.com/)

——. 2005. "Gov't Urged to Balance Intake of Post-graduate Students with Inputs." *Walta Information Center*. Retrieved October 20, 2005 (http://www.waltainfo.com/ EnNews/2005/Oct/20Oct05/Oct20e8.htm).

The World Bank. 1998. *African Development Indicators, 1998/99*. Washington DC: The International Bank for Reconstruction and Development.

——. 2001. *Africa Region Human Development Series: Education and Health in Sub-Saharan Africa, A Review of Sector-Wide Approach*. Washington, DC: The International Bank for Reconstruction and Development.

World Health Organization. 2001. "Country Progress Report: Ethiopia." (http://www. who.int/reproductive-health/mps/ethiopia_country_report.html).

Index

INTERNATIONAL STUDIES
IN
SOCIOLOGY AND SOCIAL ANTHROPOLOGY

21. FUSÉ, T. (ed.). *Modernization and Stress in Japan.* 1975. ISBN 90 04 04344 6
22. SMITH, B.L. (ed.). *Religion and Social Conflict in South Asia.* 1976. ISBN 90 04 04510 4
23. MAZRUI, A.A. (ed.). *The Warrior Tradition in Modern Africa.* 1977. ISBN 90 04 05646 7
25. SMITH, B.L. (ed.). *Religion and the Legitimation of Power in South Asia.* 1978. ISBN 90 04 05674 2
31. LELE, J. (ed.). *Tradition and Modernity in* Bhakti *Movements.* 1981. ISBN 90 04 06370 6
32. ARMER, J.M. *Comparative Sociological Research in the 1960s and 1970s.* 1982. ISBN 90 04 06487 7
33. GALATY, J.G. & P.C. SALZMAN (eds.). *Change and Development in Nomadic and Pastoral Societies.* 1981. ISBN 90 04 06587 3
34. LUPRI, E. (ed.). *The Changing Position of Women in Family and Society. A Cross-National Comparison.* 1983. ISBN 90 04 06845 7
35. IVERSON, N. (ed.). *Urbanism and Urbanization. Views, Aspects and Dimensions.* 1984. ISBN 90 04 06920 8
36. MALIK, Y.K. *Politics, Technology, and Bureaucracy in South Asia.* 1983. ISBN 90 04 07027 3
37. LENSKI, G. (ed.). *Current Issues and Research in Macrosociology.* 1984. ISBN 90 04 07052 4
39. TIRYAKIAN, E.A. (ed.). *The Global Crisis. Sociological Analyses and Responses.* 1984. ISBN 90 04 07284 5
40. LAWRENCE, B. (ed.). *Ibn Khaldun and Islamic Ideology.* 1984. ISBN 90 04 07567 4
41. HAJJAR, S.G. (ed.). *The Middle East: from Transition to Development.* 1985. ISBN 90 04 07694 8
43. CARMAN, J.B. & F.A. MARGLIN (eds.). *Purity and Auspiciousness in Indian Society.* 1985. ISBN 90 04 07789 8
46. SMITH, B.L. & H.B. REYNOLDS (eds.). *The City as a Sacred Center. Essays on Six Asian Contexts.* 1987. ISBN 90 04 08471 1
47. MALIK, Y.K. & D.K. VAJPEYI (eds.). *India. The Years of Indira Ghandi.* 1988. ISBN 90 04 08681 1
48. CLARK, C. & J. LEMCO (eds.). *State and Development.* 1988. ISBN 90 04 08833 4
49. GUTKIND, P.C.W. (ed.). *Third World Workers. Comparative International Labour Studies.* 1988. ISBN 90 04 08788 5
50. SELIGMAN, A.B. *Order and Transcendence. The Role of Utopias and the Dynamics of Civilization.* 1989. ISBN 90 04 08975 6
51. JABBRA, J.G. *Bureaucracy and Development in the Arab World.* 1989. ISBN 90 04 09194 7

52. KAUTSKY, J.H. (ed.). *Karl Kautsky and the Social Science of Classical Marxism.* 1989. ISBN 90 04 09193 9
53. KAPUR, A. (ed.). *The Diplomatic Ideas and Practices of Asian States.* 1990. ISBN 90 04 09289 7
54. KIM, Q.-Y. (ed.). *Revolutions in the Third World.* 1991. ISBN 90 04 09355 9
55. KENNEDY, C.H. & D.J. LOUSCHER (eds.). *Civil Military Interaction in Asia and Africa.* 1991. ISBN 90 04 09359 1
56. RAGIN, C.C. (ed.). *Issues and Alternatives in Comparative Social Research.* 1991. ISBN 90 04 09360 5
57. CHOUDHRY, N.K. (ed.). *Canada and South Asian Development. Trade and Aid.* 1991. ISBN 90 04 09416 4
58. RAZIA AKTER BANU, U.A.B. (ed.). *Islam in Bangladesh.* 1992. ISBN 90 04 09497 0
61. AHMAD, A. (ed.). *Science and Technology Policy for Economic Development in Africa.* 1993. ISBN 90 04 09659 0
62. VAJPEYI, D.K. (ed.). *Modernizing China.* 1994. ISBN 90 04 10046 6
63. BRADSHAW, Y.W. (ed.). *Education in Comparative Perspective.* New Lessons from around the World. 1997. ISBN 90 04 10734 7
64. UDOGU, E.I. (ed.). *Democracy and Democratization in Africa.* Toward the 21st Century. 1997. ISBN 90 04 10733 9
65. BEHAR, J.E. & A.G. CUZÁN (eds.). *At the Crossroads of Development.* Trans-national Challenges to Developed and Developing Societies. 1997. ISBN 90 04 10732 0
66. LAUDERDALE, P. & R. AMSTER (eds.). *Lives in the Balance.* Perspectives on Global Injustice and Inequality. 1997. ISBN 90 04 10875 0
67. LOVEJOY, P.E. & P.A.T. WILLIAMS (eds.). *Displacement and the Politics of Violence in Nigeria.* 1997. ISBN 90 04 10876 9
68. JABBRA, J.G. & N.W. JABBRA (eds.). *Challenging Environmental Issues.* Middle Eastern Perspectives. 1997. ISBN 90 04 10877 7
69. SASAKI, M. (ed.). *Values and Attitudes Across Nations and Time.* 1998. ISBN 90 04 11219 7
70. SPERLING, J., Y. MALIK & D. LOUSCHER (eds.). *Zones of Amity, Zones of Enmity.* The Prospects for Economic and Military Security in Asia. 1998. ISBN 90 04 11218 9
71. NANDI, P.K. & S.M. SHAHIDULLAH (eds.). *Globalization and the Evolving World Society.* 1998. ISBN 90 04 11247 2
72. ARTS, W. & L. HALMAN (eds.). *New Directions in Quantitative Comparative Sociology.* 1999. ISBN 90 04 11411 4
73. ISHWARAN, K. (ed.). *Ascetic Culture: Renunciation and Worldly Engagement.* 1999. ISBN 90 04 11412 2
74. PATTERSON, R. (ed.). *Science and Technology in Southern Africa and East and South Asia,* 1999. ISBN 90 04 11413 0
75. ARTS, W. (ed.). *Through a Glass, Darkly.* Blurred images of cultural tradition and modernity over distance and time. 2000. ISBN 90 04 11597 8
76. GERRITSEN, J.W. *The Control of Fuddle and Flash,* A Sociological History of the Regulation of Alcohol and Opiates. 2000. ISBN 90 04 11640 0
77. LEE, W.C. (ed.). *Taiwan in Perspective.* 2000. ISBN 90 04 11849 7
78. LUMUMBA-KASONGO, T. (ed.). *Dynamics and Policy Implications of the Global Reforms at the End of the Second Millennium.* 2000. ISBN 90 04 11847 0

79. HARRIS, R. & M. SEID (eds.). *Critical Perspectives on Globalization and Neoliberalism in the Developing Countries.* 2000. ISBN 90 04 11850 0
80. HOWARD, G.J. & G. NEWMAN (eds.), *Varieties of Comparative Criminology.* 2001. ISBN 90 04 12245 1
81. NDEGWA, S.N. (ed.), *A Decade of Democracy in Africa.* 2001. ISBN 90 04 12244 3
82. JREISAT, J.E. (ed.), *Governance and Developing Countries.* 2002. ISBN 90 04 12247 8
83. KEITA, M. (ed.), *Conceptualizing/Re-Conceptualizing Africa.* The construction of African Historical Identity. 2002. ISBN 90 04 12420 9
84. BERG, R. VAN DEN, *Nyoongar People of Australia.* Perspectives on Racism and Multiculturalism. 2002. ISBN 90 04 12478 0
85. DOGAN, M. (ed.), *Elite Configurations at the Apex of Power.* 2003. ISBN 90 04 12808 5
86. SENGERS, G., *Women and Demons.* Cult Healing in Islamic Egypt. 2003. ISBN 90 04 12771 2
87. WILSON, H.T. *The Vocation of Reason.* Studies in Critical Theory and Social Science in the Age of Max Weber. Edited and with a Foreword by T.M. Kemple. 2003. ISBN 90 04 13631 2
88. ZEGEYE, A. and R.L. HARRIS, *Media, Identity and the Public Sphere in Post-Apartheid South Africa.* 2003. ISBN 90 04 12633 3
89. INGLEHART, R. (ed.), *Human Values and Social Change.* Findings from the Values Surveys. 2003. ISBN 90 04 12810 7
90. BEN-RAFAEL, E. (ed.), *Sociology and Ideology.* 2003. ISBN 90 04 13104 3
91. AL-HAJ, M., *Immigration and Ethnic Formation in a Deeply Divided Society.* The Case of the 1990s Immigrants from the Former Soviet Union in Israel. 2004. ISBN 90 04 13625 8
92. AMINEH, M., *Central Eurasia in World Politics.* Conflict, Security, and Development. 2004. ISBN 90 04 12809 3
93. VINKEN, H., J. SOETERS & P. ESTER (eds.), *Comparing Cultures.* Dimensions of Culture in a Comparative Perspective. 2004. ISBN 90 04 13115 9
94. ASSIÉ-LUMUMBA, N.T., *Cyberspace, Distance Learning, and Higher Education in Developing Countries.* Old and Emergent Issues of Access, Pedagogy, and Knowledge Production. 2004. ISBN 90 04 13121 3
95. HARRIS, R.L. and M. Seid, *Globalization and Health.* 2004. ISBN 90 04 14145 6
96. DOGAN, M. (ed.), *Political Mistrust and the Discrediting of Politicians.* 2005. ISBN 90 04 14530 3
97. MÉRIOT, S.-A., *Nostalgic Cooks.* Another French Paradox. 2006. ISBN 90 04 14346 7
99. EISENSTADT, S.N., *The Great Revolutions and the Civilizations of Modernity.* 2006. ISBN 90 04 14812 4
100. NIEUWENHUYS, E. (ed.), *Neo-Liberal Globalism and Social Sustainable Globalisation.* 2006. ISBN 90 04 15159 1
101. SCHRYER, F., *Farming in a Global Economy.* A Case Study of Dutch Immigrant Farmers in Canada. 2006. ISBN 90 04 15170 2
102. SHLAPENTOKH, D. (ed.), *Russia between East and West.* Scholarly Debates on Eurasianism. 2006. ISBN 90 04 15415 9
103. DAY, R.B. & J. MASCIULLI (eds.), *Globalization and Political Ethics.* 2006. ISBN 90 04 15581 3
104. ESMER, Y. & T. PETTERSSON (eds.), *Measuring and Mapping Cultures.* 25 Years of Comparative Value Surveys. 2007. ISBN 978 90 04 15820 7
105. PATTERSON, R. (ed.), *African Brain Circulation.* Beyond the Drain-Gain Debate. 2007. ISBN 978 90 04 15885 6

www.ingramcontent.com/pod-product-compliance
Lightning Source LLC
Chambersburg PA
CBHW031325230926
51848CB00001B/92
* 9 7 8 9 0 0 4 1 5 8 8 5 6 *